P9-CRS-086

WOLF WOLFENSBERGER

THE PRINCIPLE OF NORMALIZATION IN HUMAN SERVICES

with additional texts by

B[illegible]IRJE
SI[illegible]LSHANSKY
ROBERT PERSKE
PHILIP ROOS

NATIONAL INSTITUTE ON
MENTAL RETARDATION

SPONSORED BY THE CANADIAN ASSOCIATION
FOR THE MENTALLY RETARDED

foreword

The underlying principles inherent in NORMALIZATION have lead to such recent developments as the *United Nations Declaration of the Rights of Mentally Retarded Persons* brought into being by the International League of Societies for the Mentally Handicapped.

This book is the first one to document normalization from its origins in Scandinavian services to the mentally retarded to its implications to the field of human services. The National Institute on Mental Retardation has published this text to support the current growing interest in normalization concepts and fuller integration of the retarded into the community. This concept is currently having a major impact on the pattern of programming in a number of countries. The views expressed in this book do not necessarily reflect the Institute's specific strategies, or those of its sponsor, the Canadian Association for the Mentally Retarded.

The publication of *The principle of normalization in human services*, and earlier of *Mental retardation • the law • guardianship* and *Standards for educators of exceptional children in Canada* are examples of the Institute's recently established publishing policy to bring to the attention of a wider public new concepts, innovative programs and reports of studies by the Institute itself and by others in the field of the mentally handicapped and in human services generally.

G. Allan Roeher, Ph.D.,
Director,
National Institute on Mental Retardation
November 1972

The Principle of Normalization in Human Services

WOLF WOLFENSBERGER

AND
BENGT NIRJE
SIMON OLSHANSKY
ROBERT PERSKE
PHILIP ROOS

published by

NATIONAL INSTITUTE ON MENTAL RETARDATION

through

Leonard Crainford Toronto

The principle of normalization in human services

ISBN 0-9690438-4-8
Library of Congress Catalogue Card Number 72-95107

printed in Canada 1972
reprinted 1973
reprinted 1974
reprinted 1975
reprinted 1977

designed by Leslie Smart Associates Limited
printed by Macdonald-Downie Limited
text and titles set in Times New Roman

Issued and distributed by
National Institute on Mental Retardation
York University Campus
4700 Keele Street
Downsview
Toronto
Canada

biographical notes

Wolf Wolfensberger was born in Germany in 1934 and migrated to the United States in 1950. He received a doctorate in psychology and special education from George Peabody College for Teachers, and has worked as a clinician, researcher, teacher, and administrator in mental retardation. From 1964 to 1971, he was a Mental Retardation Research Scientist at the Nebraska Psychiatric Institute in Omaha, and presently is a Visiting Scholar with the National Institute on Mental Retardation in Toronto, Canada. Recent interests include systematic planning of service systems, and implementation of the normalization principle and of citizen advocacy.

Bengt Nirje is the Co-ordinator of Training with the Ministry of Health of the Ontario Government, in Toronto. While Executive Director of the Swedish Association for the Mentally Retarded, he was one of the originators of the principle of normalization.

Simon Olshansky is the Executive Director of Community Workshops in Boston, Mass. He has served as a selective placement director for the U.S. Employment Service and as a vocational rehabilitation counsellor. Somewhat of a 'rehabilitation philosopher', he is a frequent contributor to literature.

Robert Perske is Executive Director of the Greater Omaha Association for Retarded Children in Nebraska. Former Chaplain at the Kansas Neurological Institute, he has written and lectured widely on pastoral work in retardation, and on humanization and normalization.

Philip Roos is Executive Director of the National Association for Retarded Children, in Arlington, Texas. Dr. Roos is a psychologist who has worked as an institution superintendent and in state government. He has written widely on residential aspects of retardation.

contents

prologue

In efforts to support an adaptive, communal, regulated way of life, society has developed many institutionalized ways of rendering help, assistance, or service to its individual members. These 'helping forms' are carried out primarily by professional groups (such as counsellors, educators and trainers, therapists, psychiatrists and clinical psychologists, social workers, and to some degree ministers, physicians, and nurses) and their auxiliaries, functioning through a wide range of agencies (such as courts, employment services, hospitals, clinics, schools, treatment and training centers, sheltered workshops, prisons and reformatories, and residential homes and institutions). These professionals and agencies address themselves to many human problem areas (such as delinquency and crime, mental disorder and retardation, physical and sensory disability, social incapacity, illness, poverty, and addiction and habituation to drugs), by means of numerous activities and functions (such as case assessment, diagnosis and evaluation; correction and detention; counselling, guidance, and psychotherapy; teaching and training; supervision and consultancy).

There are many continuities of training, manpower patterns, legislation, administration, and ideology in the above professions, agencies, activities, and problem areas. After all, these professions and agencies are concerned with human service to other humans, and they almost invariably render such services via societally sanctioned roles, and via a relatively small number of helping mechanisms.

Also, many benevolent, humanistic clinicians see themselves as servants of the public, offering themselves and their services in a non-controlling fashion. They see their clients as free agents, free to accept or reject the offered services. Their self-concept – in part due to the indoctrination received during training – is frequently incompatible with action perceived as controlling, directing or dictating client behavior. Yet, here it is where so many human service workers deceive themselves, because their roles are not only almost always societally sanctioned, but in an endless array of encounters between the server and the served, the server is the interpreter of and agent for the intents of society, and wields a truly amazing amount of power and control, even if he may not consciously perceive himself as so doing.

Human services fall into a number of categories, depending on whether they must be rendered, and whether they must be accepted. Both education and unemployment benefits must be rendered, but only education must be accepted. Even in services which need not be accepted, and in which the consumer has much freedom and choice, the one who renders the service is in an exceedingly powerful situation. Although the server may lack statutory power, he often exerts other types of power, since his decisions can affect the social, emotional, physical, and financial future of his client. Even in his least powerful role, he exerts a great deal of what psychologists call 'stimulus control' over his client.

Unlike education, which must be both rendered and accepted, no one is 'forced to accept' welfare payments; and even in areas as apparently non-controlling as – let us say – high school vocational counselling, the one rendering the service holds enormous stimulus control over the client who is seen as being in a position to 'take it or leave it'. Indeed, it is not too much to say that who will be rich or poor, healthy or sick, bright or dumb, honest or crooked – and even born or unborn – depends in many cases, and to a significant extent, upon the decision of human managers. The fact that this dependency is merely frequent rather than universal, and merely substantial rather than predominant, detracts in no way from the enormity of the phenomenon.

In order to speak parsimoniously about the many helping forms, functions, and manpower structures mentioned above, to underline their commonalities, and to honestly acknowledge the strong stimulus control exercised by them, this book will make frequent use of the term 'human management'. More formally, we might define this term as referring to 'entry of individuals or agencies, acting in societally sanctioned capacities, into the functioning spheres of individuals, families, or larger social systems in order to maintain or change conditions with the intention of benefitting such individuals, their family or other social systems, or society in general.' The term 'human management', it is hoped, will help to keep us humble and perceptive of what we do and are, and of that part of our functioning that we are often inclined to deny.

At this point, I want to state the three goals that this book is intended to achieve: to explain, clarify, and elaborate the principle of normalization as a system of human management; to 'translate' it from its Scandinavian origins so as to make it fully relevant to the North American scene; and to bring the principle to the attention of a broad range of human management disciplines.

In part A of the book, the normalization principle will be presented in its universal nature. Part B will contain illustrative elaborations of the application of the principle to a number of specific problem areas or issues. Since the principle has universal application in all of the human management areas discussed above, including even areas that interact with human management, such as architecture, it is to be expected that additional elaborations will be forthcoming in time. The ones presented here are intended to be primarily illustrative. In part C, some of the strategies and mechanisms for implementing normalization will be presented.

Not all the content of this book is new; some parts are adapted from previous publications, as indicated in footnotes. Material from one previous article (Wolfensberger, 1970c) was used in several chapters, and is not specifically acknowledged again.

Also, some parts of the book cover topics on which I have received considerable assistance from others. I am particularly indebted to Richard Kurtz for the discussion of deviancy in chapter 2, to Linda Glenn and Kris Rogge for work on the PASS project, which is summarized in chapter 18, and to Helen Zauha for her work in and on citizen advocacy which is summarized in chapter 17. George Thomas, former Director of the Nebraska Office of

Mental Retardation, gave much initial support both to the citizen advocacy movement discussed in chapter 17, and the development and use of PASS reviewed in chapter 18.

Wolf Wolfensberger
1972

a

defining the normalization principle and its major implications

1 the role of ideology in shaping human management models

Good ideologies rather than bad ones

Ideologies transcending empiricism but not inconsistent with it

Conscious rather than unconscious ideology

Man's behavior is in good part determined by what I want to call his ideologies. By ideology, I mean a combination of beliefs, attitudes, and interpretations of reality that are derived from one's experiences, one's knowledge of what are presumed to be facts, and above all, one's values.

Ideologies can be thought of as being 'big' or 'little'. Religions, political systems, philosophies of life, etc., these are all big ideologies, or conglomerates of ideologies. Little or at least medium-sized ideologies deal with a wide range of our functioning in our private and professional lives. For instance, we have many such ideologies in our human management professions. While the number of human management professionals and agencies is large, the services they render are profoundly affected and often even governed by a relatively small number of fundamental assumptions or concepts. Thus, in the field of mental retardation, services were for years dominated by the idea that the retarded were a menace to society. Health services of the future will probably undergo sweeping changes if the concept is generally accepted that health services are a right rather than a privilege. The list of potential examples is endless.

We not only need to recognize relatively broad human management ideologies, but also those that may be strongly held by specific professions or schools of thought, or even by specific agencies. Unfortunately, such agency ideologies are often merely agency myths or agency dogmas, and there is a point where an ideology, a myth, and a dogma merge into one. For instance, today, we recognize that the prevalent ideology of welfare agencies in regard to foster and adoptive placement of retarded infants (*e.g.* 'everybody knows you can't place mongoloids') was a dogma, and being false, was also a myth. But this ideology was powerful, and determined what was done for many decades.

Ideologies are extremely powerful forces that rule and determine a host of behaviors, both important and unimportant ones. Even scientists who pride themselves on being purely empirical in their scientific work are ruled by ideologies. Thus, Weinberg (1970) examines some of the frequently unconscious value axioms of scientists, such as 'pure science is better than applied science', or 'paradigm-breaking is better than tedious detail work'. Kuhn (1962) has rendered a widely acclaimed analysis which appears to have demonstrated that science progresses in discontinuous steps which are attained by rather radical reconceptualizations, many of which are ideological rather than merely empirical in nature. Thus, scientific theories come and go, although they are never provable, and only occasionally disprovable.

This chapter has drawn on some material published earlier (Wolfensberger, 1970a).

They come and go because of the prevailing scientific as well as social and even political ideologies. The history of science is replete with examples where even a formidable body of evidence was ignored or denied because the prevailing ideology could not tolerate or account for such evidence. Lysenkoism in Russian genetics and agriculture is an example. In medicine, the evidence against bloodletting was overpowering – yet it was practised for hundreds of years. Today, one of the most widely practised psychiatric techniques, namely psychotherapy, is supported by only scant good experimental evidence, despite more than 50 years of practice. I, too, have my trans-empirical scientific ideologies. For instance, I am most skeptical about extrasensory perception, even though the evidence for it is very strong. My scientific ideologies find it difficult to account for such evidence. Therefore, I dismiss the evidence.

If a human management assumption, concept, or ideology has rather global implication and is consistently expressed, we often refer to it as a human management 'model'. The term model here is not used in the same sense as in architecture or fashion design, but more in the sense of the word 'paradigm'. It is not necessarily something that others should model themselves after, but an example – a typical expression – of a concept or pattern.

Another way of conceptualizing a human management model is as a consistent pattern in which the behavior of persons is structured by other persons who exercise authority or strong influence over them. Human management models affect and often even dictate the location, design, and operation of human management facilities such as listed in the prologue. For instance, much has been said and written about the medical model which generally implies the perception of the consumer of a human service as a 'sick' 'patient' who, after 'diagnosis', is given 'treatment' or 'therapy' for his 'disease' in a 'clinic' or 'hospital' by 'doctors' who carry primary administrative and human management responsibility, assisted by a hierarchy of 'paramedical' personnel and 'therapists', all this hopefully leading to a 'cure'.

Not only daily management practices, but also the social organization of service systems and manpower structures are usually consistent with and related to the prevailing human management concepts and models (*e.g.* Gruenberg, 1966). This should not surprise us, because an intimate reciprocity of cause-effect exchanges often link together the social organization (*e.g.* manpower structures and training) and the management concepts in and of a field.

From the above, one might almost infer that ideologies, and human management models based upon them, are bad. This is not necessarily so. There are good and bad ideologies, and good and bad models. Some good models become bad only when they are inappropriately applied. For instance, the medical model is superb – in appropriate contexts; it has been destructive in others, as when it has been applied to certain problems which are primarily of a socio-pedagogic nature.

Perhaps it is in the sciences where the power of ideologies is to be regretted, because in contrast to human services, science is much more based in empiricism than values, and because ideologies can override facts and empiricism rather easily. However, in human management, I hope that values shall forever reign supreme, at least to a degree. Values are valuable,

paradigm – example

and our lives should be ruled by them. But at the same time, we must strive for three goals: good ideologies rather than bad ones; ideologies which either transcend empiricism or at least are not inconsistent with it; and conscious ideologies rather than unconscious ones. Below, I will elaborate upon each of these.

Good ideologies rather than bad ones

Some ideologies are obviously more adaptive than others; and ideologies differ from each other in regard to the degree to which they are consistent with the holder's other and higher-order ideologies. Yet, obviously, it is only by wisdom or hindsight that we can differentiate good ideologies from bad ones. Otherwise, there would be no bad ideologies, because everybody would embrace only the good ones.

Unfortunately, there are probably only two ways to improve the quality of our ideologies. One way is to strive with sincerity to root out all of one's unconscious ideologies which usually are unconscious only because they are 'bad'. If they were good, we would be less apt to tuck them away. Secondly, there are times when we can apply a bit of decision theory. For instance, some ideologies may be redundant but at least they will not do any harm, while others can do a lot of harm; or some may increase our options, while others reduce them. A belief in the theory that mental retardation is primarily hereditary logically leads to treatment nihilism, while an environmental theory impels toward treatment activism. If the hereditary theory is wrong but we adopt it, we lose all human values, by doing nothing where much could be done, and that is what we did for many decades. On the other hand, if we adopt the environmental theory, and it is wrong, we lose little in human values, only in money. If retarded infants can be fostered, but we do not try because we do not believe it can be done, we will have thrown away a valuable option and harmed a lot of children. If it cannot be done, but we try and fail, we have only wasted a little effort and money, and the children are no worse off than they were before.

A good contemporary example is the situation in residential services for the retarded. We have behind us 50 years of failure, and we can scarcely do worse than we have with our past patterns. Some people now say that we should not try new patterns because they are unproven. But in actuality, just about the worst that can happen is that we do as badly as in the past, while the best that can happen is a breakthrough to a new age. Thus, decision theory alone can sometimes dictate that we embrace a new ideology, tried or untried.

Ideologies transcending empiricism but not inconsistent with it

Let us compare the following two ideologies: as many of the retarded as possible should engage in work that is as culturally normative as possible; or homeless retarded children should be institutionalized because no one will foster or adopt them. The first ideology transcends empiricism. It states a principle and leaves it up to the future and empiricism to determine what 'as many as possible' or 'as culturally normative as possible' may mean. On the other hand, the second ideology is so phrased as to be directly empirically testable. There is nothing wrong with an empirically-based ideology, but it must not be inconsistent with empiricism, and the second ideology is. An example of an empirically-based ideology that is consistent with empiricism is: because most of the severely retarded, and some profoundly retarded, can perform work which, though probably sheltered, is culturally normative in quality if not always in quantity, they should perform such work rather than work which is culturally deviant.

Conscious rather than unconscious ideology

One thing that can be very bad about our ideologies is that more often than not, we are not aware of them. Sometimes we take them so for granted that we lose sight of their existence. An analogy is man's attitude toward air. He took it so much for granted that he did not 'discover' its existence until about 350 years ago. At other times, we simply are not equipped intellectually to formulate our ideologies in words. At yet other times, our ideologies are so bad that we cannot consciously face up to them.

For example, we all claim to believe in equality – and then we practise gross discrimination, but deny it because we cannot admit it and therefore do not realize that we discriminate. In our human management services, we claim to render treatment – and then we dehumanize, and yet deny that we dehumanize. Our educators call for segregated special education of the mildly retarded – and then the evidence shows that with specially-trained teachers, small special classes, and special materials, the special children learn less than they would if left integrated in large classes with regular teachers and classmates years ahead of them. But first we deny the evidence, and when we can no longer deny it, we ignore and usually repress it, and we keep doing that which makes us feel comfortable with our ideology.

There are few things more vicious, more maladaptive, more inimical to individual and collective well-being than unconscious ideologies. The fact that for 200 years, we have adhered, largely unconsciously, to racial discrimination while claiming to adhere to equality is an extreme example. It is a phenomenon that might destroy us.

In the next chapter we will review how ideologies have forged man's patterns of response to devalued groups of fellow men. The rest of the book will then be concerned with the alternative ideologies and patterns of normalization. This ideology, it will be found, is one which draws heavily on empiricism, but throughout, care will be taken to deal with values and to do so at a high level of awareness. The clash of normalization-related values with other values will be rather direct at points, and efforts will be made to sharpen rather than dull the underlying issues. Particularly sharp confrontations will be found in the issue bearing on the benefits versus the drawbacks of juxtaposing deviancy groups and in the issue of human safety and health versus the dignity of risk.

2 the concept of deviancy in human management

'I have become a stranger to my brethren
An alien to my mother's son'

PSALMS 69 8

The predominant portion of human management services is rendered by generic agencies (*i.e.* agencies not oriented toward a single condition such as mental retardation, visual impairment, *etc.*), and to typical citizens. However, a highly visible portion of human management concerns itself with individuals whom the public, or a significant segment of it, views as 'deviant'. In all likelihood, this book will be read primarily by those persons who are concerned with management of deviant behavior. Since the maintenance or attainment of nondeviant, or normative, behavior is the ultimate concern of the normalization principle, we must here explore the nature of deviance before we can profitably discuss the principle itself.

The social definition of deviancy

The concept of deviancy has been elaborated in the recent past by social scientists, and it is a very useful one. A person can be said to be deviant if he is perceived as being significantly different from others in some aspect that is considered of relative importance, and if this difference is negatively valued. An overt and negatively valued characteristic that is associated with the deviancy is called a 'stigma'.

Some sociologists (*e.g.* Farber, 1968) do not consider the terms 'deviant' and 'deviancy' as appropriate for some groups, such as the retarded, because to these sociologists, the definition of deviancy implies an intent to be deviant. I find this definition to be very weak, since it would necessitate the determination of the presence or absence of intent in each individual instance, and in practice, this would imply reliance on a mentalistic and intangible construct that is rarely ascertainable in a convincing manner.

It clearly must be kept in mind that deviancy is of our own making; it is in the eyes of the beholder. An observed quality only becomes a deviancy when it is viewed as negatively value-charged. And the same quality that may be negatively valued in one culture may be positively valued in another. Obesity in women is a good example, being valued in some mid-eastern cultures. As a German proverb proclaims: what is an owl to one person is a nightingale to another.

Handicapped individuals are frequently perceived as deviant. One only needs to consider the history of attitudes toward and the management of the mentally retarded and disordered; the visually, aurally, physically, or speech handicapped; the cosmetically disfigured; the aged and epileptic; and the

I acknowledge the strong influence which the sociologist Richard Kurtz has exerted upon the formulation of this chapter which has drawn partly upon an earlier publication (Wolfensberger, 1969b).

delinquent and legal offenders. Even those whose differentness may not constitute a disability may be perceived as deviant, for instance those who are unusually tall, short, thick, or thin; members of ethnic, racial, or non-conformist minorities; and even those who stand out because of special talents, high intelligence, or virtue.

The generality of attitudes toward deviancy

Too often, we are only concerned about attitudes toward one type of deviancy, perhaps the type that is of primary concern in our own work. Yet frequently, the attitude that we may see expressed toward a person with a certain deviancy may not really be specific to that deviancy at all; such an attitude is very apt to be part of a more generalized attitude-complex about a group of deviancies, or perhaps about deviancy in the broadest sense.

We should keep in mind that such assertions have considerable empirical and historical evidence behind them. Persons rarely appear to be prejudiced against only one type of deviancy. For instance, English (1971) showed that negative attitudes toward blindness were related to similar attitudes toward racial and ethnic minorities. Adorno, Frenkel-Brunswik, Levinson, and Sanford (1950) identified an 'authoritarian personality' type that is particularly apt to be prejudiced. Also, history shows that different types of deviancies were often managed in very similar ways, and that a wide range of deviancies may elicit similar responses or expectancy patterns from people.

To explain such generalization of response, Wilkins (1965) suggests that our attitudes toward deviance derive from the platonic notion that goodness, truth, and beauty are related to each other, and that any deviations from norms *i.e.* truth are 'errors' which, by analogy, must be related to evil and ugliness.[2] For instance, a person may react with similar emotions toward retardation as he does toward blindness, delinquency, and senility.

In early New England, the Puritans looked with suspicion on any deviation from behavioral norms, and irregular conduct was often explained in terms of evil supernatural powers, such as witchcraft. There is reason to believe that retarded and/or disordered persons were tortured, hanged, and burned on this suspicion. Later in New England, records show that lunatics, 'distracted' persons, people who were *non compos mentis,* and those who had 'fits' were all classed together, and perhaps with vagabonds and paupers as well. Connecticut's first house of corrections in 1722 was for rogues, vagabonds, the idle, beggars, fortune tellers, diviners, musicians, runaways, drunkards, prostitutes, pilferers, brawlers – and the mentally afflicted. As late as about 1820, the retarded, together with other dependent deviant groups (such as aged paupers, the sick poor, or the mentally distracted) were publicly 'sold' ('bid off') to the lowest bidder, *i.e.* bound over to the person who offered to take responsibility for them for the lowest amount of public support (Deutsch, 1949).

[2] This view may go back even further than Plato. In the Old Testament (Leviticus 21, 16-18), '. . . the Lord spoke unto Moses saying "Speak unto Aaron saying whosoever of thy seed in their generations it be on whom there is any blemish shall not approach to offer the bread of his God. For whatsoever man it be on whom there is a blemish shall not approach: a blind, or a lame man, or one that hath a flattened nose or a man one of whose limbs is too long".'

The tenth (1880) United States census first combined 'defectives, dependents, and delinquents' for reporting purposes. In its reports, the Public Health Service combined criminals, defectives, and delinquents as late as the 1920's. Between about 1875 and 1920, one of the most important organizations of human service workers in the United States was the National Conference on Charities and Correction, and in its proceedings during this time span, it often grouped the idiotic, imbecilic and feeble-minded with the deaf, dumb, blind, epileptic, insane, delinquent and offenders into one general class of 'defectives'. Few of us today are aware of the fact that the more contemporary term 'mental defective' was coined to distinguish the retarded from these other 'defectives', and it is no coincidence that there were many public institutions serving both the retarded as well as epileptic nonretarded. During the eugenic alarm period (*circa* 1890-1925), an incredible variety of deviancies were believed to be associated with retardation; indeed, they were seen to be caused by it: illness, physical impediments; poverty; vagrancy; unemployment; alcoholism; sex offenses of various types, including prostitution and illegitimacy; crime; mental illness; and epilepsy. All these were called the 'degeneracies'.

'The chronic insane, the epileptic, the paralytic, the imbecile and idiot of various grades, the moral imbecile, the sexual pervert, the kleptomaniac; many, if not most, of the chronic inebriates; many of the prostitutes, tramps, and minor criminals; many habitual paupers, especially the ignorant and irresponsible mothers of illegitimate children, so common in poor houses; many of the shiftless poor, ever on the verge of pauperism and often stepping over into it; some of the blind, some deaf-mutes, some consumptives. All these classes, in varying degree with others not mentioned, are related as being effects of the one cause – which itself is the summing up of many causes – 'degeneracy' ' (quoted by Johnson, 1903, p. 246).

The first institutions for the retarded in North America were built (*circa* 1850-1870) in a period of optimism regarding mental disorder and the education of the deaf and blind, and many facilities for these other deviant groups were erected at that time. The later disillusionment about retardation was also not isolated, but part of a more generalized aversion toward, and virtual persecution of, deviancies. Isolated and segregating farm colonies were a logical development in the history of residential institutions of many types.

During the early part of the century – a very chauvinistic period – numerous writers claimed that a large proportion of the retarded and otherwise degenerate came from foreign-born stock, contributing to the call for more restrictive immigration laws (Wolfensberger, 1969b). This is perhaps an extreme example of how retardation was linked in the minds of many to other types of deviance. One could go on endlessly demonstrating the point that societal responses toward one type of deviancy were not specific, but were part of a more generalized pattern of response toward deviance.

Major historic roles of deviant persons

When a person is perceived as deviant, he is cast into a role that carries with it powerful expectancies. Strangely enough, these expectancies not only take hold of the mind of the perceiver, but of the perceived person as well. It is a well-established fact that a person's behavior tends to be profoundly affected by the role expectations that are placed upon him. Generally, people will play the roles they have been assigned. This permits those who define social roles to make self-fulfilling prophecies by predicting that someone cast into a certain role will emit behavior consistent with that role. Unfortunately, role-appropriate behavior will then often be interpreted to be a person's 'natural' mode of acting, rather than a mode elicited by environmental events and circumstances. There is profound truth in what Shakespeare said.

> 'All the world's a stage,
> And all the men and women merely players.
> They have their exits and their entrances;
> And one man in his time plays many parts'
>
> *As you Like It.* Act II Scene VII 139-142

When we review history and literature, it becomes apparent that regardless of time or place, certain roles are particularly apt to be thrust upon deviant persons. The way in which these roles transcend time, distance, and culture is remarkable. Most of these socio-historical role perceptions reflect fairly clear-cut prejudices which have little relationship to reality. However, as with many prejudices, the lack of objective verification is not a crucial element in the shaping of a social judgment or social policy. The major roles to be reviewed below include those of the deviant person as subhuman, a menace, an object of dread, a diseased organism, an object of ridicule, an object of pity, an eternal child, and a holy innocent. Most of these roles will be discussed again in chapter 6, where the architectural design implications of various role perceptions are reviewed.

THE DEVIANT INDIVIDUAL AS A SUBHUMAN ORGANISM

Historians and sociologists have long recognized that deviant subgroups within a culture may be perceived as not fully human. To this day, for example, there are large segments of our population which deny full human status to members of certain minority groups, such as Negroes and Indians. Even ordinary army recruits may be said to need 'being broken' or tamed, like wild beasts or horses. But the retarded are particularly apt to be unconsciously perceived or even consciously labelled as subhuman, as animal-like, even as 'vegetables' or 'vegetative'. The literature of retardation is richly endowed with allusions to the alleged subhuman nature of retarded individuals, and with labels that suggest subhuman status. The term 'garden variety' retardation, widely used by professionals in the past to refer to so-called cultural-familial retardation, has definite vegetative connotations.

It is interesting to note that the vegetable concept may, in part, have been derived from an inappropriate transfer of the medical concept of 'vegetative functions'. In medicine, the 'vital functions' controlled by the autonomic nervous system and/or the hypothalamus may be referred to as 'vegetative'. These functions, which include temperature, heart rate, blood pressure, respiration rate, *etc.* are possessed by all humans and most animal species, and yet the concept of vegetative functions is sometimes translated into the social context in such a way as to abrogate even animal, not to mention human, qualities.

One historic perception of the malformed child as a nonhuman entity is expressed in the common myth of the changeling (Haffter, 1968), deposited in lieu of the real human infant either by good fairies (*e.g.* in Ireland), or by evil spirits or the devil (*e.g.* in central Europe). For instance, Martin Luther, in describing what appears to have been a severely or profoundly retarded child, denied the child's humanity and interpreted him as a changeling as follows: 'Eight years ago, there was one at Dessau whom I, Martinus Luther, saw and grappled with. He was twelve years old, had the use of his eyes and all his senses, so that one might think that he was a normal child. But he did nothing but gorge himself as much as four peasants or threshers. He ate, defecated and drooled and, if anyone tackled him, he screamed. If things didn't go well, he wept. So I said to the Prince of Anhalt: 'If I were the Prince, I should take this child to the Molda River which flows near Dessau and drown him.' But the Prince of Anhalt and the Prince of Saxony, who happened to be present, refused to follow my advice. Thereupon I said: 'Well, then the Christians shall order the Lord's Prayer to be said in church and pray that the dear Lord take the Devil away.' This was done daily in Dessau and the changeling died in the following year.' When Luther was asked why he had made such a recommendation, he replied that he was firmly of the opinion that such changelings were merely a mass of flesh, a *massa carnis*, without soul. 'For it is the Devil's power that he corrupts people who have reason and souls when he possesses them. The Devil sits in such changelings where their soul should have been!'[3]

A recent children's book in a Scottish setting (Duncan, 1965) incorporates a pseudohistorical retarded character by the name of 'Simon the Changeling', in connection with the old myth of some infants being 'touched' by the fairies or 'little people'.

Deutsch (1949) pointed out that the mentally disordered were often apt to be stripped of their human attributes, together with their rights and privileges as human beings. Logically, if one dehumanizes a person who once had reason but lost it, then it is even easier to dehumanize a person who never possessed much reason in the first place, such as a retarded individual. For instance, a comment in the *Atlantic Monthly* (October, 1967, p. 49), called for '. . . . sacrifice of mentally defective humans, or human vegetables . . .' to provide organ transplants and '. . . increase the intellectual betterment of mankind . . .'.

Mowrer (1965) proposed that operant conditioning is so effective with autistic children because it is also effective with animals, and the autistic individual 'is least removed from the 'animal level' ' (p. 208). In a footnote, he then also referred to the good results of these procedures with retarded children. Dehumanization of the retarded is so accepted, even in this day, and even by workers in the field, that we can witness a public statement by a contemporary superintendent of a state institution referring to some of his retarded residents as '. . . so-called human beings . . .' '. . . below what we might call an animal level of functioning . . .' (*Frontiers of Hospital Psychiatry*, 1968, *5*(1), 5-6).

[3] There are several versions of this account, derived from the various editions of Luther's Tabletalks, *e.g. Luther's Works*, Vol. 45, Fortress Press, Philadelphia, 1967, p. 396; and Aurifaber, Jr., *Tischreden*, Vol. 5, Weimar Edition, p. 9. In all editions, the account is item No. 5207.

Some of the implications of the subhuman role perception to human management are obvious. Aside from these obvious points, the following corollaries of the subhuman perception are of note: attribution of animal-like qualities or even skills; belittling of the learning capacity; abrogation of a sense of esthetics; need for extraordinary control, restriction, or supervision; denial of citizenship rights and privileges, which may partially explain why, since about 1900, retarded residents in public institutions have been treated in a fashion that today is being (or will probably soon be) ruled illegal or unconstitutional; abrogation of human emotions, sensibilities, shame, and even sensation and perception.

In regard to the last point, the idea that the mentally afflicted lack sensory acuity, *e.g.* that they are insensitive to heat and cold, was popular into the mid-1800s (Deutsch, 1949). This myth resulted in their often being denied heat during the winter for their cold institution cells, and may well have contributed to the image of the retarded as insensate vegetables. Indeed, even new buildings designed specifically for the disordered did not provide for heating of the residents' cells, nor were their windows glazed (Tiffany, 1891). Parallels to this interpretation of a devalued group as being insensate nonhumans can be found even in contemporary society. As recently as 1972, the South African government was planning to build high-rise housing for nonwhite laborers, in which these laborers would be 'kept' segregated by sex, four persons to a room, and without any heating (*Time*, May 15, 1972).

Devaluation of a human being into a subhuman role is so contrary to other ideals and values which a perceiver may hold as to prohibit the conscious recognition and labelling of the dehumanization. Therefore, it is important to be aware that while many persons hold subhuman perceptions, they cannot admit these perceptions to their own awareness because the implied interpretation of a human being would clash with other, concurrently held, perceptions and values. Thus, it is very common to encounter a person who dehumanizes a group of devalued individuals without being conscious of the meaning of his overt behavior and the reality of his attitudes. Only by understanding this process of repression of an unacceptable impulse can we also understand certain dehumanizing behaviors, or why some dehumanizers are remarkably unaware that their behaviors and attitudes are dehumanizing and are perceived to be so by others.

Vail (1967) has probed this problem with considerable sophistication. For instance, how can the fact be explained that individuals who, by all ordinary criteria, can be described as model citizens, suddenly become the cold-blooded killers of millions. This can only be understood if one understands the reality and process of the dehumanization of devalued individuals. The explanation is that if an organism is perceived as being not fully human, then it does not matter whether this organism is destroyed, dislocated, disowned, or otherwise used at the convenience of those perceived to be human. Animals are thus used all the time.

What is remarkable is that individuals who are relatively moral in every other sphere of their lives are capable of imposing nonhuman role perceptions upon certain groups, and are then very readily capable of treating such groups no better than animals. Only this reality can explain how otherwise moral and loving individuals can be unfeeling and dehumanizing human managers in certain spheres of their functioning. For example, this has not been an unusual phenomenon with many superintendents of institutions. It explains a phenomenon such as the senior personnel of an institution with about 75 years of experience in work with retarded children designing a new building for severely handicapped children which has toilets that are too large and high to be usable by such children, and soap dishes and towel racks attached so high on the wall as to be unreachable by the children. Had the designers been charged with planning a building for human children, they would have anticipated such problems; designing for entities perceived to be nonhuman, it was impossible for the designers to muster the empathy necessary to anticipate this problem, even with generations of experience behind them.

Only by fully understanding the dynamics and the accompanying unconsciousness of dehumanization will one be able to fully perceive and relate to the symbolic ways in which dehumanization often manifests itself. For example, there are many documented instances in which a parent has destroyed his handicapped child. The motives have been varied, and have included disappointment, frustration, hostility, pity, *etc.* However, it is not often that a middle-class parent not merely destroys his own child, but also commits the highly symbolic act of discarding the child literally in the garbage, as has happened recently in a large North American city.

As Buddenhagen (1971) points out, there may be similar symbolism in the fact that severe aversive punishment is particularly apt to be used with the retarded, and perhaps for reasons which are not quite conscious. With less impaired individuals, we are much more apt to use rewards, and while it might take some ingenuity to devise an appropriate reward system for the profoundly retarded, such ingenuity is probably quite within the scope of ability and grasp of most experimenters. Thus, their sometimes too ready recourse to severe aversive stimulation when dealing with the profoundly retarded may well derive from an unconscious perception of these individuals as nonhuman.

Similarly, the use of the electric cattle prod to administer aversive stimuli in the shaping of the behavior of the profoundly retarded may carry with it profound symbolic meaning. Assuming for the moment that the administration of electric shock were more humane than permitting the person to engage in extreme self-destructive behavior – as some of the profoundly retarded and disturbed may do – one can still ask the question why such stimuli are not administered in a fashion which strips the symbolism of animal-handling and particularly of 'dumb cattle' from the methodology that is chosen.

Finally, Rowland and Patterson (1971) suggest that past and recent efforts of prominent scientists to explain the social problems associated with certain minority groups as being due to genetic intellectual inferiority is merely a sophisticated way of interpreting such minority groups as subhuman.

THE DEVIANT INDIVIDUAL AS A MENACE

Unknown events or objects, if alien enough, tend to arouse negative feelings in both man and beast. Man's history is filled with incidents of man's persecution of fellow men of different features, skin pigmentation, size, shape, language, custom, dress, *etc.*, and it is apparent that man has been very apt to see evil in deviance. Therefore, it is not surprising that one role perception prominent in history is that of the deviant person as a menace. He might be perceived as being a menace individually, because of alleged propensities toward various crimes against persons and property; or he might be perceived as a social menace because of alleged contribution to social disorganization and genetic decline. This role perception has been a very prominent one during the so-called genetic scare or alarmist period (*circa* 1890-1925) when most of society's problems were attributed to inherited defect.

THE DEVIANT INDIVIDUAL AS AN UNSPEAKABLE OBJECT OF DREAD

Somewhat related to other role perceptions of the deviant person as subhuman or a menace is the perception of him as a dreadful entity or event. In some respects, this role perception is similar to the one of 'Man as other' defined by Vail (1967). Man as changeling, discussed earlier, may fit here, as may perceptions of a deviant person as sent by God as a punishment for the sins of his parents, discussed further below.

THE DEVIANT INDIVIDUAL AS AN OBJECT OF PITY

Frequently, a deviant individual is viewed as a person who is handicapped because of a misfortune for which he bears no responsibility, and who therefore should receive special attention, services, *etc.* The deviant person may even be seen as 'suffering' from his condition, even though such an interpretation may be highly subjective and even inaccurate. While there may be made efforts to relieve this alleged suffering, the person may also be seen as possibly unaware of his deviance. Much as in the sick role perception, the pitied person is likely to be held blameless for his condition, and perhaps unaccountable for his behavior. He is very apt to be viewed with a 'there but for the grace of God go I' attitude.

Usually, this form of the pity perception is benevolent and is accompanied by compassion and acceptance, although it may be devoid of respect for the deviant person. However, there also exists another variant of the pity perception, upheld more by a sense of duty than compassion. Particularly persons possessing a strongly moralistic conscience but not much genuine humanism are apt to perceive deviant persons as objects of sour charity. This attitude can be likened to the one widely held in the Victorian age toward orphans, and is epitomized by the Victorian response to Oliver Twist's request for 'more'. While the affected person was usually (but not necessarily) viewed as innocent, his parents often were not. Thus, the advent of a handicapped child was sometimes interpreted as a punishment for parental sins, and occasionally, the handicap was even attributed to a sin committed by the handicapped person himself prior to the presumed onset of his impaired condition.

For instance, colonial New Englanders often looked upon handicaps as the consequences of a stern providence meting out judgment for wickedness. According to Suraci (1966), such a view is quite common today in the Puerto Rican subculture in New York City. Where such a view prevails, the family members of a malformed or impaired person are likely to feel shame, and outsiders are more apt to be contemptuous rather than sympathetic toward them and the handicapped individual. Any charity extended with such views can be expected to be cold, and the person receiving such aid might be labelled rather aptly a 'burden of charity'.[4] Thus, the sour humanist may look upon a deviant recipient of services as a 'kept' object of charity, and while such charity clients may be seen as entitled to basic assistance and sustenance, they are not seen as entitled to anything interpretable as luxuries, frills, or extras. The object of such charity is expected to be grateful, and to work as hard as possible for his 'keep'.

As Coll (1969) pointed out, the Puritan Ethic had a strong influence in the formulation of the 'less eligibility' doctrine in the history of welfare services and charitable agencies. The doctrine states that no matter what the need of a person may be who is supported by public funds, assistance to him must be below the level of the lowest prevailing wage.

THE DEVIANT INDIVIDUAL AS A HOLY INNOCENT

In a number of cultures and eras, deviant individuals, particularly the mentally afflicted, have been accorded a religious role interpretation as the special children of God, as saints, or as holy or eternal innocents. Those incompetent to perform everyday tasks might be perceived as having religious thoughts on their minds, or as being endowed with saintly powers. It may also be believed that such persons have been sent by God for some special purpose. Perceived in a religious light, the afflicted are usually seen as incapable of consciously or voluntarily committing evil, and consequently they may be considered to be living saints. Religious role perceptions of some kind were reportedly prevalent among the Eskimos, North American Indians, and Arabs; and in Russia, Central Asia, and medieval Europe.

The first institution founded for the disordered in the Western world (Valencia, Spain, in 1410) was intended by its originator, Father Juan Gilabert Jofré to be 'for the innocent ones, that is, the insane', and it was called the 'Hospital of Innocents'. In France, the retarded person has been referred to as 'l'enfant du Bon Dieu'. In English, the term 'Christling' or 'God's Infant' might be used (Norris, 1963-64). Even a theater review in *Time* (December 8, 1967) referred to the main character in 'Pantagleize' by Ghelderode as 'a fool in Christ, one of nature's eternal innocents'. In the Gaelic tongue (at least as spoken in Ireland), the retarded may be referred to as 'innocent', 'artless', 'guiltless', and even the contemporary term for a retarded person translates as 'one of God's people' (Kidd, 1970). In Russia, the retarded were called 'holy idiots' (Edgerton, 1970).

At times, deviant persons have been perceived as not merely incapable of sin, but as actually being representative of, or possessed by, a sacred spirit. In such cases, a certain awe or even cult may surround such persons, as was reportedly the case among some North American Indian tribes. A person perceived in such a way may be quite valued, and he or his family may be perceived as specially favored by the Lord. To this day, certain Central American Indian cultures perceive their albino members as being on special terms with the sun god, and as being less inclined to commit evils (Shatto and Keeler, 1971).

[4] Here, the burden of charity is discussed as a variant of the pity perception. However, the two roles almost could be given co-equal standing, as is done in the chapter on 'Additional architectural-environmental implications of the normalization principle', because the two perceptions can lead to quite distinct management implications.

Vanier (1971) relates the story of an Algerian who said to the parents of a retarded child 'How lucky you are to have a child like that. We believe that a family that has a child like that is blessed by Allah.' In the Arab world, the word 'saint' may actually be used for persons of altered mind, including the retarded, disturbed, epileptic, and religious ascetic. The term 'marabut' might be applied equally to the lowly retarded servant girl or to a respected saintly figure (Edgerton, 1970).

Jewish tradition, like many, is divided as to attitudes toward handicap. While one current of attitudes is very devaluing, another provides a positive and religious interpretation. Thus, the following ancient Hebrew prayer, over 3000 years old, is intended to be said upon encountering a deformed person: 'Praise to you, Lord God, king of the universe, who varies the forms of thy creatures.' A Jewish proverb states that 'the power of prophecy is given to children and fools.'

In Western culture, the holy innocent perception is still particularly prevalent in Catholicism. There is a 'Prayer for Holy Innocents' in the Roman ritual, and one encounters many poems on the theme, such as the much-publicized 'Heaven's Very Special Child'. One recent article by a Catholic nun is entitled 'The Religious Education of the Holy Innocents', and another one (Anonymous, 1970) 'The Saint in our House'.

The holy innocent perception is one of the most benign role perceptions in human management. However, it has one element that is objectionable. It implies a reverse form of dehumanization, by elevating a human being almost above the human level, and by suggesting a 'little angel' status. Vail (1967) subsumes such role perceptions in his profoundly insightful conceptualization of 'man as other'.

However, the perception of the holy innocent must be differentiated from the interpretation of the impaired person as innocent but not necessarily holy. This is a perception forcefully synthesized by Vanier (1971), and if applied with discretion to some impaired persons (such as to some of the retarded), it may be quite accurate for them. This interpretation is based upon certain child-like traits which may be found especially in retarded persons, without implying that such persons are either holy or eternal children. In other words, selectively applied, this perception can be a highly realistic one which, in a sensitive and properly motivated person, can elicit a rich and enriching response style toward the perceived person.

THE DEVIANT INDIVIDUAL AS A DISEASED ORGANISM

An additional historically prominent role perception is that of the deviant individual as sick, *i.e.* as an incumbent of what sociologists refer to as the 'sick role'. Much has been said and written about the medical model which generally implies the perception of a deviant person as a 'sick' 'patient' who, after 'diagnosis', is given 'treatment' or 'therapy' for his 'disease' in a 'clinic' or 'hospital' by 'doctors' who carry primary administrative and human management responsibility, assisted by a hierarchy of 'paramedical' personnel and 'therapists', all this hopefully leading to a 'cure'. Conditions which have been widely subsumed under such a model include homosexuality, mental disorder, mental retardation, stuttering, alcoholism, and drug addictions.

When a deviant person is thus seen as sick, then education, work, and recreation can come to be interpreted as educational, industrial, and recreational therapy; those who 'administer' such therapy (perhaps in 'doses' rather than lessons, *etc.*) may be called therapists; finally, there often exists a pessimistic preoccupation with the issue of curability versus incurability because of the perceived 'chronicity' of a condition.

Perceived as sick, the deviant person may be seen as entitled to the privileges, as well as subjected to the demands, that have been proposed by Parsons (1951; Parsons & Fox, 1958) as characteristic of the sick role generally, and as partially verified empirically by Gordon (1966). The privileges include exemption from normal social responsibilities, and recognition that the condition is not the individual's fault; the demands are that the individual must want to get well or at least better, and must seek suitable and appropriate remedy for his condition.

It should be noted that the disease model can be expressed in two variants, one of these embodying the best tradition of medical service to fellow humans, and the other one being concerned with health but not with human values. The latter model can be likened to veterinary medicine, and is particularly apt to be encountered in residential institutions.

THE DEVIANT INDIVIDUAL AS AN OBJECT OF RIDICULE

This role perception is closely associated with another one in which men are perceived as 'trivium' (Vail, 1967), *i.e.* as unimportant or not to be taken seriously. Thus, for many years, the Negro was virtually always depicted by the mass media, such as movies, in the role of a servant; a comic figure (*e.g.* the eye-rolling superstitious porter); or, at best, a light entertainer. Similarly, the retarded have frequently been cast into the role of village idiots, and in folk humor they are almost without exception depicted as an object of ridicule. A relatively recent manifestation of this role perception is the so-called moron joke of a few years ago, and an outstanding depiction of the retarded person as an object of ridicule was contained in the award-winning film *Charly*, based on Keyes' (1966) book *Flowers for Algernon*.

In medieval society, the retarded and deformed achieved some distinction as court fools or court jesters who would dress in garish costumes and engage in comic and silly antics for the merriment of the high-born. Thus, Horsfield (1940) relates that 'the court of Philip IV of Spain, 1621-65, was crowded with a horde of zanies, jugglers, tumblers, clowns, buffoons, jesters, an incomparable assortment of dwarfs, in fact almost every sort of person that might be included in fooldom. This motley pack was probably unequalled in any other time or country, except perhaps by that at the court of the Aztec king, Montezuma. These individuals, most of whom were probably mentally deficient folk, many with marked physical defects, were gathered from the highways and byways of the kingdom and brought to the palace, primarily for the amusement of royalty. At the court of Montezuma, these unfortunates were housed after the manner of a modern park zoo' (p. 152).

THE DEVIANT INDIVIDUAL AS AN ETERNAL CHILD

A very strong role perception of some deviant individuals is that of persons who are and perhaps always will be much younger than their age. For instance, the book *The Child Who Never Grew* by Pearl Buck (1950) and a Canadian film entitled *Eternal Children* render such a depiction of the retarded person. A recent article (Fendell, 1969) is entitled 'Israel's Eternal Children'.

Generally, those who hold the eternal child role perception do not place strong or even reasonable developmental and adaptational demands upon the person so perceived. Instead of expecting the person to adapt to the environment, those who see him as a child would adapt the environment to him. For example, Eaton and Weil (1955) report that when a child is recognized as retarded among the Hutterites, extensive adjustments are made in his social environment. His baptism may even be 'cancelled', so that he can do no wrong as an adult. In no case is the retarded person institutionalized, as happens in the mainstream North American culture when the social systems surrounding a retarded person cannot or will not adapt to his limitations.

Societal management of deviancy

When we review society's efforts to handle deviancy, we can readily classify these efforts into four categories: destruction of deviant individuals, their segregation, reversal of their condition, or prevention thereof.

In the past, some kinds of deviance were seen to be the work of the devil or other malignant forces. As such, the deviant person was perceived as evil too, and was persecuted and destroyed in order to protect society. Destruction of the deviant has often been advocated – even today – for reasons related to self-preservation or self-protection. For instance, many societies have condoned the destruction of weaker, less adequate, or handicapped members. This was true of ancient Greece and Rome, of the Eskimos and bushmen, and of Nazi Germany. In North America, the increasing sentiment for, and legalization of, abortion of high-risk fetuses can be viewed, at least in part, as a variant of this theme.

As a more humane alternative to destruction, the deviant person who is being perceived as unpleasant, offensive, or frightening can be segregated from the mainstream of society and placed at its periphery. We have numerous examples of this: we segregate the Indian in reservations, and the Negro in the ghetto; the aged are congregated in special homes, ostensibly for their own good, and these homes are often located at the periphery of, or remote from, population centers; the emotionally disturbed and the retarded are commonly placed in institutions far in the countryside; and we have (or have had) 'dying rooms' in our hospitals to save us the unpleasantness of ultimate deviancy.

Deviance can be seen to be someone's fault or perhaps a sign that the deviant person's parents had sinned and were therefore being punished by the Lord. The belief that blemished offspring is a punishment for parental wrongdoing appears to be deeply ingrained in the unconscious of the people. Often, this belief is overtly expressed. It is a belief that had been held by Howe (a leading American pioneer in the field of blindness and mental retardation) and was repeatedly expressed by him. Another early authority on mental retardation (Greene, 1884, p. 270) said: 'Our wards are innocent of crime or fault. In the large majority of instances, they are the feeble and deformed expressions of parental sins or sorrows.' Parental alcoholism, for instance, was widely believed to be a major cause of retardation (*e.g.* Kerlin, 1886, p. 297). In fact, many deviancies were perceived to be due to a person's own sins. Howe asserted that even retardation might result from a person's own wrongdoing (Howe, 1848, 1852, 1866), *e.g.* 'It appeared to us certain that the existence of so many idiots in every generation must be the consequence of some violation of the *natural laws;* – that where there was so much suffering, there must have been sin' (1848, p. 4). Perceived to be the result of sin, deviance is something to be ashamed of, hidden, and 'put away'. Thus, the Puritans held views very much along these lines (Deutsch, 1949).

The third and fourth alternatives for handling deviancy are to reverse or prevent it. Reversal is generally pursued by means of education, training, and treatment, which may also apply to prevention. Since deviancy exists by social definition, it can also be prevented or reversed by social redefinition, *e.g.* by not attaching negative value to certain types of differentness. For instance, medieval Catholicism and the more contemporary Hutterites (Eaton & Weil, 1955) did not place excessive value on intellectual achievement, and therefore were less likely to view a retarded person as deviant.

In essence, prevention and reversal of deviancy are what this book, and normalization, are all about. As the reader will find, the means encompassed to achieve these goals will be not only physical and psychological, but will also include methods of social redefinition.

3 the principle of normalization as a human management model: evolution of a definition

A reformulation of the normalization principle

Until about 1969, the term 'normalization' had never been heard by most workers in human service areas. Today, it is a captivating watchword standing for a whole new ideology of human management.

To the best of my knowledge, the concept of normalization owes its first promulgation to Bank-Mikkelsen, head of the Danish Mental Retardation Service, who phrased it in terms of his own field, as follows: 'letting the mentally retarded obtain an existence as close to the normal as possible.' Bank-Mikkelsen (1969) was instrumental in having this principle written into the 1959 Danish law governing services to the mentally retarded.

However, it was not until 1969 that the principle was systematically stated and elaborated in the literature by Nirje (1969b), who was then executive director of the Swedish Association for Retarded Children. This elaboration was contained in a chapter of the monograph *Changing Patterns in Residential Services for the Mentally Retarded* (Kugel & Wolfensberger, 1969), sponsored by the President's Committee on Mental Retardation. This systematic description was not only the first one in English[1], but even had to be translated into Swedish in order to become the first major treatise on the topic in the Scandinavian literature. In this 1969 chapter, Nirje phrased the principle as follows: 'making available to the mentally retarded patterns and conditions of everyday life which are as close as possible to the norms and patterns of the mainstream of society' (p. 181).

Although the normalization principle had not yet been systematically presented in the Scandinavian literature until 1970, its significance had been widely recognized before that, and in 1967, a new, far-reaching Swedish law governing provisions and services for the mentally retarded was developed from it and became effective in 1968 (Swedish Code of Statutes, 1967 (4), dated December 15, 1967). Parts of this law were presented and discussed in the above-mentioned chapter by Nirje (1969b).

Nirje's chapter was mostly concerned with the implications of the normalization principle to the design and operation of residences for the retarded; however, the relevance of the principle beyond residential aspects, and even beyond mental retardation to deviancy and human management in general, was clearly recognized and stated. In a synthesizing chapter in the same book, Dybwad (1969) pointed to the principle as a major emergent human management concept, while also elaborating further on some of its implications to the location, design, staffing, and operation of residential services.

[1] The first major statement of the normalization principle in the British literature was contained in a three-article symposium in the December 1970 issue of the *Journal of Mental Subnormality* (Gunzberg, 1970; Nirje, 1970; Zarfas, 1970).

A reformulation of the normalization principle

For purposes of a North American audience, and for broadest adaptability to human management in general, I propose that the definition of the normalization principle can be further refined as follows: 'Utilization of means which are as culturally normative as possible, in order to establish and/or maintain personal behaviors and characteristics which are as culturally normative as possible.'

From the proposed reformulation it is immediately apparent that the normalization principle is culture-specific, because cultures vary in their norms. For instance, normalization does not necessarily mean that human services should resemble Scandinavian services. It does mean that as much as possible, human management means should be typical of our own culture; and that a (potentially) deviant person should be enabled to emit behaviors and an appearance appropriate (normative) within that culture for persons of similar characteristics, such as age and sex. The term 'normative' is intended to have statistical rather than moral connotations, and could be equated with 'typical' or 'conventional'. The phrase 'as culturally normative as possible' implies ultimately an empirical process of determining what and how much is possible.

Since deviancy is, by definition, in the eyes of the beholder, it is only realistic to attend not only to the limitations in a person's repertoire of potential behavior, but to attend as much or even more to those characteristics and behaviors which mark a person as deviant in the sight of others. For instance, wearing a hearing aid may be a greater obstacle to finding and keeping a job than being hard of hearing (Kolstoe, 1961).

It is for this reason that the proposed reformulation implies both a process and a goal, although it does not necessarily imply a promise that a person who is being subjected to normalizing measures and processes will remain or become normal. It does imply that in as many aspects of a person's functioning as possible, the human manager will aspire to elicit and maintain behaviors and appearances that come as close to being normative as circumstances and the person's behavioral potential permit; and that great stress is placed upon the fact that some human management means will be preferable to others. Indeed, sometimes a technique of less immediate potency may be preferable to a more potent one, because the latter may reinforce the perceived deviance of the person, and may be more debilitating than normalizing in the long run.

The distinction between 'elicitation' and 'establishment' of normative behavior on the one hand, and 'maintenance' on the other hand, has a number of implications. For instance, the term 'maintenance' underlines not only the importance of supporting behavior that is normative (or as normative as possible) in a person who previously behaved in a deviant (or more deviant) manner, but also the necessity of assisting some persons who have never been perceived as deviant from coming to be so perceived.

The normalization principle can be viewed as being neutral as to whether a specific deviant person or group *should* be normalized. That decision must be based on criteria and values which exist independent of the normalization principle. Here it is useful to recall that our society considers it appropriate that normalizing measures be *offered* in some circumstances, and *imposed* in others.

The normalization principle as stated is deceptively simple. Many individuals will agree to it wholeheartedly while lacking awareness of even the most immediate and major corollaries and implications. Indeed, many human managers endorse the principle readily while engaging in practices quite opposed to it – without being aware of this discordance until the implications are spelled out. Then a manager may find himself in a very painful dilemma, endorsing simultaneously a principle, as well as practices opposed to it.

In the next chapter, some of the major corollaries and implications of the normalization principle will be elaborated. The reader may find himself just as surprised by some of these as this writer was.

4 typical programmatic and architectural implications of the normalization principle

Having stated, reformulated, and somewhat explained the normalization principle, we will now examine in more detail what it means to translate it into action. After trying unsuccessfully to differentiate between programmatic and architectural implications, I will elaborate on both of these concurrently, although additional architectural and residential implications will be covered in chapters specific to these issues. Also, the entire issue of societal integration will only be touched upon in this chapter and elaborated at length in the next one.

The levels and dimensions of the normalization principle

One can conceive of the implications of the normalization principle as falling into two dimensions and three levels of action. *Table 1*. One dimension is concerned with the structure of interactions that involve deviant or potentially deviant individuals directly, while the second dimension is concerned with the way such persons are interpreted to others. Another way of putting this is to say that both dimensions deal with the structuring of a deviant person's environment, one dimension involving the person directly, the other involving the way this person is symbolically represented in the minds of others. Of great importance to the latter are labels, concepts, stereotypes, role perceptions, and role expectancies that are applied to a person, and that often determine the circularity between his own self-concept, the way others react to him, and the way he is likely to respond.

Role perceptions and stereotypes are known to exert considerable influence on behavior. For instance, normalized and normalizing role expectations have been used with great effectiveness in treating members of the armed forces who display mental disorder (Talbot, 1969). However, only through some very recent research has the full power of the feedback loop between role expectancy and role performance been brought into sharp focus. The work of Rosenthal and Jacobson (1968), which suggests the power of role perception in the development of children, is one of the more spectacular examples. It is consistent with and explains a number of other research findings. For example, it appears quite consistent with the well-documented fact that retarded children who are placed into special classes underachieve grossly when compared to their retarded peers who are carried along in regular classes, even without any special attention.

The immediacy of contact with, or interpretation of, (deviant) individuals can be divided rather meaningfully into three levels. The first level involves individual human managers with individual (potentially) deviant persons. The second level is concerned with the immediate (primary) and intermediate social systems that act upon a person; such systems include the (deviant) person's family, peer group, classroom, school, neighborhood, place of work, or service agency. The third level concerns itself with the larger relevant societal social systems, such as the school system of an entire province, state, or nation, the laws of the land, and the mores of a society. Below, implications in each of the six categories summarized in *Table 1* will be discussed.

TABLE 1

A schema of the expression of the normalization principle on three levels of two dimensions of action

Levels of action	Dimensions of action	
	Interaction	Interpretation
Person	Eliciting, shaping, and maintaining normative skills and habits in persons by means of direct physical and social interaction with them	Presenting, managing, addressing, labelling, and interpreting individual persons in a manner emphasizing their similarities to rather than differences from others
Primary and intermediate social systems	Eliciting, shaping, and maintaining normative skills and habits in persons by working indirectly through their primary and intermediate social systems, such as family, classroom, school, work setting, service agency, and neighborhood	Shaping, presenting, and interpreting intermediate social systems surrounding a person or consisting of target persons so that these systems as well as the persons in them are perceived as culturally normative as possible
Societal systems	Eliciting, shaping, and maintaining normative behavior in persons by appropriate shaping of large societal social systems, and structures such as entire school systems, laws, and government	Shaping cultural values, attitudes, and stereotypes so as to elicit maximal feasible cultural acceptance of differences

NORMALIZING ACTION ON THE PERSON LEVEL

The interaction dimension

On the first level of the interaction dimension (*i.e.* the person level), the normalization principle would dictate that we provide services which maximize the behavioral competence of a (deviant) person. Indeed, much of the programming offered by human management fields and agencies would fall into this general category.

However, we appear to be much more effective in shaping skills to be physically adaptive than in shaping them to be socially normative, or in shaping their *habitual* normative exercise. For instance, the normalization principle demands that a person should be taught not merely to walk, but to walk with a normal gait; that he use normal movements and normal expressive behavior patterns; that he dress like other persons his age; and that his diet be such as to assure normal weight. Too often, we may content ourselves to teach a handicapped child to walk, but we may be relatively unconcerned when the child develops a quite preventable idiosyncratic gait which elicits or reinforces a perception of deviance. We may teach a retarded young adult how to use a deodorant – but then fail to convert this skill into the adaptive habit it tends to be. Thus, we must direct much more conscious effort to this issue than we ordinarily do.

Obviously, the design of a human management-related building can have much to do with the shaping of both skills and habits of its users. For instance, buildings can make, or fail to make, developmental challenges and demands; they can elicit adaptive decision-making and enhance independence, or impose dependency. Life space should be zoned so as to encourage rather than discourage individuals from interacting in small groups at least part of the time, in contrast to space which implies interaction in large groups only, or which discourages almost all interaction. Even in the presence of other design elements which permit use of the building by the severely physically handicapped, many residential and educational human service buildings should have stairs and not merely ramps, and residential facilities generally should provide residents with access to the controls that adjust room and water temperature; turn lights on and off; open and close windows, blinds and curtains; and flush toilets. To do otherwise deprives residents of culturally normal opportunities, restricts their range of learning opportunities, and fosters non-normative dependency.

The interpretation dimension

The interaction dimension just reviewed implies that we teach a person to habitually exercise those behaviors which elicit social judgment even if they have little practical problem-solving value. These behaviors include etiquette, and may be related or attached to other normative skills of dressing, grooming, walking, talking, eating, *etc.*

However, there are situations where a person's public image does not (alone) depend on what he is or does, but on how those around him 'present' him. In either case, a person's image depends greatly on the actions of those who exercise 'managerial' controls over him, and therefore the manager should take steps to minimize the probabilities that the person for whom he has responsibility presents himself to the public in a fashion that is apt to lower what we might call the 'perceived deviancy threshold'. For instance, while a moderately retarded adult can be taught to dress himself habitually in a normative fashion, a moderately retarded child still has to be dressed by others, or told what to wear. A retarded adult living independently in society may indulge himself and become deviantly obese, and there may be little we can do about it. However, a mildly retarded adult in a community hostel or supervised apartment will usually still be under agency management, and his diet can be regulated to some degree.

Similarly, where a person's appearance is less determined by himself than by the manager, it is important to attend carefully to such things as the grooming and hairstyle that we might confer upon such a person. For example, we could give a young man with Down's syndrome a 'soup bowl' haircut which accentuates his perceived deviancy in the sight of others, or a haircut which minimized the cranial and facial stigmata of mongolism. Cosmetic surgery can often eliminate or reduce a stigma, and can be as effective in enhancing a person's acceptability as teaching adaptive skills, changing his conduct, or working on his feelings. In other words, the probabilities should be minimized that a citizen can identify on sight, as being different, a person who is already deviant, or who is apt to be so labelled in the future.

Labels can be as powerful as appearances. The type of public response to the aforementioned young man with Down's syndrome will depend significantly on whether we introduce him to the public as 'Mr. Smith' or 'Joseph Smith'; somewhat condescendingly as 'Joe'; perhaps derogatorily as 'Joe, the mongoloid'; or contemptuously as 'a mongolian idiot'.

The question may be raised why it is so important to reduce the perceived deviancy of a person who may already be clearly identified as deviant. The answer is that there are degrees of deviancy, and every additional measure of deviance becomes an additional social handicap, further reducing a person's self-image, and increasing the likelihood that he will emit non-normative maladaptive behavior.

NORMALIZING ACTION ON THE LEVEL OF PRIMARY AND INTERMEDIATE SOCIAL SYSTEMS

The interaction dimension

On the level of primary and intermediate social systems in the interaction dimension, we would not work with (deviant) individuals directly, but through those social systems which act rather closely upon them. The importance and cost-efficiency of shaping social systems can not be overemphasized. If the system is maladaptive, all the efforts of the clinicians interacting with clients on the person level can be vitiated. This has often been the case in residential institutions where the systemic structure has vastly reduced the effectiveness of dedicated workers.

In an interesting study (Rubin & Balow, 1971), it was found that of 967 children who had been tested as being essentially normal during kindergarten, 41% were classified within three years by the school system as having appreciable problems or as requiring special services. Twelve per cent had been made to repeat a grade. Phenomena such as this strongly suggest that systems often are in greater need of diagnosis, treatment, and reshaping than the individuals they purportedly serve.

Examples of working through a social system rather than with the afflicted directly would include counselling the family of an impaired person; or performing environmental manipulations of his family social system, as we would if we helped the family obtain a home that was physically more suitable for the rearing of a handicapped child. We might help his school to start a special class into which he might fit, counsel his teacher, or prevail upon some appropriate governing body to replace (with a new and more competent director) the director of an agency that had served the person poorly in the past.

Similarly, in order to accomplish the greatest amount of normalization, both by encouraging deviant persons to imitate nondeviant ones, as well as by shaping the stereotypes held by the public of various deviant groups, deviant individuals should have maximal exposure to the nondeviant, and minimal exposure (or juxtaposition) to workers, volunteers, or other individuals who are perceived as deviant themselves by a significant proportion of the public.

In typical community life, social interaction with one's everyday contacts brings with it innumerable occasions and role expectancies that have implications to the normalization process. Unfortunately, a person identified as deviant is often further 'dehabilitated' by being deprived of these normalizing social contacts, or by being cast into social roles where he is actually expected to act deviantly.

For instance, by placing a deviant client among other deviant clients, we may reduce his social contacts with nondeviant persons. Often, we compound this problem by permitting some or even most of the staff working with a deviant group to be deviant. Thus, a common phenomenon in human management is for deviant persons to drift into employment where they work with clients who are deviant themselves. A teacher who cannot cope with regular pupils may be given a special education class; a physician who does not have a licence to practise in the community (usually because of inadequate training or skill, language problems, alcoholism, drug addiction, physical or mental problems, *etc.*) may be permitted to practise in an institution for the retarded or disordered; convicts may be placed into training or work with the mentally retarded; retarded workers may be placed as aides in homes for the aged; aged pensioners may be asked (even against their will) to become boarding home operators for convicts (*e.g. Toronto Star*, April 5 and May 8, 1972); *etc.*

Usually, human managers defend such juxtaposition practices on the grounds that the deviant worker can make a contribution by such an arrangement, that he can be habilitated by it, *etc.* However, when a person is perceived somewhat (or definitely) as a deviant 'reject' by society, and is then placed into a position where he administers services to other persons similarly perceived, it is inevitable that members of the public conclude consciously or unconsciously that the deviant individuals who are being served are of low value. For instance, a teacher who is not good enough to work with my normal child may be good enough to teach someone else's retarded child; or a retarded orderly would scare me in a general hospital, but is good enough to take care of someone else's old mother.[1] Thus, a juxtaposition of deviant workers with deviant clients devalues both of them, but particularly so the client. Inevitably, this devaluing perception will induce the public to emit behavior toward the deviant client group that is more likely to be 'dehabilitating' than normalizing.

[1] It is interesting to note the tortuous reasoning that must make up for the twisted attitudes that support the wide-spread custom of placing retarded persons as workers into nursing homes for the aged. And yet, if a retarded worker is good enough to be a competent orderly in a nursing home – as is often the case – then he is usually also good enough to work in a general hospital (*e.g. Anonymous*, 1971).

Also, when deviant individuals work for and with other deviant persons, or when deviant persons socialize intensively and perhaps exclusively with each other, it is almost inevitable that a climate or subculture of deviancy is created which exacerbates rather than reverses the deviancy of those within this climate or subculture. Finally, at a given time, a person generally has the potential of forming a limited number of social ties and meaningful relationships. Usually, he will fill his 'relationship vacancies' with people he encounters in the social systems close to him. The likelihood of filling one's relationship needs with deviant persons is probably in direct proportion to the percentage of such persons in one's social systems. Thus, if we surround a deviant client with deviant workers, or vice versa, the chances of each group to socialize with nondeviant persons is lowered. The perceived deviance of both groups is likely to increase, and even their adaptive behavior often decreases. Far from being habilitative, the chances of habilitation for either group, especially the much larger client group, is likely to be reduced by such measures.

It follows that instead of there being mutual benefits, both groups may actually lose – if not in each specific instance, then at least in the long run of societal processes. Normalization principles would thus not only argue against the juxtaposition of deviant workers with deviant clients, but would demand that as much as possible, deviant individuals be surrounded by nondeviant ones. By the same logic, those who serve a group of deviant clients should meet at least the same standards of qualification as are applied to persons who work with comparable nondeviant groups.

Buildings should be so designed and located as to be physically integrated into the community, encourage maximal social integration of the persons served in and by them, and provide client-users with a wide range and large number of normalizing experiences. Since a neighborhood or community can only integrate a limited number of deviant persons at any one time, the size of a facility should be such as to congregate no more deviant client-users than can readily be absorbed in and by the surrounding area, services, resources, social life, *etc.* This means that hostels and other group residences have to be small, and in most cases, several residential units of small size should not be placed too close together. For instance, instead of putting two sheltered hostel-apartments for four retarded adults each in one apartment house, more integration would be achieved by placing the apartments into separate apartment houses some distance apart.

Smallness of size, in turn, dictates that residential services should be specialized[2] for specific types of problems and/or groups. Unlike the all-purpose institution, a small group residence is usually incapable of rendering appropriate services simultaneously to infants and the aged, the near-independent and the totally dependent, the well-behaved and the uncontrolled, the blind and the deaf, *etc.* At any rate, services for children and adults ordinarily

[2] The concept of 'specialization' will be encountered in several chapters of this book, and is given a meaning that differs slightly from its more common one. In the context of normalization, specialization does *not* necessarily refer to more skilled manpower use, but to more clearly identified management models and perhaps problem (but not necessarily impairment) targets. For instance, a residence operated on a child development model may actually require very little advanced manpower, and it may serve children who, despite a wide range of disabilities, have similar essential needs.

should be physically separated anyway, both in order to reduce the probability that children will imitate the deviant behavior of their elders, and because services to adults and children are generally also separated in the mainstream of society. These and certain other implications specific to the structure of residential services will be elaborated in other chapters.

Normalizing dispersal of specialized residences generally means that the location, distribution, and concentration of facilities should follow the prevailing population distribution. Thus, service facilities, and even group residences, must not only be dispersed across communities within a region, but also within specific communities. For example, one of the first comprehensive community service plans based on the normalization principle (Menolascino, Clark, & Wolfensberger, 1968, 1970) envisioned as many as fifty small, dispersed, specialized residences, hostels, and apartments for the mentally retarded of Douglas County in Nebraska (an urban area containing the city of Omaha and a population of about 400,000). By means of such a specialized dispersed system, it is planned to eliminate entirely the need for traditional institutional residences, even for the most severely impaired.

In regard to size of a facility or client group, it is important not merely to consider the ability of the surrounding social systems to absorb deviant individuals, but also the size of a grouping that tends to create clannishness, exclusiveness, and inward-centeredness. Members of small groups tend to gravitate outward and to interact with other social systems; as group size increases, this tendency diminishes. The sheer size of the group may create mutual barriers of attitudes; and a person in a large group may find too many of his social needs met too conveniently to motivate him to reach out for normalizing socialization.

In regard to the physical and contextual separation of age groups, strong rationales can be derived from both the interaction and interpretation dimensions.

First of all, in regard to the juxtaposition of children and adults, we must remember that many normative services for children in the mainstream of society are separate from services for adults. Furthermore, deviant adults are only rarely and in limited ways appropriate role models for children. Often this is true because today's adults did not receive the kinds of services we can offer to the children of today and tomorrow. Thus, we do not want the children to acquire some of the less adaptive characteristics of the casualties of yesteryear, but want them to be exposed as much as possible to healthy normal children of their own or similar age, or to adults who are appropriate models for their development.

Additionally, when a service for children and a service for adults are placed in close context to each other, they are often under the same administrator, and/or experience a lot of social interactions of each other's staff. A common example is a sheltered workshop in the same building and under the same management as a program for children. In such situations, the director usually will be either adult- *or* child-oriented, and the program toward which he lacks proper orientation suffers. If he is adult-oriented, the children's program will suffer, as it has typically to this day in psychiatry generally, which is overwhelmingly adult-centered. If he is child-oriented, the adults will be apt to be cast into children's roles. Similarly, the virtually unavoidable close interaction between the staff of the children's program and the adult clients will tend to denormalize the adults by imposing the eternal child role upon them. As a result, the adults in such a setting will be perceived by the public to be little differentiated from children.

Finally, the optimal physical locations and juxtapositions of children's and adult services are often quite different. By selecting the same site for both, one of the services is often disadvantaged in regard to the most normalized location for its particular mission and identity.

For the sake of continuity, one of the principles relevant to the juxtaposition of aged with mature or young adults will here be drawn forward from the interpretation dimension in the next section. If we place impaired adults in a setting or grouping perceived to be specific to the aged (such as a nursing home), it is virtually inevitable that in the perception of many – if not most – observers, the younger impaired adults will be identified with the aura of hopelessness that is unfortunately imposed upon the aged ones. This means that it is much more adaptive to integrate one or a few aged persons among younger ones (in order to acquire *their* aura) than vice versa.

The underlying principle to all of the above juxtaposition issues is that any negative aura (identity, role expectancy, *etc.*) attached to a setting or a particular group will be transferred upon a minority within that setting or group. The aura can rarely be reversed by adding a valued minority to the setting or group. It is much more powerful both in terms of public perception and direct behavior modification to include a devalued person or minority in a mainstream (or even valued) majority, than to mix devalued groups with each other, or to place a valued minority with a devalued majority. One of the recurring and stronger findings of social psychology is that deviant members of a group are much more likely to change their behavior to meet the standards and norms of the group and especially its model members than the other way around (Berelson & Steiner, 1964).

The interpretation dimension

On the same level, in the dimension of interpretation, considerable thought must be given to how service facilities, and the groups of clients they serve, are named or labelled. For instance, Outwood (in Kentucky) is a very unfortunate name for an institution for the retarded. The name of a possible facility should be carefully considered so as to promote a role perception of its client-users that is nondeviant, or at least minimizes the perceived deviancy. Thus, even words such as 'retarded', 'crippled', 'handicapped', *etc.* should probably be avoided in facility names. In fact, some facilities might fare better staying unnamed altogether, perhaps being referred to informally according to the street or area in which they are located, *e.g.* the 'Harney Street Hostel', or the 'Bellevue Heights Workshop'. Similarly, the labels applied to groups of clients by an agency are very important. For instance, adults should not be referred to as 'children', 'kids', or 'inmates'; but as 'men', women', 'clients', 'citizens', 'trainees', 'workers', 'residents', or 'guests', as the case may be, all these latter terms lacking stigma, conveying respect, and being more normative. The term 'patient' should only be used in contexts that are unequivocally medical, and in which the various obligations and privileges of the sick role are appropriate for the persons served (Parsons & Fox, 1958).

Even the symbols surrounding a potentially devalued person or group should be carefully considered. These symbols may be both transmitted and received unconsciously, but nevertheless tend to suggest or perpetuate social perceptions. When cattle prods are used to train the retarded or severely disturbed, a conscious or unconscious perception of the trainees as 'dumb cattle' is apt to be reinforced. Even well-intended symbols can be ill-chosen, as in the song 'Hi, Look Us Over' (from the film of the same title on the Canadian Special Olympics), in which the retarded invite the public to 'put us in clover, not behind a fence'.

An implication of particular poignancy is that contrary to common belief, a staff-to-client ratio that is any higher than necessary is undesirable. A high staff ratio can imply an interpretation of the client as being more deviant than he is, and can thus be denormalizing under certain circumstances. This is also one of the reasons why service facilities (especially residences) should 'specialize'. We should group clients so that each group can be served with the minimum feasible number of restrictions and personnel.

In many instances, a normalizing measure falls into both dimensions of the person level, or into both the person and primary-intermediate level of the interaction dimension. In consequence, a measure may serve the function of shaping a normative skill while simultaneously creating a normative role perception in an observer which, in turn, elicits additional normative behavior from the deviant client in a beneficial circularity. Some examples of management with such dual impact follow.

> Normalization means living in a bisexual world. This has differing implications in different service settings. In children's programs, it means that men as well as women should be involved. For adults, especially in residential services, it usually means that the building and the social structure should produce at least as much mingling of sexes as in a hotel. There are only a few contexts – many of these in adolescence – where activities are normally sex-segregated.
>
> The daily routine of clients as well as client groups should be so structured as to be analogous to that of comparable nondeviant persons of the same age.
>
> A physically or mentally handicapped adult, even if severely impaired, should be engaged as much as possible in work that is culturally normative in type, quantity, and setting. Even if conducted in sheltered settings, work should be culturally typical adult work, rather than involving activities commonly associated with children, with play, with recreation, or with leisure; and sheltered workshops should resemble industry.
>
> An important aspect of normalization is to apply health, safety, comfort, and similar standards to human management facilities and programs as they are applied to comparable settings for other citizens. This has implications primarily to residential facilities, such as institutions; and even more particularly to publicly operated services which, in many jurisdictions, may and do operate below the standards prescribed by law and/or regulation for private facilities. However, it also has implications to clinics and other settings. For instance, reception and waiting areas should be as comfortable, attractive, and private as typical citizens might encounter in comparable community services.

Also, in regard to physical facilities, thought must be given to the 'building perception', *i.e.* the way the physical facility is likely to be perceived by the public. The external appearance or context of a building, even if it is perfect in terms of internal arrangements, can exert a detrimental effect upon citizens' response to the persons associated with this building. For instance, a building that looks like a prison or that was recently used by disturbed individuals is apt to elicit associations not conducive to integration of subsequent client-users of the building. Positive or negative associations affect not only outside observers, but also those who work with the client who is being perceived.

Architecture speaks a powerful language, and can shout out loud interpretations of the client-users of buildings. For instance, putting a drain in the middle of a living room floor (as in some institutions) interprets the person who lives in such a room as an animal who must be 'kept' and cleaned as in a zoo. A non-enclosed toilet says that its user has no human feelings of modesty. Bars on the windows, or even an isolated location of a building, suggest that the building's inhabitants are a menace to society. However, since group residences in particular imply an agency context, and since buildings generally interpret their users almost invariably in a social-systemic rather than individual context, the architectural implications on the person level are virtually indistinguishable from those on the level of primary and intermediate social system.

NORMALIZING ACTION ON THE SOCIETAL LEVEL

The interaction dimension

On the societal level of the interaction dimension, we might work to change the entire school system of a province, state, or even nation, rather than merely changing one class or one school. For instance, many authorities have stated that our present school system unconsciously encourages teenagers from lower-class and disadvantaged backgrounds to drop out. To change such practices, we may have to change laws, perhaps reform teacher training institutions, revise funding and taxing patterns and priorities, *etc.*

The interpretation dimension

Perhaps the major challenge in the interpretational dimension of the societal level is to achieve a redefinition of deviancy, and to foster greater acceptance of some behaviors or characteristics considered deviant today. Normalization can be enhanced by encouraging currently normative citizens to broaden the range of what they consider to be normative. To cite a simple example: to wear a business suit to an important reception or social affair would probably have been perceived as deviant behavior in the past; however, if a number of prominent individuals or a significant minority of persons wore business suits or other more casual attire to such events, such behavior would no longer be considered deviant. Thus, citizens in the mainstream of a culture can do much toward the eradiction of harmless deviancy by adopting habits and lifestyles which are somewhat more tolerant and casual than some of those of the past, many of which have been entirely due to historical accident and convention, and are entirely neutral from a moral viewpoint.

Teaching, exhortation, demonstration, and life-style modelling may be necessary to convince the public that deviancy is of our own making, and is often harmless. We should work for greater acceptance of differentness of modes of grooming, dressing, speaking; of skin color, race, religious and national origin; of appearance, age, sex, intelligence, and education. Also encouraged should be greater acceptance of the physically and sensory handicapped, the epileptic, the emotionally disordered, and perhaps the sexually unorthodox. Here, it is important to recall that societal response to deviancy tends to be general, rather than specific to a particular deviance. By furthering societal acceptance for one type of differentness, we are also and indirectly gaining increased acceptance for a group in which we have a particular personal or professional interest.

Concluding comments on the normalization principle

There are, of course, innumerable other implications from the clinical level to the level of large social systems. The examples given here represent only a selected and arbitrary sampling. However, they underline that many major and minor practices that are currently accepted and not found objectionable by proponents of other human management systems are, in fact, quite inconsistent with the principle of normalization.

The normalization principle has powerful theoretical force vis-a-vis other human management systems, and despite its late emergence, considerable empirical evidence – primarily from social psychology and related fields – can be marshalled in support of it. However, upon first superficial exposure to the principle, one may well ask how it differs from a number of other approaches.

The difference lies in the simplicity, parsimony, and comprehensiveness of the principle. It subsumes many current human management theories and measures – but goes beyond them in stipulating other measures that have been neglected so far. And the principle is easily understood once one has opened one's mind to it.

There are some persons who react to the normalization principle with indifference. I view such reaction as being due either to lack of understanding of the principle, defensiveness about being associated with practices which violate the principle, or attempts to project an air of blasé sophistication. It should, however, be obvious already that even some enlightened human management systems, such as the 'therapeutic milieu', have either been fragmentary in their conceptualization, or have failed to incorporate features which clearly flow from the normalization principle.

Perhaps in no other human management aspect is the above point brought out more clearly than in regard to the corollary of integration of the deviant with the nondeviant. While the strongest arguments for integration can be made on the intermediate level of the interaction dimension of the normalization schema, considerations derived from other levels and dimensions appear to provide additional support for integration practices. Our typical past failures to implement such integration imaginatively, systematically, and aggressively is proof of the fact that we have not really either conceptualized or embraced an ideology of normalization. Thus, the blasé sophisticate's claim that normalization is merely a new name for old beliefs and practices, or for existing systems, is patently false.

I firmly believe that the normalization principle, simple and uncomplicated as it is, is the human management principle that is most consistent with our socio-political ideals and current psycho-social theory and research on deviancy, role performance, and other social processes. I further believe that the normalization principle is so self-evidently valid as well as 'right' that it may well become universally accepted in all areas of human management.

This chapter is intended to translate the principle into some specifics, and to summarize certain major implications. Some of these implications require additional and more detailed treatments, especially as provided in the next three chapters.

5 societal integration as a corollary of normalization

In the preceding chapter, maximal integration of the perceived or potential deviant person into the societal mainstream was established as one of the major corollaries of the principle of normalization. Such integration can be achieved in many areas, and in many ways. One major paradigm is to obtain services from generic agencies which serve the general public, rather than from specialty agencies which serve only or primarily groups of individuals perceived as deviant.

For instance, visually limited children were once educated almost entirely by special schools or at least special classes. Today, they are increasingly educated in the regular classroom by regular teachers who receive special orientation and support from resource rooms and resource teachers. In their general practice, general medical practitioners handle psychiatric problems which were formerly the almost exclusive province of specially-designated mental health personnel. Retarded children who were once placed into special institutions are increasingly placed into ordinary foster homes. The list could go on at some length.

In the past, generic services were often denied to special groups on the basis of two arguments. One was that since the generic agency did not possess the necessary specialized skills and resources, the person with a special condition would be *better served* by a special service. The second argument was that certain deviant individuals *should* be segregated from the mainstream of society, and be served apart – even if not always expertly. People who were different should remain 'with their own kind' – to use the popular expression. It is important to recognize that the first argument was primarily an empirical-technical one, but that the second one was largely value-based.

Today, we can marshal powerful empirical and programmatic arguments in favor of the tenet that segregated services, almost by their nature, are inferior services. This holds true not merely for racial segregation, where this principle was most forcefully promulgated by the courts; it also holds true for segregation of other minority-deviancy groups.

Programmatically, segregation is particularly self-defeating in any context that is claimed to be habilitational, which includes special education. If we are serious about working for the goal of preparing a person toward independence and normative functioning, then we must prepare him to function in the context of the ordinary societal contacts which he is expected to have and to handle adaptively in the future. One of the basic principles of education, in the broad sense, is to 'educe' (lead forth) the learner stepwise into the context in which he is to function; and to bring about this education as early as possible, because the earlier a behavior is learned, the more likely it is to persist. Also, early learning is usually easier than later learning.

Here is where much of our habilitation human management, and especially traditional special education and rehabilitation, have been weak. Too often, training took place in one context, which was an artificial, segregated, and non-normative one; and at the end of the training period, there came a precipitous transfer into realistic normative societal settings. Perhaps our so-called 'corrective' services are the most extreme example of this practice. The fact that our failure rates have not been higher than they have been is more due to the resilience of man than the merit of our practices. To conclude, programs that fail to incorporate a relatively demanding pace of carrying clients stepwise and increasingly into culturally normative (and therefore, by definition, culturally integrated) contexts and activities are, by their very nature, not genuinely habilitational.

This much for the programmatic-empirical argument. However, the arguments involving primarily issues of values have also changed, as our conception of the privileges and obligations of citizenship have changed in recent years. Indeed, we have seen develop almost a preoccupation with issues of right and justice, apparent in a wide range of events and movements among which are the following.

The intense controversy over the justification of various types of wars and weapons, as exemplified by the controversy over the war in Vietnam and the use of weapons such as napalm.

The concern with American intervention into the internal affairs of other countries, as evidenced by the uproar over Project Camelot where a social science experiment carried out by US investigators in a South American nation had to be abandoned.

In the United States, intense public discussion over an equitable draft system.

The continuing battle over the proper definition and enforcement of civil rights, especially in relation to discrimination because of race or sex. We probably have only seen the beginning of a redefinition of the role and rights of women in our society.

Increasing definition of the rights of the accused, and of the proper and improper use of police powers.

Proposals to institute systems of compensating victims of crime.

Demands that large private corporations develop socially-relevant corporate responsibility, adopt more democratic and less secretive governance procedures, and include consumer representatives on their governing boards.

Concern over the unequal distribution of wealth and opportunity in our society, and action on many levels to do something about it.

Redefinition of numerous human services, including medical care and welfare benefits, as a right rather than a privilege.

Demands that the Scandinavian system of the ombudsman be vigorously implemented in Canada and the United States.

Widespread concern over the conduct of scientific research involving human subjects.

Extensive re-examination of the use of psychological tests in education, industry, and elsewhere, culminating in congressional hearings, new administrative rulings, and new laws.

Concern over invasion of privacy on the part of government, industry, or agencies – a concern which has also resulted in various governmental actions.

Soul-searching regarding the rights of man has even generalized to animals, as can be noted in the public controversy over legislation regulating the handling and use of animals for research purposes.

To the above list, other items could readily be added. One of these is of prime relevance here, and that is the new belief that unless a person is a proven menace, he cannot be separated from society by fiat, perhaps merely because his presence is inconvenient or unpleasant. Our society is becoming more pluralistic, and even the armed forces have had to accept a soldier's right to wear sideburns and peace medals. Also, that a deviancy is harmful and warrants denial of societal participation must now be painstakingly proven – individual by individual; such a judgment can no longer be imposed upon a class of persons. Admission, and even commitment, to an institution can no longer be equated with loss of citizenship rights, as was almost universally the case in the past, especially in the field of mental retardation. Even the fact that parents can no longer be held responsible for the support of handicapped children who have attained the legally-defined age of adulthood bespeaks subtly of a new legal interpretation of the handicapped adult as an adult rather than an eternally-dependent child – even if he should require legal guardianship throughout his adult life.

It is apparent that today, neither programmatic nor value-based rationales are sufficient to justify a segregationist service structure. However, it has not always been the majority that has excluded the minority; on many occasions, a minority has deliberately cut itself off from the mainstream. Such self-elected segregation may have been motivated by the fear of mainstream demands; by the desire to continue an established power and bureaucracy structure that might become redundant through integration; and by the fear of change and of rejection. For instance, many leaders in mental retardation have been afraid to give up their special programs and merge their clients into generic and/or public programs for fear that once their special program was discontinued, the other program might begin to exclude the retarded clients who would then be without service altogether. In some version or other, fears like this are encountered again and again – and they are often justified. This is why one of the later chapters will address itself to administrative safeguards for integrative services.

The two integrations: physical and social

If integration is one of the major means for achieving and acknowledging societal acceptance, as well as for accomplishing adaptive behavior change, then we must distinguish between and elaborate upon its dimensions and components. First of all, let us define integration as being the opposite of segregation; and the process of integration as consisting of those practices and measures which maximize a person's (potential) participation in the mainstream of his culture.

For a (deviant) person, integration is achieved when he lives in a culturally normative community setting in ordinary community housing, can move and communicate in ways typical for his age, and is able to utilize, in typical ways, typical community resources: developmental, social, recreational, and religious facilities; hospitals and clinics; the post office; stores and restaurants; job placements; and so on.

Ultimately, integration is only meaningful if it is social integration; *i.e.* if it involves social interaction and acceptance, and not merely physical presence. However, social integration can only be attained if certain preconditions exist, among these being physical integration, although physical integration by itself will not guarantee social integration.

PHYSICAL INTEGRATION

Social integration takes place on the 'person level' and involves the close interaction of (potentially) deviant individuals with those who are not so perceived. However, physical integration generally involves buildings or at least 'settings', *i.e.* a physical setting which permits or facilitates social interaction. In the context of this discussion, the building will probably be one in or through which human services are mediated.

Physical integration (or segregation) of a service facility is determined primarily by four factors to be discussed below: its location (in the sense of distance from resources and social groupings); its physical context to other facilities and settings; access to it; and its size (in the sense of number of (deviant) persons grouped together in or by the building). This fourth point is sometimes also referred to as dispersal.

Location The center and emphasis of services generally should be at the community level where the persons are to be served, and the structure such that the (deviant) persons may remain in or be absorbed into the prevailing social, economic, educational, *etc.* systems. Unless it is distinctly desired as part of an appropriate human management model or rationale, as perhaps in the case of a retreat camp, physical isolation of settings is one of the conditions to be avoided.

Physical context The type of area in which the program is to be located should be consistent with the type of service to be provided, *e.g.* vocational services in industrial park areas, hostels in residential areas, *etc.* Services in upper lower-class neighborhoods of medium density population with a large array of resources (post office, stores, restaurants, libraries, churches, playgrounds, movies, *etc.*) will, in all likelihood be capable of absorbing deviant persons at a relatively high rate, while thinly-populated upper-class suburban areas beyond walking distance from community resources would probably be less suited.

Access It should be kept in mind that elements in addition to distance can determine access. Among these are availability and convenience of transportation means and routes, and other circumstances which can be highly specific.

Size or dispersal The normalization principle dictates here one of its major corollaries: every effort should be made not to congregate deviant persons in numbers larger than the surrounding (community) social systems can absorb and integrate. This principle implies that instead of single large facilities, a larger number of modestly-sized facilities usually permit greater normalizing dispersal within as well as between population centers, especially so in the larger communities. Dispersal is particularly important for the numerically most-needed programs, and especially for residential services.

Services should be dispersed across a region consistent with population patterns, and so located as to enable all clients to take full advantage of other existing community resources. Programs should be so developed as to break up, or prevent the establishment of, excessively large service facilities.

While the four elements of location, relationship, access, and size (dispersal) tend to be related to each other, there can also be some independence among them. For instance, a facility could be very close to other resources, and yet access to it may be very difficult to attain. Conversely, a physically distant facility might be close to several major means of access such as expressways, rail transportation, *etc.*

SOCIAL INTEGRATION

Integration can be facilitated (or inhibited) not only by physical but also by social circumstances. A service could conceivably be optimally integrated physically, and yet suffer from extensive social segregation. For instance, despite optimal location, such factors as agency policy, service structures, and/or social circumstances might still keep a deviant person out of the cultural mainstream, and segregated from normative and normalizing social intercourse. Thus, a person needs not only to be *in* but also *of* the community.

It would appear that once physical integration exists, social integration (or segregation) will be determined by at least four factors: program features affecting social interactions; the labels that are given to services and facilities; the labels and terms applied to the clients; and the way in which the service building is perceived.

Program features A few examples may suffice. Handicapped children should be integrated into generic developmental day care and, as much as possible, into regular classes. Vocational training need not always be conducted in special workshops but can often be carried into generic programs, as well as into the mainstream of business and industry itself. With special efforts, deviant individuals who are frequently provided with recreation in segregated fashion can often be enabled to participate in regular recreational activities in which they interact with other typical recreating citizens. And special support and training will enable many handicapped persons to utilize ordinary community transportation, rather than requiring special car pools, segregated buses, and other extraordinary means. The list of integrating opportunities is virtually endless – limited more by the ideology and the imagination of programmers than the extent or type of an individual's deviancy.

Labelling Social integration will also be affected by the way in which clients and their families, as well as the service locations and facilities involved, are named or labelled. Thus, the labelling of persons as 'retarded', 'patients', 'inmates', *etc.*; the name of a possible site; and the name of a possible facility should all be carefully considered so as to promote a role perception of the client that is nondeviant, or that at least minimizes the perceived deviancy.

Building perception In regard to the facility specifically, some thought should be given to the 'building perception', *i.e.* the way the physical facility is likely to be perceived by the public. The external appearance or context of a building, even if it is perfectly suitable in terms of internal arrangements, can exert a detrimental effect upon citizens' response to the persons associated with this building. For instance, a building that looks like a prison or that was recently used by disturbed individuals is apt to elicit associations not conducive to integration.

It should be kept in mind that the four factors specified above affect not only outside observers, but also those who work with the client who is being perceived.

Current integrative opportunities

Below, I will briefly discuss some program areas (especially education, work, and housing) in which the time appears to be propitious in North America for major normalizing restructuring of prevailing service patterns, via the process of integration. There probably are other areas, but the ones discussed here can serve as examples.

INTEGRATION IN EDUCATIONAL PROGRAMS

For a long time, the idea has prevailed that special education is and must be synonymous with segregated education. The realization is now growing that this need not be so. Indeed, we are finding, on the one hand, that segregation often brings with it a lowering rather than an improvement of standards; and on the other hand, that by the very nature of things, integrated education has certain normalizing features which can make it better than segregated education.

Educational integration, at this time, would affect primarily early childhood (so-called preschool) education, but also education in the traditional sphere, and in the rapidly expanding area of vocational education, all discussed below.

Integration in early childhood education In this area, particularly, we are used to thinking mostly in terms of day care centers, nurseries, kindergartens, *etc.* which either serve only the handicapped, or at best have special and segregated sections for them. And yet, it is probably on this very level that integration should be achieved most urgently, and can be most easily.

Early integration is relatively easy because: very young children are less perturbed by individual differences; early education programs tend to be more apt to have groups of mixed ages and sizes anyway; and such programs are oriented to more individualized handling than the regular schools are for older children. Among major benefits of early integration are the breaking down of social barriers and stereotypes, not only in our young future citizens, but even in our current fellow-citizens – their parents.

Already, one can see many early education programs which have included small numbers of handicapped children – although sometimes more by oversight than by design. In almost every instance of early integration that I have encountered, I have been impressed with the smoothness of the integration process, and the amount of progress made by the handicapped children involved. Particularly at this age level, normal peers seem to constitute non-threatening models from which the handicapped (especially the retarded) children learn much more than they typically do from their impaired peers.

Maximal integration in traditional education On this topic, so much has been said that only brief recapitulation is necessary. Most of the mildly impaired and retarded can function in regular grades if special additional services (*e.g.* resource rooms, resource teachers) are provided. This is also true of many severely handicapped children, such as the deaf or blind, and others who may have some very severe and rare handicaps (*e.g.* Mullins, 1971). Other severely impaired children, such as the severely retarded, can function in special classes that are integrated into regular schools, rather than in special classes grouped together and/or placed in separate wings or even separate schools. Secondary work-study programs, which often use only in-school or sheltered workshop assignments for their work training, need to emphasize assignment in business and industry instead.

Integration in vocational education Legislation as well as attitudinal changes are presently opening up new integrative vistas in vocational education. These opportunities need to be pursued vigorously. There exists now the option to do – within the mainstream of the rapidly expanding vocational education field – much of what was previously done in the specially-designated and stigma-attached field of rehabilitation, or on the side-tracks of secondary special education.

Concluding comments on integrated education It is both salutary and gratifying to note that in the future, integrated special education will become better, and easier to accomplish, as all education becomes special education, *i.e.* as we move more and more from lockstep teaching to individualization of the learning-teaching process. Vast improvements in the educational manpower structure have already taken place, and such improvements make for better and more individualized education. Other developments – almost certain to be even more significant – will be the increased availability of new and better educational aides, the routine use of computer-assisted and computer-managed instruction, and new administrative methods of structuring the educational process. As all education becomes special, grade levelling and grade grouping of children – as we now know it – will disappear, and integration will no longer present the problems it does today.

INDUSTRY-INTEGRATED WORK STATIONS

For many years, we have aspired to the establishment of more vocational service centers ('workshops') which would offer vocational evaluation, training, long-term employment, and possibly other vocation-related services, either to the handicapped in general, or to special handicapped groups. For instance, it was widely felt that the problems of the retarded were such as to require separate (segregated) work centers, and the need for workshop places for the retarded was sometimes estimated to be as high as 1.4 for every 1000 population (*e.g.* Goodwill Industries of America, 1961). The concept of 'integration' was used mostly to refer to integration of one handicapped group with other groups perceived as deviant, as in a generic (Goodwill-type) workshop.

Actually, from a normalization (though not always economic) viewpoint, there is little to be gained by favoring a generic (*i.e.* all-handicapped) over a specialty (*e.g.* all-retardation) workshop. In the generic center, a deviant person would still be grouped with others similarly perceived (*e.g.* the retarded, blind, deaf, physically impaired, emotionally disturbed, alcoholic). On the other hand, integration of a deviant worker or work trainee with typical workers in business and industry would constitute a major normalizing advance.

The time has come to establish the *functions* of the 'sheltered workshop' right in the work community, right within the confines of specific firms, right on the work floor. Service systems can rent floor space from factories, often for nominal sums. 'Segregated' work space can serve for initial placement of trainees or workers, with integration being restricted to space and functions associated with the time clock, the toilets, and the cafeteria and/or canteen area. After a period of transition, some handicapped workers can be integrated into the midst of the work floor. Many such workers eventually will achieve a normative level of production, and will become eligible to be hired by that firm or elsewhere in the job market.

Establishment of work stations in industry can reduce the need for special and segregated services considerably. For instance, as late as 1968, the plan for comprehensive mental retardation services in Douglas County (where Omaha, Nebraska, is located) called for five vocational service centers with a total of about 340 places (Menolascino, Clark & Wolfensberger, 1968). Today, the staff of this service system believes that with the establishment of a number of industrial work stations, one or two vocational service centers for the retarded within the county may suffice.

Industry-integrated work training and/or sheltered work is not new. It has been practised successfully – though only sporadically – in the past, both in North America and elsewhere. But now, the time has come to implement this option systematically and massively.

INTEGRATING RESIDENCES FOR SPECIAL-NEED GROUPS

Where possible, the utilization of the much-neglected options of adoptive, foster, and boarding placement for handicapped children (even the profoundly retarded) is most desirable. These various approaches have been extensively discussed in the recent literature. However, in addition to these opportunities, much community integration of the retarded, the emotionally disordered, *etc.* can be achieved by developing small group residences, such as home-like hostels and highly dispersed special apartments.

Even where community-integrated group residences are considered and established, the possibility is seldom considered that in addition to integrating the group residence into the community, integration can also be achieved *within* the residence itself (*e.g.* Colbert, 1969). Such internal integration can be brought about in a number of ways. For instance, two or three mature college students might share an apartment with two or three retarded persons who are working in competitive industry or in sheltered situations. A college might lease some rooms or a wing of a dormitory, to be used by retarded young adults on a temporary basis while they are under training in a vocational center. Hostels might serve both handicapped and homeless non-handicapped children, instead of only the handicapped. Public housing might be designed from the very beginning to accommodate both the impaired and the unimpaired (*e.g.* Klein & Abrams, 1971). Finally, there is little reason why many of the institutionalized aged cannot be placed into ordinary (but good) nursing homes.

The objection is sometimes heard that the handicapped do not want to live integratedly. Often, this is a defensive claim, advanced to avoid having to pursue such integration. A recent survey of 658 handicapped persons (Columbus & Fogel, 1971) certainly suggests that lack of opportunity is a larger factor than lack of desire.

MISCELLANEOUS AREAS READY FOR INTEGRATION

It is absurd to build expensive dental suites and surgical operating theaters specifically for the retarded or emotionally disturbed, as is done in so many institutions. Teeth and appendices can be excised just as readily in ordinary community hospitals and dental offices if a little care is taken in the planning and social interpretation of such procedures.

Today, we conduct special camps for the handicapped, reserve bowling alleys for occasions when the handicapped bowl by themselves, and reserve swimming pools on a similar basis. Other examples of segregation in recreation can readily be cited. Often, such segregation is practised not intentionally or from lack of alternatives, but from a neglect to pursue a strategy of integration consciously and systematically.

Instead of reserving an entire bowling alley or a block of adjacent lanes, why not reserve a few lanes dispersed among other lanes? Similarly, by going swimming in small groups, one need not reserve an entire pool. With a few extra counsellors, a modest number of handicapped persons can be integrated into regular camping activities. In Stockholm, there are about 25 social clubs for young people in which the membership is balanced evenly between the retarded and the non-retarded, and in which the retarded learn to acquire a vast range of normative skills and behaviors by imitating their non-retarded age peers.

Nowhere is integration more appropriate than in those atmospheres where the essence rather than the accidents of man's nature is emphasized, and where man is even interpreted as possessing similarities to God, *i.e.* in religious worship and instruction. Here, much integration can be accomplished by thoughtful planning. Of course, no community has enough churches to integrate the thousands of retarded or disordered who may be congregated in a nearby institution. In religion, as elsewhere, integration is only feasible if the persons who are perceived as deviant are dispersed.

CAUTIONS

Sometimes, integration is easier than we think, and sometimes harder. For instance, we thought we had achieved a great deal of integration in our first hostels for retarded adults in Omaha. Each hostel was ideally located in lower middle-class neighborhoods, near community resources and transportation routes. The residents took the public bus to the workshop, and went to ordinary neighborhood and community recreation sites and events. However, in the hostel, all residents were retarded; on the way to the workshop, they went together in groups, which had an isolating effect; at the workshop, the fellow-workers were retarded; going in small groups to recreation was, again, isolating; and the same was true for church. Thus, the residents still ate, worked, played, worshipped, and slept primarily in contact with other retarded persons. They were integrated physically, but not socially. Reflection on this phenomenon underlines the need to train the handicapped not to commute and recreate in groups; to set up one-to-one as well as group peer relationships with non-handicapped age peers; and to develop work settings where work can be sheltered, but where the workers immediately surrounding the handicapped person are not handicapped, *etc.*

Conclusion

Integration is one of the most significant corollaries of normalization, having vast programmatic and architectural implications. It is for this reason that it is given extensive and repeated treatment in several chapters of this book.

b

application of normalization principles to specific problem and service areas

6 additional architectural-environmental implications of the normalization principle

Human services are generally rendered inside of buildings, and these buildings often affect the way these services are or can be rendered, how these services are perceived by the public, how the public perceives the recipients of these services, and how the recipients perceive themselves. Thus, the design, location, and history of a building interact most intimately with the nature, quality, and direction of any service that may be associated with it. In this chapter, then, specific building-related issues not adequately covered in the preceding chapters will be discussed in the light of the normalization principle.

Among the factors that bear upon the resolution of architectural issues, there are at least three:

> certain local phenomena, circumstances, limitations, opportunities, *etc.* which may include terrain, availability of sites and building materials, local cost factors, manpower phenomena, and many others;
>
> mandates or limits imposed by codes, standards, and regulations, both local and national: especially prominent here are fire, health, and safety codes; usually, local codes parallel national ones, but may be even stricter: presumably, codes and regulations are based upon the needs of the users of a building, but frequently this is not so;
>
> problems which arise from
>
> > the special needs of the special persons who are the recipients of the services rendered in or via a building; and
> >
> > the way these persons may be perceived by the public.

This chapter, of course, is concerned primarily with the problems arising from this third source; in modern human management, it ultimately should control the other two much more than *vice versa.*

The meaning of a building

To begin with, we must recognize that buildings have many symbolic meanings, and many purposes other than or in addition to those that are overtly stated or even privately admitted. Often, a building has a much louder and more honest voice than the men who may talk to us about it and its purpose.

Samuel Gridley Howe was probably the most remarkable and foresighted figure in the American history of special education. In 1866, he gave the

Parts of this chapter have been adapted from an earlier publication (Wolfensberger, 1969b).

dedication address at the cornerstone-laying of a new institution for the blind in Batavia, New York. By that time, he had been instrumental in founding the early US institutions for both the blind and retarded, had been superintendent of the first such public institution for the retarded (in Massachusetts), and had already perceived and accurately defined most of the shortcomings under which residential institutions were to labor for the next 100 years. To capture fully the eloquence of Howe's statement on the language of architecture, several excerpted passages, pp. 13-16, from his 1866 dedication address follow.

'Language is of vast extent, and speech is only one of its powers. By speech and by print, men of our generation hold intercourse with each other. There are, moreover, some sorts of language by which the generations of men hold intercourse with other generations, and by which they converse across centuries and cycles of time. Among the various forms of language between generations, and between the ages, monuments hold a high place.

'As men and women unwittingly, and sometimes unwillingly, reveal their character and even their secret motives of action, by the sort of language which they use, so the generations unwittingly reveal the prevailing ideas of the men who lived in them, by the works which they leave behind them. Consider the Pyramids of Egypt, and read the speech which they utter. . . . What say the ten million cubic feet of solid masonry, enclosing two or three small chambers, whose entrances are so narrow that the enclosed sarcophagus must have been placed therein before the walls were built; and those entrances afterwards closed up by huge blocks of stone, too heavy to be moved by any common force? What does all this tell? What is the language of that generation, spoken by the tongues of the pyramids to this generation?

'It is, that the monarchs were absolute, selfish, cruel and short-sighted. That they built these vast monuments to preserve their fame from oblivion, and their bodies from disturbance. . . . The monuments tell us, moreover, that the people must have been ignorant, oppressed, and like 'dumb, driven cattle'.

'They tell us, that great multitudes of men and women were driven in from towns and villages, to toil and moil, and lift stones and carry sand for weeks and months; and when some had died and all were exhausted, then that fresh gangs were driven in to take their places.

'And so of smaller monuments, whether the triumphal arch, where the chained captive walks sadly behind the sculptured conquerors; or the storied column, with its winding procession of battles, assaults and sieges, leading up to the proud victor standing self-glorified on the top. And so of those which tell a better story – the aqueducts, the fountains, the bridges, the canals, the docks and the like.

'If we study the monuments which a generation built, and the kind of men in whose honor they raised statues, we may learn much of the character of the people themselves.

'You are assembled to lay the foundations of a monument which will speak to future generations; and although what you grave upon the cornerstone, and what you put within it, should never be seen, the monument itself will talk to future generations; and what will it tell them?

'It will disclose that the physical condition of the human race in this country was imperfect and unfavorable and that there were born to this generation, and expected to be born in the next, . . . children, numerous enough to form a persistent class. That children of this class were not only loved and cherished by their parents and kindred, but also cared for by the public. That there was no Mount Taygetus[2] here, on which to expose them, with other infirm folk, to perish or be devoured, but asylums into which they were gathered and nurtured.

'It will prove that the social and political union which here leagued three million people into one powerful State, was formed and maintained not only for defense against enemies, for common commercial interest, for great enterprises, for social prosperity and enjoyment, nor yet for mental culture and high civilization of the many, but also for the protection and care of the weak and infirm. That the State of New York, which could dig out a navigable river clear across her broad land, which had just armed and sent forth three hundred thousand sturdy soldiers to serve the common country and the cause of humanity, that this great State, while holding on in her high career of material prosperity, and providing schools for all the children, took thought also, that not even the . . . little ones should be neglected.

'In such language will be the building, those foundation-stones you this day lay, speak to many generations in coming time.

'But, while thus noting with pleasure and even excusable pride, the humane impulses which prompt and which will carry forward the work, pardon me if I utter a word of warning.

'Good intentions, and kind impulses, do not necessarily lead to wise and truly humane measure.

'Nowhere is wisdom more necessary than in the guidance of charitable impulses. Meaning well is only half our duty; thinking right is the other and equally important half.'

A later superintendent from Massachusetts offered an equally relevant insight.

'This history of the development of the human race has been most enduringly written in its architecture. A study of the architecture of a people reveals their dominant thoughts and ideals. The caves of the cave-dweller suggest man's early struggle for existence against wild beasts; the tents of the ancient shepherds the nomadic traits of these people in their moving from place to place in search of food for their flocks. The religious fervor of the middle ages is unmistakably recorded in the cathedral monuments of Europe. The creative and commercial ideals of nations are accurately recorded in their factories, warehouses, docks, highways, and office buildings, and their warlike instincts are well gauged by their forts, armories, battleships, tanks and aeroplanes; their educational interests by their schools and higher seats of learning; their interest in the sick and handicapped are clearly recorded in their hospitals and eleemosynary institutions' (Wallace, 1924, p. 256).

Human management buildings, like other buildings, can project many meanings. Certain of these meanings are of particular relevance to our discussion. At least three such relevant meanings can be readily recognized in human management facilities: the building as a monument, as a public relations medium, and as a medium of service. Each will be discussed briefly.

[2] The mountain upon which the Spartans abandoned infirm or unwanted infants.

THE BUILDING AS A MONUMENT

Buildings are often erected, consciously or unconsciously, as monuments. In human management facilities, this is especially likely to be true of administration and medical treatment units. The monument may be to a governor, minister, prime minister, *etc.*; a famous man; a foundation donor, or donor dynasty; or an administrator or professional who may want to achieve identity or 'immortality' through this monument-building. Common examples of the latter are the aged superintendent or administrator who wants to make one last, only, or major contribution before he retires or dies.

While such aspirations often result in genuine benefits to mankind, they can also pervert the consciously verbalized or officially defined purpose of the building. For example, in order to fulfill its function as a monument, the building may be erected in a locality not consistent with normalizing and optimal program development; available funds may have been so plentiful as to result in a building that is either larger than optimal or overequipped; limitations of funds may result in a building so small as to require wasteful duplications and adjustment later; the ambitions of the initiator may require a free-standing building where an additional wing or floor on existing buildings would have been preferable; or the concepts which the initiator imposes upon the building plans may force future human services into undesirable and hard-to-remedy patterns.

Examples of the latter are donations of facilities such as swimming halls, medical buildings, churches or institutions. The existence of such facilities often makes it very difficult later to establish a pattern of increased and integrating use of the community for recreation, medical services, and church attendance. Similarly, an expensive new service building designed to serve large numbers of residents can become a great obstacle to reduction of an institution to a smaller size consistent with normalizing dispersal.

'Let us remember that our purpose is not to build costly monuments, at the expense of the taxpayer, to architects, legislators and governors or indeed to ourselves, . . .' (Kirkbride, 1916, p. 256).

THE BUILDING AS A PUBLIC RELATIONS MEDIUM

A building, or an entire facility, can become a medium of public relations. While such a medium may produce desirable and beneficial results in the long run, the public relations function may also be irrelevant and even detrimental to the welfare of client-users. A number of examples follow.

The building may function as an advertisement for the architect. There are many instances of widely acclaimed buildings which had serious functional shortcomings.

Innovations in design may become means of aggrandizement or advancement to staff or administrators. Real benefits of novel designs may be blown up beyond all proportion. Other widely-hailed design innovations may later be recognized as gigantic and foreseeable errors. For example, one institution for the retarded in the late 1950's erected a new showcase nursery in which the infants' cribs had solid, visually attractive, and expensive marble sides, and wire mesh fronts. Among other things, this obviously could lead to injuries, especially to children with seizures. Soon after construction, the cribs had to be rebuilt at great expense. This was hailed as another dynamic innovation rather than as rectification of a predictable blunder.

A building may be a public relations tool for a governmental or political body. The building may be designed to win votes or good will, to gain power by providing employment opportunities and/or patronage, *etc*. Again, such buildings may do more harm than good. Erection of large institutions in isolated areas has often been prompted by such public relations, rather than service, considerations.

THE BUILDING AS A MEDIUM OF SERVICE

A building may truly be intended to be primarily a medium of human service; however, this intent by itself does not ensure that the actual service rendered will be appropriate in type and quality. Many human service buildings fail to offer either.

The focus of convenience of a building

Before we can move on to other matters, it is important to recognize that a building also can tell us much about the question for whose convenience it was designed. Social norms demand that when a human service building of some sort is constructed, we must pretend and proclaim that the building is designed for the convenience of the prospective client-users. In reality, the building may be designed to serve the convenience of the builder or architect. If buildings are erected with public funds, the convenience of the community can easily become a primary consideration. If the prospective client-users belong to a deviant subgroup that requires special management, then the building may be designed for the convenience of the 'manager' rather than the 'managed' client-user.

THE CONVENIENCE OF THE ARCHITECT

Some buildings are designed for the convenience of the architectural agent. Such buildings may have required the least imagination, planning, and work from the architect or engineer, while perhaps resulting in the largest profit to him. Many ill-designed, ill-constructed buildings and building complexes bespeak an utter disregard for the prospective client-user. This is especially true of residential buildings. However, the building as a monument to the architect, though perhaps well-designed for external beauty and effect, may also fall into the 'convenience of the architect' category, if client-user welfare is neglected.

THE CONVENIENCE OF THE COMMUNITY

The location of a large proportion of institutions has been determined by economic considerations. Institutions were often placed in areas where jobs were needed, and site selection became a very political matter. In many instances, institutions were located by the accident of land donations by job-hungry communities. Locations of this nature were not only ill-advised as far as the client-users were concerned, but often also inconvenient to their families. Furthermore, they resulted in professional and scientific isolation of the staff.

To locate any human service agency with the needs of the server rather than the served in mind is analogous to requiring people to eat in order to provide employment to cooks.

THE CONVENIENCE OF THE STAFF

Many buildings, when entered, leave little doubt that staff convenience was paramount in the designer's mind. Characteristic elements may include the following.

'Segregated' staff lounges to which caretakers withdraw for meals, coffee, rest, *etc.*

Air conditioning for staff, but not for client-users.

Caretaker stations which provide maximal visual control over client-user areas, while minimizing staff involvement; the glass-enclosed nursing station is a classical example.

Services such as classrooms, beauty shops, barber shops, and therapy areas that are located inside of residential buildings, saving staff the effort of dressing residents, escorting them to other buildings, or arranging for them to leave the grounds.

THE CONVENIENCE OF THE CLIENT-USER

It is not always possible to design a human service building only with the convenience of the intended client-users in mind. Staff are also human, and cost is a justifiable element of importance. However, when all is said and done, surely the client-user should be the most important consumer of the building; otherwise it is a matter of eating to support cooks. The building should reflect this client-centeredness.

Architectural implications of certain role perceptions of the client-users of buildings

Having reviewed the symbolic meanings and the focusses of convenience of buildings, we can now analyze a given human management environment in terms of what it says about its client-users.

In the chapter on 'The concept of deviancy in human management', we reviewed eight major social roles into which deviant individuals have frequently been cast. These were the roles of the deviant individual as subhuman, a menace, an object of dread, a diseased organism, an object of ridicule, an object of pity, an eternal child, and a holy innocent. Some of these role perceptions have highly specific and clear-cut implications as to the location, design, and operation of the building in which persons so perceived might be served, *i.e.* to the human management model that prevails. This is especially true of residential facilities such as hospitals, prisons, institutions, hostels, boarding schools, camps, *etc.* Elsewhere (Wolfensberger, 1969b), I have attempted to demonstrate how some of the above role perceptions have shaped the entire history of the management of the retarded in United States society since about 1850, including the evolution of the prevailing institution system.

Within a facility, role performance of client-users is influenced not only by the interpersonal stimuli to which these clients might be exposed on the part of the personnel, the public, and each other, but also by the opportunities and demands of the physical environment. For instance, the environment can very clearly express the expectation that a client-user will act out violently, is not supposed to assume any responsibility for his actions, *etc.* By the same token, the physical environment may impose a demand for controlled and highly socialized behavior which is clearly communicated to the prospective client-user. Thus, the building can usually tell us whether it is appropriate for the mission as stated by a human interpreter.

In order to illustrate the effect one's perception of a deviant group has upon one's approach to the location, design, and operation of facilities – and especially residential facilities – let us examine some typical implications of those deviancy role perceptions which, by their nature or through historical events, have found clear-cut architectural-environmental expression. Specifically, this will involve the following role perceptions: subhuman, menace, sick, pity, burden of charity, object of ridicule, eternal child, and holy innocent. The burden of charity perception, previously discussed in conjunction with the pity perception, will be treated separately because of its distinct implications here.

THE DEVIANT INDIVIDUAL AS SUBHUMAN

The atmosphere and design of a building can very clearly express an expectancy that the client-user will behave in a subhuman fashion, no matter how vociferously the staff may deny adherence to dehumanizing attitudes. Such expectancies are implicit in any of virtually hundreds of dehumanizing practices encountered in institutions and enumerated by Vail (1967). Some of the more common expectancies will be listed and briefly elucidated here.

The perception of the deviant individual as an animal usually implies an expectation that he behave in a primitive, uncontrolled fashion. Thus, the environment may be designed to be 'abuse-resistant', which implies measures such as:

- walls, floors, *etc.* made of material that is indestructible;
- unbreakable, shatterproof, or wire-enmeshed glass in windows and partitions;
- installation of the sturdiest, most heavy-duty furniture and equipment;
- minimization of moving parts;
- high ceilings, and/or recessed or specially shielded or laminated light fixtures, to minimize damage from thrown objects;
- extensive soundproofing to muffle the (animal?) sounds which client-users are expected to emit; such soundproofing may even be installed in areas designed for clients quite capable of considerable adaptive behavior;
- television sets protected with wire screens, recessed into protective housing, and/or placed above reach.

A presumably subhuman individual is usually perceived as being potentially assaultive, destructive, and lacking in self-direction and constructive purpose; this necessitates restricting his movements, both to control him more easily, and to protect either the human from the subhuman or one subhuman from another. This characteristically leads to a number of measures:

locked areas and living units;

locked areas within locked areas; in the case of children or the physically handicapped, door knobs may be set high and above reach, or complicated release mechanisms may be installed: this permits staff to perceive the facility as 'open' even though it is *de facto* locked;

doors made from heavy material; bedroom doors that can be locked only from the outside, and often open outward, rather than inward as in most homes or offices;

barred windows; more sophisticated but equally effective are reinforced window screens, or so-called security screening, which are incredibly strong but which are not readily identified by an observer as being extraordinary; and windows so small or subdivided that a person cannot slip through them;

outdoor activity areas enclosed by either high walls; or high, strong fences; or by both;

> (Often, these areas are quite small (and therefore easier to control), and not sufficiently large (or equipped) for adequate exercise. Such small areas again permit the staff to engage in conscience-salving self-deception. I once inquired of a nurse whether the semi-naked retarded children in her locked living unit were ever dressed and taken outdoors. She assured me that the children were dressed and taken for outdoor walks every day. The woman was not hypocritical; she was only rephrasing reality so that she could live with it. The reality was that these moderately to severely retarded ambulatory children did not leave the building confines for months, perhaps years, at a time. 'Dressing' meant putting on more clothes than merely underpants and diapers; and 'going for a walk outdoors' meant being turned loose in large groups with minimal supervision in a small outdoor enclave enclosed by high brick walls on two sides and high wire fences on the other two sides.)

a fence or wall surrounding entire buildings or even an entire facility complex;

segregation of the sexes: such segregation may assume absurd proportions (and more clearly reveal the underlying ideology) when practised with infants and children, or with the aged.

A typical programmatic, rather than architectural, expression of the subhuman view surrounds the 'feeding' of clients. To this day, food and drink may be served in unbreakable tins reminiscent of prison riot films of the 1930's. Knives or forks may be prohibited; in turn, this necessitates the serving of special foods, such as finger foods or soft homogenized pap that can be spooned. The latter situation is particularly apt to be encountered in institutions for the retarded.

Since the perceived subhuman is not believed to be capable of making meaningful choices, he is permitted minimal control over his environment. This typically implies the following:

switches controlling the lights in client areas such as 'dayrooms', sleeping quarters, toilets, *etc.* are made inaccessible to clients by placement in staff control areas such as nursing stations, by placement in locked cabinets, or by keying (*i.e.* a key is required to turn a light on or off);

water temperature in lavatories, showers, *etc.* is controlled by thermostats: the water flow may be controlled by caretakers by means of removable and portable handles;

temperature, humidity, and air movement controls are locked or keyed; radiators are locked, recessed, or screened;

residents may be forbidden to carry matches or lighters.

In residences, perception of the deviant individual as an animal implies an emphasis on efficient 'keeping' of clients, rather than on interaction with caretaker personnel. Consequently, the environment is designed for efficient supervision.

Caretakers work behind isolating (protective?) partitions which keep out residents and perhaps even their sounds, but permit extensive or complete visual monitoring; today, this might even include closed circuit television. A stated rationale here may be that isolation makes for greater efficiency in certain caretaker tasks such as visual supervision, record keeping, and administration of medications.

Residents sleep in large dormitories, with no or only low partitions between beds. Lights may burn even at night to facilitate supervision. If bedrooms exist, they may lack doors.

Caretakers engage excessively in tasks minimizing chances for interaction. For example, supervisory staff may be isolated in a separate building. Living units on a campus may be widely dispersed and removed so that ready interaction between staff and residents is difficult to achieve; in one such widely dispersed residential complex I have known, low staff interaction with residents was partially due to the fact that walking was both time-consuming and often not feasible due to bad weather, and driving was inconvenient because of lack of parking space near the residential units. Even staff meetings and in-service training activities can become an unconscious legitimization of noninteraction with residents.

There is much emphasis on use of drugs (chemical straight jackets?), rather than human interaction, to control and shape behavior.

The placement of residential centers far from population centers and towns can, in some cases, be a correlate of a 'keeping' or 'controlling' desire.

Subhumans are perceived to 'live like animals', *i.e.* to soil themselves and their habitat. This results in design of an environment that can be cleaned easily, frequently, efficiently, and on a massive scale:

walls and floors may be made of a material that is virtually impossible to 'deface', *i.e.* scratch, soil, stain, *etc.* and that can be hosed down (as in a zoo); there may be drains in the floors of living areas;

beds or bed stalls may be designed to be picked up and immersed in cleaning solutions in their entirety by means of cranes;

bathing facilities may be designed for efficient cleaning of large numbers of clients by small numbers of caretakers; there may be slabs, hoses, and mass showers, rather than installations conducive to self-conducted cleansing or the learning thereof.

Typically, subhumans are either not expected to learn or develop appreciably, or their growth potential is seen as so small as to be irrelevant, since it will never lead to complete 'humanization'. In other words, the state of subhumanity is perceived as being essentially permanent, or at least to last as long as the person resides in the building. In consequence, the environment may be designed to maintain a client's level of functioning at best, but not necessarily to provide opportunities for further growth and development.

Animals have no rights; it follows that deviant individuals perceived to lack humanity are also perceived to lack certain rights. Among these are the rights to privacy, property, communication, and individuality.

The right to privacy Bedrooms often lack doors, not to mention that the bedrooms themselves may be lacking. Where doors exist, they almost always have window panes or so-called 'Judas-windows' (complete with wire-enmeshed glass or peepholes). Private visiting space may be nonexisting. Toilets and showers may lack partitions, curtains, or doors. There may be physical continuity between space for living, elimination, and bathing. I have seen modern intensive treatment buildings for the disordered in which the showers were openly (and visibly) accessible from the 'day room'; and I have visited new institutional buildings for the retarded that had huge 'picture windows' between the 'day room' and the toilet.

The right to property Residents may have few or no possessions. Often they have little or no space to store possessions, or lack ready access to such space and control over it. Residents may be denied the privilege of locking up their possessions, carrying the key, and using it without restrictions. They may be denied personalized clothing, and residents of the same size (sometimes of various sizes) may share the same supply of clothes. All of these points have implications to architectural design, especially regarding space allocations and selection of built-in furniture. Residents may be seen as not entitled to payment for their work, or to carry actual currency even if they do own money. 'Poverty in a mental hospital is no less dehumanizing than in a slum . . .' (Bartlett, 1967, p. 92).

The right to communicate freely There may be censorship of incoming and outgoing mail, although some forms of censorship may not be perceived as constituting censorship. Telephone usage may be severely restricted. Visiting is often restricted for several weeks after admission.

The right to individuality As described so well by Vail (1967), clients are regimented and managed in groups, even where individual management might be feasible. For example, residents are mass-showered even where individual showering is feasible; residents may even be mass-toileted, which accounts for the fact that some living units for the retarded have many more toilet seats than would be needed for, say, an equivalent-sized college dormitory.

The assumption that deviant individuals lack esthetic sensibilities is a subtle but important corollary of the subhuman view. This corollary results in the creation of unattractive environments, since funds spent on beauty are seen as wasted. The drab, monotonous design and furnishing of many human management residences (sometimes in contrast to staff living quarters) is usually a testimony to this view. Rarely does one see furniture that is both comfortable and attractive in lines and color in institutions for the disordered and retarded, and even yet more rarely is there culturally-typical (at least middle-class) zoning of living space so that the furniture reflects the mood and function of different living areas in an attractive fashion. The degree to which a deviant client can appreciate beauty is really only one of two important issues involved here. The second important issue is that observers' (*e.g.* the public's or employees') attitudes are shaped by the context in which deviant individuals are presented to them. For example, to deprive a deviant person's environment of beauty is likely to predispose an observer to view him as subhuman.

Caretakers sometimes claim that drabness is due to lack of funds, but this is often untrue because much beauty can be provided at little or no cost. In my own institutional work, I recall trying to mount attractive pictures on walls of several retarded children's living units that had a severely deprived atmosphere. There was no support for this project from the institutional power echelons; nursing and housekeeping services objected to the 'defacing' of the walls; and the pictures which actually got put up were pulled down (by personnel) within days. It is quite possible that a human manager's compulsion to preserve a drab environment is motivated by his malignant need to maintain a difference between him and those he perceives as so different as to be no longer human.

A 1964 prospectus, written by the staff of an institution, contained the following instructions to an architect regarding the design of a new residence building for 'trainable' retarded adults and young adults: 'All interior wall surfaces shall be of a smooth material, and without wall projections other than those specifically stated. All thermostats should be protected with a guard to avoid tampering. Window areas shall be kept consistent with patient needs. Excessive window areas are not desirable. Consideration should be given to using shatterproof glass in patient areas. Door louvers in patient areas should be made of a steel material to withstand patient abuse. Mechanical and electrical equipment and controls throughout the building shall either be tamperproof or located outside the patient areas. Maximum water temperatures for bath and lavatories must be automatically controlled to eliminate the possibility of scalding. Switches in large patient areas shall be located on the outside of the rooms. A cubicle measuring 24" x 12" x 12" should be provided for each patient.'

While such instructions are not conclusive evidence that the instructors held a 'subhuman' view of the retarded, such instructions certainly appear to be consistent with such a view. Today, individuals of the type for whom this environment was designed live in small homelike community hostels, generally in a lower middle-class atmosphere, but not one too much different from the homes of most readers of these lines.

THE DEVIANT INDIVIDUAL AS A MENACE

A building environment based upon the menace perception has much in common with the subhuman model. Certain features, such as segregation from the community, as well as segregation of the sexes, are likely to be accentuated. Since the menace model may ascribe a certain willfulness and evil intent to the deviant individual (in marked contrast to the medical (disease) model), an element of vindictiveness and persecution may enter into his management, and some of the protective features even inherent in the subhuman model may be omitted. Otherwise, building features of both models have much in common.

THE DEVIANT INDIVIDUAL AS AN OBJECT OF PITY

One human management model is based upon the image of the deviant individual as an object of pity. This 'pity image' will tend to be expressed in a paternalistic environment which shelters the client against injury and risk, and which will make few demands for growth, development, and personal responsibility. Both these features may imply infantilization, and lack of risks and environmental demands such as stairs, sharp edges, hot water, hot heaters, and electric outlets, as discussed previously.

While the pity model has some features in common with the disease and subhuman models, there are important differentiating features. The benevolent version of the pity model strives to bestow 'happiness' upon the person, often by emphasizing recreational programs, religious nurture, and activity for its own sake. This, in turn, is likely to result in allocation of generous space and facilities for music, arts, crafts, parties, picnics, and worship (*e.g.* a chapel on the grounds or in the building).

It is no coincidence that the pity model shares features with the subhuman model: it has many similarities to Vail's (1967) definition of the 'man-as-trivium' (*i.e.* a human being who is not taken seriously or given importance) mode of dehumanization.

THE DEVIANT INDIVIDUAL AS SICK

One of the role perceptions of great impact upon environmental design and operation is that of the deviant individual as sick. When the client is viewed as a diseased organism, his service facilities are structured on the (medical) hospital or clinic model. This model tends to have the following characteristics.

> The facility is administered by a medical hierarchy: the chief administrative officer (*e.g.* the superintendent) is a physician, with a hierarchy of other physicians under him, and a hierarchy of nurses under them. Concern about authority lines tends to result in a tightly controlled perpendicular administrative structure rather than a flexible subunitized one.
>
> The facility is identified or even labelled, at least in part, as a clinic or hospital, *e.g.* a public institution for the disordered may be called a hospital (*e.g.* 'state hopistal'); a common name for public institutions for the retarded is 'hospital and school'.
>
> Living units are referred to as nursing units or wards.
>
> Residents are referred to as patients, and their condition is identified as being a 'disease' that requires a 'diagnosis' and 'prognosis'.
>
> Resident care is referred to as nursing care.
>
> Case records are referred to as charts.

Hospital routines prevail. For example, residential admission procedures may require days or weeks of 'observation' and residence in an 'infirmary' or similar unit prior to 'diagnosis' and to assignment to regular living quarters. Daily routines may resemble hospital routines in regard to rising, body inspections, sick call, charting, *etc.*; indeed, the daily schedule may revolve around the hinge of medication schedules. Dispensing of medication, in turn, may become the model for intake of all nourishment, and for other 'treatments' as well. Such other treatments, even if 'administered' in the form of education, may be referred to as 'dosages'. Usually, there is at least moderate emphasis upon convenience of 'nursing care'.

Concern with professional symbols and status differentiation often encountered in a hospital atmosphere may be expressed by features such as presence of hierarchical staff lounges, showers, and private toilets. There may be separate vending machines (and areas) for staff and 'patients'. Staff and client-users may eat in separate areas, requiring separate dining and sometimes even cooking facilities. Caretaker personnel may wear uniforms. Even professional and semiprofessional personnel may wear uniforms, coats of different colors, badges, name plates with academic degrees listed, and similar insignia of their role and rank.

Architecturally, a prominent place is given to the space (locus) from which human management is 'dispensed'. Often, this means a 'nurses station' is given a central and perhaps large space. This space is often so designed as to afford maximal surveillance of the client area with minimal engagement therewith, reflecting both the assumption that 'nursing manpower' is very limited, and that 'nursing personnel' must perform many functions (*e.g.* charting) which require seclusion from the 'patient'. This seclusion may be perceived necessary either because of the confidentiality of the activity to be performed, or because of the tranquil setting it requires. Status concerns may also have a bearing on the design (spaciousness, sumptuousness, or exclusivity) of the human management locus.

Nonmedical personnel may emulate the medical role, *e.g.* social workers and psychologists may wear white coats or jackets, and prestigious professionals may be referred to as 'doctor' even if they do not possess a doctorate degree.

Human management programs are referred to as 'treatments' or 'therapy', *e.g.* recreation and work assignments may become recreational and industrial therapy. Even ordinary schooling may become educational therapy.

Physicians, whether qualified or not, make decisions about nonmedical matters, *e.g.* clients' rights and privileges; visits; work assignments; discipline; inclusion in school, training, and other programs. Even if these decisions are made by nonmedical personnel because of temporary or permanent lack of physician manpower, this may be perceived as delegation of medical authority, and as such is interpreted as undesirable and transient.

Departments with the greatest affinity to medicine are given priority in program development, *e.g.* dentistry, orthopedics, and physical therapy may receive stronger support than behavior shaping, education, *etc.*

Physical and medical techniques are more likely to be used in managing the behavior of clients than other techniques. Thus, disturbed clients are more likely to be physically restricted or settled with drugs than to be counselled or trained; persons with seizures may be placed on anticonvulsant medication with little thought given to environmental manipulation of seizure-precipitating events, or to educating the person to develop preventive behavior habits.

There exists an excessive abhorrence of any chance or likelihood of injury to the client. On the one hand, this is exemplified by *lack* of stairs and steps, sharp objects and corners, conventional electrical outlets, and access to conventional hot water faucets. On the other hand, it is exemplified by the *presence* of special features such as ramps, screening of radiators, and screened stairways (if any).

A disease conceptualization of deviancy tends to result in a management dilemma. On the one hand, such a conceptualization often results in pursuit of treatment that is hoped to result in cure; on the other hand, unless a 'cure' is seen as likely, the management atmosphere is often permeated with hopelessness and treatment nihilism. In other words, the disease conceptualization tends to be correlated with inappropriate extremes of management attitudes. This appears to be one reason why the quality of service for individuals with conditions that have been defined as 'chronic' is often very poor in those residential facilities which operate on a medical model.

THE DEVIANT INDIVIDUAL AS A BURDEN OF CHARITY

Charity clients are seen as entitled to food and shelter, but not to anything interpretable as luxuries, frills, and extras. A residence based on this model will be austere and lacking in privacy, individuality, and opportunities to have personal possessions. The resident is expected to be grateful, and to work as much as possible for his 'keep'. An example of a Victorian 'burden of charity' view is found in the following quotation taken from the Massachusetts report at the 1890 National Conference on Charities and Correction. 'As to the State schools, it recognizes the value only of such teaching, mental or manual, as shall develop the boy or girl and tend toward an honest and respectable life outside the institution.' 'It disapproves of extravagant or luxurious appointments in institutions, as foreign to the spirit of true charity. The inevitable weakening of character by life in institutions, the arrest of development, must be prevented, if possible, by some hardships and privations, such as these boys and girls would be sure to encounter in their own homes or those to which they would be sent' (Reports from States, 1890, p. 329).

Again, much of the physical environment implied by this model will be similar to that of the subhuman model; however, there are certain differentiating architectural and program implications. In a residence built on the charity model, there will be less emphasis upon segregation from the rest of society. There will be a grim and unimaginative emphasis upon eventual self-sufficiency, and while there will be little stress upon environmental enrichment as a means of fostering development, education and training in traditional occupational skills may be strongly valued.

THE DEVIANT INDIVIDUAL AS AN OBJECT OF RIDICULE

The role of the object of ridicule generally does not have architectural implications. But there have been exceptions.

Montezuma, the last of the Aztec kings, kept an extensive zoo in Mexico City which made considerable impression upon the Spanish chroniclers who accompanied the conquistador Cortes. It is noteworthy that in the same building in which the beasts were kept and displayed, he also 'kept' men and women who were crippled, deformed, dwarfed, hunch-backed, and albinos. At times (apparently especially at meal time), some of these persons played the role of jesters, amusing Montezuma and his court, who might feed them left-overs from his table (de Fuentes, 1963, p. 40; Diaz Del Castillo, 1956, p. 210).

Similarly, at the Royal Bethlehem Hospital in London, popularly known as 'Bedlam', the curious public in the 1700's would pay their coins to go and stare and laugh at the writhing and screaming of the chained inmates. 'Up to so late a date as 1770, this famous hospital was still regarded as the raree show of the city, superior even, in the attractions it offered the pleasure-seeker, to a bull baiting or a dog fight. No more diverting entertainment could be devised by the average citizen for guests visiting him from the country than to take them, for a hearty laugh, to Bedlam, to see the madmen cursing, raving, and fighting. There was to be had on show St. Paul or Julius Caesar chained to the wall, or Semiramis or Joan of Arc ironed to the floor, while the general throng, left more at liberty, were guarded by brutal keepers, ready on the slightest provocation to knock them senseless with heavy clubs. The annual fees derived from this public entertainment amounted to several hundred pounds. No one seems to have felt any pity for the poor wretches. The abyss which opened up between them and ordinary humanity was too deep and wide for any sympathetic imagination to span. A madhouse was a menagerie, nothing more; and it was as legitimate to look through the bars at one class of wild beasts as at another' (Tiffany, 1891, p. 61).

THE DEVIANT INDIVIDUAL AS AN ETERNAL CHILD

The role of the 'eternal child' 'who never grows' plays only a minor part in shaping environmental models, but occasionally it can be discerned quite clearly, especially in the field of mental retardation. Here, adults are frequently placed into environments more suitable for children. In fact, adults may be housed with children, and subjected to the same forms of address, rules, and general management. A very common phenomenon is the decoration of the environment with children's pictures and themes.

THE DEVIANT INDIVIDUAL AS A HOLY INNOCENT

The holy innocent perception is frequently fused with the eternal child model, but has probably had a stronger influence on residential service ideology than is realized – albeit in a subtle way. The holy innocent was generally considered to be harmless, or was indulged much like a child. His presence may even have been valued, as it made the beholder feel a bit closer to heaven and to God. Thus, this role perception tended to inhibit the development of specially-designated residential facilities, as the innocent were gladly accepted and integrated into the family, and into the heart of the community. A contemporary example is the Hutterite communities in the United States and Canada, studied by Eaton and Weil (1955). In these communities, not one retarded person had been institutionalized on a long-term basis; instead, they were accepted and integrated into the community life.

While the holy innocent perception has generally inhibited the development of residential placement, it did not prevent it altogether. If residential placement was achieved, however, it tended to be of a very special kind. It might involve placement of persons in a childlike role in godly homes; as menial workers in religious communities such as monasteries; or as workers in nursing homes or hospitals run by religious orders. One variant of this practice exists in the Belgian town of Geel where, since the Middle Ages, thousands of the mentally handicapped have been boarded in an atmosphere of sheltered benevolence in ordinary homes, and have the liberty of the city. The presence of a religious shrine to St. Dymphna – long believed to be the patron saint of the mentally afflicted – gave rise to this practice.

CONCLUDING COMMENTS ON ROLE PERCEPTIONS

Other roles are conceivable, but historically have not had much of a bearing upon residential models. The models are presented above in order to sharpen the ability of an observer to assess, perceive, and interpret human management buildings and programs. Obviously, some environmental features can be associated with more than one model (*e.g.* the subhuman and menace, or subhuman and ridicule). On the other hand, the persistent emphasis on, or systematic combination of, numerous features can very readily reveal the model that is dominant. An interesting and worthwhile project would be to develop a quantitative instrument which assigns weights to different features, and which permits one to draw a profile of a building's implied role perceptions. The highest peak or peaks on this profile would then define both the nature and extent of the models and role perceptions implied.

Generally, the models sketched above constitute models that are to be avoided, but this does not necessarily tell us what models to construct. The remainder of this chapter will address itself to some alternative architectural implications of the normalization principle. Some repetition of points brought out in other chapters will be unavoidable, but the repeated elements will be presented in contexts that bring out new implications.

The implications of the normalization principle, with special reference to internal design of buildings

The foregoing discussion should have made abundantly clear that in order to define an architectural environmental challenge in human management, it is necessary to stipulate clearly the human management model to which one wishes to adhere. By a human management model I mean a consistent set of assumptions and/or facts about the persons to be served, the persons serving them, and the means and measures by which the servers serve the served.

The model considered axiomatic to the discussion here assumes that even though recipients of human services may be viewed as deviant by large segments of the public, they are not animals, vegetables, or objects; and they are neither angels nor devils, but human beings. As human beings, they are also viewed as citizens in the socio-political-constitutional sense, and therefore endowed with certain socio-political-constitutional rights; as individuals; and as capable of growth and adaptation, even if profoundly handicapped. As adaptive human beings, they are viewed as deserving of challenges for growth, *even if these challenges imply a measure of risk and discomfort.*

Actually, any of the three role perceptions of the deviant individual as either a fully-human being, an adaptive person, or a citizen would be quite sufficient as a base for successful and enlightened management. If the individual were perceived as a fully-human being, we would want to share with him all those privileges and attributes we ordinarily perceive as common to humanity. If we perceived him as an ever-adapting organism, we would provide him with those societal services which would come close to developing and maintaining his full potential. And if we perceived him as a citizen in the legal sense, we would accord him those rights which, in the spirit as well as the letter of our constitutions and laws, are his, but which have been denied him to a significant degree.

O. R. Lindsley once said (1964) that our society is willing to spend money on the design of environments that maintain life, but not on those that maintain dignified behavior. Of all management models, the normalizing-developmental one is probably most likely to provide the framework for a cathedral of human dignity.

Normalization principles require that individuation, growth challenges, respect for rights, *etc.* must be recognized in and supported by a delicate interplay between programs and physical environments. Buildings are part of the physical environment, and they appear to have at least six characteristics of particular importance to the implementation of the principle of normalization: location, physical context, size, access, appearance, and internal design.

Immediately, the reader will recognize that several of these characteristics, *e.g.* location, context, access, and size, are the same elements that have already been discussed in the chapter on 'Societal integration as a corollary of normalization' as determining the degree of physical integration. There is no point in repeating this material here, except to underline that physical integration must be one of the major goals in the design of the vast majority of human service buildings.

The appearance of the building also has been discussed in the above chapter, under the topic of social integration, and in connection with the concept of 'building perception'. It should be noted, however, that while appearance has objective dimensions, perception is more subjective; it is nonetheless real and must be considered. Internal design, then, remains to be discussed in some detail.

Staffing, program structure, social atmosphere, and other variables can all affect the quality of a human management service. One additional variable of relevance here is the internal physical environmental design of the setting.

As mentioned earlier, this design can elicit and support many maladaptive behaviors, or it can enhance and support physical as well as personal growth, competence, privacy, comfort, esthetic experience, and individuality.

Perhaps most immediately, desirable features would include adequate warmth and ventilation; a cheerful, colorful decor; and absence of noxious odors and excessive or constant noise. Where counselling is rendered, there should be privacy. Privacy can also be expressed in toilet design, and in living arrangements of residential buildings. Furniture and waiting areas should be comfortable, and there should be decorations such as curtains, pictures, sculptures, plants, *etc.*

A very important part of the normalization principle is to enable persons to experience the rhythm of the day and the year, the change in weather and in seasons. This is particularly critical for children, and particularly for children who have difficulty in experiencing and/or learning, such as children with sensory, emotional, and intellectual impairments. In consequence, modern buildings which reduce contact with the outdoors (as by small or unopenable windows), or even eliminate it (by having no windows) may, despite their increasingly normative presence, violate certain normalization principles. This, by the way, provides another example of an instance where one of two normative means may be much better than the other.

Where a building is intended for client-users who need to learn or experience nature's rhythms, there should thus be provisions such as large (perhaps low) windows, windows which are openable, and outdoor spaces which are readily accessible and which permit the 'capture' of seasonal changes, *i.e.* via plants and grasses, rain spouts, *etc.*

Absence of desirable features may sometimes be dictated by circumstances, but they should not merely be the result of lack of ideological commitment. Rarely is their absence due to lack of funds, because ingenuity and commitment can offset lack of funds in most instances. Also, it is often much more expensive to design non-normalizing buildings than normalizing ones.

Normalization, and especially beautification, of the interior of human management buildings is one of the areas in which managers have much to learn from the Scandinavians. In fact, many of us must first experience Scandinavian settings before we fully understand this issue.

The building codes versus the normalization principle

This chapter is addressed primarily to those architectural challenges of the normalization principle that arise from the needs of clients, or the way clients are likely to be perceived by others. I will only comment briefly here on other architectural challenges which are artifacts of such circumstances as building codes.

There is an urgent need to revise building and related codes so as to make them consistent with the principle of normalization while, at the same time, maintaining appropriate standards. At present, these codes do not distinguish adequately between different groups of residents, and they impose extreme hospital- and institution-like standards on too many small community group residences for the handicapped, and even on nonhandicapped persons living in groups in agency contexts. It is remarkable that such an agency-operated group home can be subjected to institutional codes, even though the home may contain no more residents than are found in many large families with small children who may be less capable than handicapped adults. However, revision of codes may take years, and may be only partially successful. Therefore, it is of greatest importance that where new construction is essential, we design buildings which meet the various codes while still maintaining both normative appearance and atmosphere.

I am pleased to be able to report that an Omaha architect is currently evolving designs for hostels for the severely and profoundly retarded that contain some ingenious features.

Even the strictest codes will be met, and will be met in such a fashion that an unskilled observer would not be apt to distinguish the hostel from ordinary community housing.

The hostels will be designed on a modular plan so that elements such as live-in staff suites, single and double bedrooms, bathroom units, and kitchen, dining, and social area units can be adjoined to each other in a number of ways. The building can be on two levels (basement and main floor), or on three. By incorporating only a few bedroom modules, the hostel can be very small, and by adding such modules, it can be increased in size. To accommodate building lots of different sizes, modules can be added on in different configurations. Also, there will be a number of options for window placement and roof lines, depending upon the neighborhood and the other options that have been incorporated.

Hostels incorporating various options and modules can be built in large numbers across a town, and even the country, without being monotonous in design.

The hostels are so designed that with minor modifications, they can be used for either children or adults, and possibly even for more specialized purposes such as habit shaping and perhaps even crisis assistance units.

Since the basic plans for each module and for a number of module combinations will be available, local builders will only need to incur minor expenses in modifying the plans for any one particular hostel.

Since new service needs and concepts may render the hostel obsolete in a relatively short time, the design will be such as to permit easy conversion of the building into several self-contained apartments for ordinary community use.

The cost of such a hostel will be much higher than that of ordinary community housing, but will still be below that of institutional space.

Here, truly, we have an instance where a major architectural challenge of the normalization principle is being met creatively and effectively.

Conclusion

Cruickshank and Quay (1970) observe that when one considers how many billions of dollars go into the construction of human management buildings, it is remarkable how little research has been done to support the many premises and assertions that determine environmental design. Some such avenues of research are then suggested by these authors.

However, as long as it is still a matter of ideologies being pitted against ideologies – some perhaps with trans-empirical implications – I submit that the humanness of a previously devalued person will not be full acknowledged, or his normalization attained, until significant numbers of valued members of society are willing to share their lives with him. This sharing must take place in both residential as well as nonresidential contexts. Thus, a crucial test of the adequacy of the design of a building is whether most valued members of society would gladly use it in the fashion and for the length of time the designers or human managers had planned to have it used by devalued (deviant) persons.

This principle holds particularly true for residential settings. Such settings must be designed to promote, elicit, and support integrated living by handicapped and nonhandicapped, deviant and nondeviant persons. This can be achieved by thoughtful location, access, physical context, size, appearance, and internal design of a building. More and more, we must design such residences in a fashion which does not make it a burden for ordinary citizens to live there. To the contrary; if anything, such buildings should be attractive enough to make life-sharing a pleasure. Nowhere in environmental design is the principle of 'doing unto others as we would have them do unto us' more poignant than in housing for long-term residential service, as for the aged, retarded, chronically ill, *etc.* Every designer and human manager should be prepared to live himself in the housing he would impose upon others.

As in the past, we undoubtedly will continue to schedule conferences about architectural problems in this field and that, such as mental health, rehabilitation, mental retardation, *etc.* Frankly, I am getting a bit tired of one recurring feature of these conferences: the endless presentation of ground plans, drawings, and pictures of planned or completed facilities which are primarily monuments to the architect. In the residential area, I am especially tired of attempts at improving institution buildings without, however, getting away from the institution model.

I am also somewhat tired of the explicit or at least frequently implicit argument that the architect is merely someone else's tool, and if this someone else specifies the construction of an institution or an institutional building, the architect cannot do much about it except to make the building as little institutional as possible. While I concede some validity to the argument, I reject the buildings thus designed; and no matter how cleverly they may be designed, I am compelled to call them what they are: institutions!

Too many architects today are still prepared to accept missions which the young generation will probably judge to be immoral. Is it still moral to design new skyscrapers for downtown Manhattan? Was it moral for the architects who recently went on trial in Austria to design 'better' concentration camps during the Hitler regime? With all that we know today, is it still moral to design 'better institutions'? Architecture cannot escape its social responsibilities, and there comes a point where an architect must refuse a lucrative commission to build what should remain unbuilt – just as there comes the moment of morality to the soldier at My Lai, to the industrialist who pollutes his community, or the teacher or psychologist who labels a child into exile from the mainstream of his peers.

Architects also need to internalize that their professional behavior will be influenced by their unconscious personal attitudes toward handicap. Architects, like other citizens, carry with them certain stereotypes and role expectancies in regard to deviant groups. For instance, I have found again and again that when architects are told that retarded individuals will reside in a building they are to design, with the best will in the world, they simply seem unable to keep themselves from designing dehumanizing features into the building. Thus, these features are not always the fault of the programmer who furnishes specifications to the designer.

Nowhere was this driven home to me more forcefully than in Sweden where I visited a series of apartments which were used as hostels for the retarded – even the severely retarded. These apartments were very normalizingly dispersed within apartment houses inhabited by ordinary citizens, but a curious phenomenon could be discerned: the most normalizing atmosphere existed in those apartments which had been rented in culturally typical fashion from the owners. However, in a few instances during the design of the apartment houses, certain apartments had been designated beforehand as specifically for the retarded, and lo and behold, upon being so designated, certain heavy-duty features had been added immediately in the design phase and installed during construction. These heavy-duty features gave these apartments an unmistakable non-normative and even slightly dehumanizing and institutional flavor.

Thus, there exists among architects what could be called a noble myth. This myth is that those who commission a building should give complete specifications and descriptions regarding the intended function and use of the building, and then cease at playing architect, leaving the rest up to him who, if these specifications and descriptions are well done, will then design an environment consistent with these. This is simply not true, and architects should deeply introspect upon their deep-seated attitudes toward the persons for whose use they set out to design a building.

The time has come to adopt the normalization principle in environmental design of human services, and to apply our pragmatic ingenuity to implementing it. Particularly in the design of residential buildings, this requires that the architect confront and accept three challenges:

to desist from the design of traditional institutions and institution buildings – as one would from the design of concentration camps – even if it means loss of business and income;

to apply his talents to the design of small but highly specialized residential buildings;

to accept the fact that residential buildings for most deviant individuals require no unique design features, and the modification of existing community housing is often preferable to new construction.

And this last implication asks of architects that they practise a self-disciplined ascetic abstinence from the urge to build.

7 additional implications of the normalization principle to residential services

Many human management systems have residential components. In some fields, these are minor, *e.g.* in lower education; in others, they are major. Particularly, there are four areas of human management in which residential services are a major component – if not in terms of the proportion of individuals served, then at least in terms of their sheer numbers nationwide, and in terms of the significance of residential services in the tradition of the area. These four areas are mental retardation, mental disorder, geriatrics, and correction. However, it is amazing how similar residential service problems are, regardless what group of clients is involved: the retarded, disordered, blind, deaf, delinquent and legal offender, aged, orphaned, homeless, *etc.* It is also surprising how powerfully the normalization principle can apply to residential services in any area, underlining once more both the universality as well as parsimony of the principle.

Other chapters in this book have touched upon normalization implications to residential services, especially so the preceding one. However, some points relevant to residential services bear repeating or elaborating, and additional ones need to be presented.

Residential services can be subdivided into individual and group placements. Individual placements would include adoptive, foster, or boarding homes for one person, or at most a very few. Group placements would include boarding schools, most jails, institutions, hospitals, *etc.* One general difference between individual and group placements is that the individual placement involves a home that has the primary purpose of housing one or more additional persons who are adults and who do not provide domiciliary services to others as a primary pursuit. In contrast, most group residences exist primarily for persons under human management. Those who work there and perhaps live there do so primarily in order to serve the group residents. This is a statement one could not even make about a mother of ten children, even if her home were large.

Individual placement into culturally normative homes presents some normalization challenges, and some of these will be covered later in this chapter. However, far greater challenges, almost inseparable from architectural ones, are presented by group settings which will be covered first. Too often, group residences are institutions, and we need to distinguish clearly in our minds between institutional and other group residences.

Normalization implications to group residences

WHAT IS AN INSTITUTION?

Both the 5,000-place institution as well as the 5-place hostel are residential services; what makes us apt to label one as an institution, and the other one as something else? Obviously, definitions are arbitrary. We are free to define institutions in such a way as to reflect the typical citizen's opinion of what an institution is; we can impose an arbitrary definition that is more scientific or technical; or we can combine elements of both approaches.

Goffman (1961) rendered a brilliant analysis of what he called 'total institutions', which he defined ultimately in terms of the barriers which exist between them and the outside, especially the barriers to departure. I suspect that even without awareness of this definition, most citizens today would similarly define an institution largely on the basis of features that emphasize separateness from the community mainstream. Yet, as attractive and useful as this definition has proven to be, I feel that such a barrier is merely a common rather than essential feature of an establishment that might be defined as a total institution, and that appears to typify so many of our traditional human management residential services. It seems to me that ultimately, an even more useful definition would be based on the *deindividualization* that permeates the atmosphere of a residential community. More of the features commonly associated with an institution appear to be corollaries of deindividualization than of separation from the 'outside'. Such corollary features include the following.

An environment that aims at a low common denominator among its residents – for instance, because a few or occasional residents may be unstable or destructive, *all* residents may be subjected to an environment that appears necessary and/or appropriate to the few or occasional ones. We are all familiar with the locked doors, heavy-duty construction and furnishings, and socio-behavioral surveillance, structure, and restrictions imposed on a group for the sake of a few of its members. That deindividualization can be a more significant feature than confinement is apparent from the fact that physical restraints, even when used, are usually quite unnecessary and often even ineffective in maintaining separateness and confinement.

Congregation of persons into residential groups larger than those typically found in the community – in North American society, the most typical grouping residing together in the community is the nuclear family, which rarely exceeds six to eight members.

Reduced autonomy of residents, and increased regimentation, generally including mass movement and mass action on the part of the residents, and regimentation of their routine – again, very extensive regimentation can be attained even when there is no physical and even little social barrier to departure. The voluntary deindividualization, regimentation, and separateness of monasteries is a good example.

Ordinary citizens sleep, study, work and play in separate contexts and settings, and in each setting, they tend to interact with a different group of fellow citizens; in institutions, these settings tend to be physically fixed under one roof or on one contiguous campus, and sometimes programmatically unified in terms of environmental and supervisory structures. Also, the same group of persons tends to interact with each other in each such setting, resulting in an inward directedness. Again, these features greatly reduce opportunities for individualization.

Thus, it is necessary to distinguish between institutions and other group residences. In the subsequent discussion, the term institution refers to a deindividualizing residence in which persons are congregated in numbers distinctly larger than might be found in a large family; in which they are highly regimented; in which the physical or social environment aims at a low common denominator; and in which all or most of the transactions of daily life are carried out under one roof, on one campus, or in a largely segregated fashion.

FIVE MAJOR IMPLICATIONS OF NORMALIZATION

Aside from innumerable fine points of programming, the normalization principle suggests or even dictates that group residential services have certain gross characteristics, among these being integration, smallness, separation of the domiciliary function, specialization, and continuity, all to be discussed below.

Integration

In many provinces, states, and countries, a large percentage of residential services is provided either in relatively isolated areas, and/or far away from major population centers. Obviously, such a situation violates the principle of integration which demands that residential services, like all services, generally need to be community-integrated and dispersed so that residents will intermingle with typical citizens in typical activities.

The above needs to be considered carefully in deciding upon the nature and location of a residential unit or complex. For example, residential units generally should be within easy walking distance to major community services such as shopping centers, public libraries, post offices, churches, schools, and recreational resources such as movie houses, bowling alleys, *etc.* They should also be accessible to various transportation alternatives to facilitate entry in and contact from the community, and they should have ample parking. Unfortunately, many current residential services, even if located very favorably, still encourage segregation rather than integration of residents.

So much has been said about integration in this book that little needs to be added, except to reemphasize the profound implications which the integration goal has on the type of client grouping, and on group and facility size.

Smallness

A problem of concern in many countries of the world is the typically large size of residential facilities in many fields, especially in mental health and mental retardation. In this regard, the following points are now increasingly accepted (*e.g.* Fairweather, Sanders, Maynard, Cressler, & Bleck, 1969; Ullmann, 1967).

Large size does not necessarily result in economy of operation.
Sometimes, large size results in uneconomical operations.
Large facilities result in inward rather than outward direction of both resident and staff socialization, and therefore they foster insulation from society, 'institutionalization' of attitudes and behavior, and often result in longer duration of stay of residents.
If it is desired to create an atmosphere of continuity between a residential service and the local community, then a residential facility should have no more residents than the surrounding community can readily

'absorb' in terms of recreation, transportation, shopping, socialization, and tolerance of perceived deviancy.
The management of large numbers of individuals, especially if these are of reduced behavioral adequacy, is difficult and perhaps impossible without regimentation and loss of individuality; thus, in large facilities, dehumanizing management tends to develop.

Even by itself, the goal of integration almost automatically implies that services, and especially residential services, be small, since neighborhoods and communities cannot absorb large numbers of deviant individuals. Exempted to some degree from this principle are certain generic residential services whose clients are not perceived as deviant, *e.g.* general hospitals, and residential services which, by their nature, cannot or must not aspire to integration, *e.g.* detentive facilities.

Separation of the domiciliary function

A major residential corollary of normalization is the separation of the domiciliary function. In the mainstream of society, a residence is merely a domicile, and formal education, work, medical treatment, and many recreational, social, and friendship transactions are carried out elsewhere in places such as schools, training centers, offices, clinics, churches, playgrounds, bowling alleys, bars. *etc.* Since these locations are typically separate from the residence, the same separation should be attained for human management residences, if at all possible. Thus, when we offer residence, treatment, education, work, religious nurture, and recreation all on one campus (as we commonly do in residential treatment and service centers), or even under one roof, we often denormalize. In fact, when we also offer virtually total medical care as well as a significant amount of restriction, then we have fused the roles of community, home, school, hospital, and jail into one single entity, and too often, the lowest common denominator – usually the jail elements – prevails and sets the tone for everything else.[1]

There appear to be only two types of residential services in which the domiciliary function must be fused with other types of management. One is for individuals who require major medical services (perhaps actual maintenance of life) which necessitates that typical non-domiciliary transactions be brought to or near the bed. The second is for individuals requiring detention. Even among groups whose behavior may be very significantly impaired, *e.g.* the mentally retarded and disordered, there are very, very few persons who would fall into either of these two categories.

Separation of the domiciliary function is one more expression of the management concept that human services should not provide more support and shelter than a client needs. Too often, when a person needs support or shelter in one sphere of his functioning, human management services have supported and sheltered several or all. Again, institutional practices are an

[1] Just as these lines were being written, I experienced a poignant reminder of the almost invariably unconscious mixing of models that should not be mixed unless unavoidable. I received an advertisement from a residential center which defines its goals as 'medical, educational and residential care of handicapped infants and children'. The word 'detentive' was missing – but the picture showed a brown brick building in what appeared to be a rustic setting, with a sturdy fence around it.

example: because a person may have needed a sheltered domicile, he was not only given such domicile in the institution, but was usually also separated from his ordinary school or work, his recreation, worship, and many other societal functions. In the institutions, these functions were often denied; provided in a sheltered, controlled, and segregated fashion; or conducted in societally non-normative fashion.

To offer all services under one roof is convenient – although not always as economical as claimed. However, this convenience should be sacrificed if a useful principle is at stake. We should ask ourselves at all times whether any service provided in conjunction with a residential service would not be provided in a more normalizing fashion by drawing on extra-residential and community resources, thereby increasing the resident's integration and habilitation.

Thus, among other things, the normalization principle demands that as few central services as possible be provided as part of a residential unit. In other words, professional offices, educational space, treatment areas, *etc.* generally should not be in the same building that serves as a home. Residents should go to regular community resources and services, such as kindergarten, school, other education, shopping, most medical and professional services, movies, bowling, swimming, and most other recreation. Only to the degree to which no alternatives are possible should such services be provided even on the same 'campus'.

Specialization

Specialization of the residential management model has many normalizing features. For instance, it helps in the separation of the domiciliary function. Also, it separates age groups to some degree; in society, we rarely find individuals of divergent age groups living in one home, except within nuclear families. Indeed, the nuclear family of today rarely even spans more than two generations. In order to individualize management, specialization also separates those groups that require entirely different types of environment. For instance, it imposes the medical model only upon those who definitely need it. Further specialization reduces other undesirable types of heterogeneity of client groups. To repeat an earlier example, in many of our institutions, those who need detention or a high degree of structure and supervision are housed in the same living units as those who do not, but because of the needs of the less advanced residents, *all* residents are subjected to a high degree of structure, supervision, and perhaps even detention. This is merely one instance of the type of protective overkill that is common in many deindividualized heterogeneous groupings. Finally, in many areas, specialization is the only way to operate small facilities economically.

As desirable as the specialized model is, managers should remain alert to the need to integrate residences as much as possible into the community. In fact, there is no reason why many residences cannot be specialized as well as integrated. Despite my objections to the term 'halfway house', and its commonly associated conceptualization of a very limited range of residential options, the book by Raush and Raush (1968) on this topic documents a number of systematic attempts to integrate clients with other citizens in residential settings.

Further details on the residential specialization concept are available in

Dunn (1969), Dybwad (1969), Governor's Citizens' Committee (1968a, 1968b), Menolascino, Clark & Wolfensberger (1968, 1970) and Wolfensberger (1969c). I will return to this topic in the next chapter.

Continuity

In order to make a specialized system of small domiciliary units work, there must be continuity between different types of residences, and between domiciliary and nondomiciliary functions. In some instances, this will imply an administrative continuity which assures program continuity.

A continuum of living facilities will provide many more options than exist now, so that individuals can be moved along the continuum of supervision as needed, and in either direction. Thus, an adult client may start out under intensive observation and in individual and group management at a central facility. He might then be moved to a hostel from which he attends a community sheltered workshop half-day, spending the other half-day in an intensive personal management program at the central treatment facility or some other meeting point. Eventually, he may move to another hostel which he leaves every day for competitive employment, until he becomes fully independent in both work and residence.

Conversely, an adult with minor impairment may come to live at a minimal supervision hostel while continuing to hold his regular job. If he becomes more impaired, he may be moved to a more intensively supervised hostel or even a central treatment center.

The vast majority of chronically and severely impaired persons who make up the long-term residents of our public institutions are ideal candidates for sheltered community hostel living. Some require the services of hostels that function much like nursing homes. Others could be infinitely better served than they are now by living in hostels from which they (if they are adult) attend all-day sheltered work. The waste of human resources practised by our institutions is socially inexcusable.

Too often, the literature refers to halfway houses, or even 'the' halfway house, as covering the gap between institutional and independent living. Such a conceptualization is clearly inadequate. It will take different types of intermediate residences in different fields, but in some fields (mental retardation, mental health), more than a dozen types each are needed.

Concluding statement regarding the five major implications

It can be seen that the above corollaries of normalization are intimately interrelated. Integration requires smallness, which implies both dispersal and specialization. All three require a separation of the domiciliary function. Specialization further implies a continuity of options, also required by individualization of management which, additionally, needs continuity of movement and function between different types of services.

SPECIAL CONSIDERATIONS FOR DIFFERENT AGE GROUPS

Residential services for children

Residential services to children generally should be clearly separated from services to adults. To serve both children and adults in the same facility is increasingly recognized as having many drawbacks. It does not parallel most accepted patterns of analogous services to individuals not defined as deviant in society; and to treat deviant children and adults in the same context provides the children with inappropriate adult models and, on the other hand, diminishes the dignity of the adult resident by casting him into a role not sufficiently demarcated from a childlike one.

If at all possible, residential treatment services for children should be based on small home-like units of four to eight children each. Normalization principles would strongly suggest that these units function in typical family homes or apartments. A 'ward' is a poor substitute for normality. A compromise for some circumstances is a complex of cottage-like units, or use of multiple apartments in an apartment house.

Also, if at all possible, most children's residences should have live-in houseparents as the primary contact personnel, rather than a series of persons, often with limited job stability, rotating through three shifts a day and various weekend and relief shifts. If a houseparent system is not possible, a compromise between the houseparent and the traditional shift system should be established, as exemplified in *Project Re-Ed* for disordered children (*e.g.* Bower, Lourie, Strother, & Sutherland, 1969; see also the entire March 1969 issue of *Mind over Matter*). Traditional, essentially hospital-derived, shift systems are extremely unsatisfactory for children, although some type of shift system can work very well if it is superimposed upon a houseparent or at least a 'day parent' base.

As much as possible, children in special residence should be enabled to mingle with children of the community, and should go to school in the community – even if this means attendance of community special education programs. Too often, and without compelling reason, children's residences have adopted the traditional residential school model, which contributes strongly not only to segregation but often also to the formation of a subculture milieu. Again too often, this subculture is not one that prepares the child for optimal adaptation to the main culture later in his life. The devastating effects of all kinds of segregation should be apparent to everyone by now.

Residential services for adults

The major invariant activity and mission of adults in our culture is work. This is likely to remain the case in the future, despite some predictions to the contrary. Therefore, adults in special residential management should be enabled to engage, as much as possible, in work that is adult in nature and connotation, is productive and remunerative, and adheres to a schedule that can be considered normative.

There is generally a good reason why an adult is under special residential management. Usually, the reason is some kind of impairment, in a broad sense. Thus, the work activities of residents should and must be graded along a continuum. Some residents will hold a full-time competitive job in the community, and the residence should provide only a minimum of needed support, shelter, and/or companionship. Other residents may work competitively in the community but only part-time, and receive other treatments the rest of the time. Yet others may work under sheltered rather than competitive conditions, full or part-time, and some may not work at all – hopefully only temporarily. However, it is fully to be expected that sufficient sheltered workshops and other sheltered employment opportunities will be developed, beyond any extent most people can currently imagine.

Particularly in large population centers, sheltered living residences could be graded rather easily from those with minimal supervision to those with more intensive supervision. These gradations must be much more extensive than the frequently encountered institution/halfway house/independence trichotomy. An extreme type of minimal supervision might involve dispersed apartments in which residents live like ordinary apartment dwellers except for certain central services such as occasional walk-in supervision. In family-type residences, there would be much more intensive interaction between residents, and more socialization.

Some sheltered living units could be located so that residents would have access to training workshops, vocational training centers, and similar agencies. Thus, young adults would have an opportunity to attend such services to receive vocational preparation, and the atmosphere in this particular type of hostel could be structured so as to have a strong vocationally-centered emphasis. However, easy access does not mean adjacent locations, which often violates normalization principles.

In a normalizing program scheme, there is need not only for meaningful work, but also for recreation, each to be conducted at appropriate places and times. I doubt, however, whether there will be as much, or even any, use of occupational and recreational therapy as generally conceptualized and practised at present. Both of these 'therapies' are frequently dehumanizing: occupational therapy by substituting largely meaningless activity for meaningful work, and recreational therapy by substituting childlike play for adult work. In both cases, the client is engaged in activities which are only valued by society if they are performed in certain contexts. Persons performing these activities in un-normal contexts, at un-normal times, and in un-normal amounts, are doing things which are either not generally valued, or which may even be devalued, and consequently the persons so engaged are not valued either.

Residential services for the aged

Old age is a great leveller. Persons who once were disordered, retarded, or well-adjusted and highly contributive citizens all may be equally disabled in their old age, and require similar types of care.

Increasingly, there is sentiment (which happens to be consistent with normalization principles) that the aged person who was deviant in his younger days and who needs a special residential service in his old age should be integrated into homes for the aged which are located in or near his home community.

Great progress has been made in placing aged residents of our public mental institutions into nursing homes. However, considerable further progress is indicated. I suspect that a much larger number of institution residents could be placed into such homes, and that they could be placed closer to their home communities than in the past. However, a great deal of work remains to be done to assure adequate and humane programming in services for the aged throughout North America. At present, the situation is a national disgrace, and in many instances we have emptied large isolated human warehouses only to create small isolated ones. Above all, we need citizen advocacy, integrative safeguards, and accountability systems, such as discussed in the last part of this book, in order to assure that normalization will be achieved for the aged as much as for other groups.

In the chapter on 'Implications in the field of mental health', more will be said about the normalizing effect of work upon adults. At this point, it will only be mentioned that many adults in special residence, by the very fact that their functioning has been reduced so as to require this type of service, are in financial straits. This presents a problem, since poverty in our culture can be destructive of one's self-concept, demoralizing, and dehumanizing. This implies that managers should be very concerned with the owning and earning capacity and behavior of clients. As much as possible, clients should be provided with ownership, not only of their own possessions, but also of their life space in the residence. Furthermore, work generally should be provided not only as a normal adult activity, but in many cases also as a means of transmitting money to the residents. At the very least, the resident generally should have, and control in adult fashion, enough money (not scrip or credit!) to be able both to indulge his minor whims (refreshments, snacks, smokes, small gifts) as well as feel the satisfaction of earning. In Danish and Swedish human management services, clients who are impecunious or cannot earn money are provided generous allowances so as to increase dignity, assist in realistic social training, and foster independent choice behavior.

Considerations for all age groups

Residential services should be alert to measures which simultaneously are behavior-normalizing as well as image-normalizing. A normal rhythm of the day means that most people should not have to rise significantly earlier than typical fellow citizens, or have to go to bed at odd hours. It also means that they should be able to eat their meals at normal hours; few citizens eat their supper at 4:30 or 5:00 p.m., as do clients in many of our residential facilities. Not only can abnormal schedules foster abnormal habits, but they also can make a person appear odd.

Most people go on a vacation trip once a year, which breaks up the routine of life. Few things are as monotonous as long-term residence in a special facility. It is thus normalizing to provide annual trips for such residents to the usual tourist and vacation places. In Scandinavia, even the severely retarded are taken on vacation trips – often abroad. Although cost may be a problem, at least some arrangements can be made, even if it is only a trip of two to three days' duration to a vacation home owned by the facility.

Normalization also dictates that a person should be as independent, free to move about, and empowered to make meaningful choices as are typical citizens of comparable age in the community. As much as possible, his wishes and desires should carry the same weight as they would in ordinary circumstances outside of a human management context. This means that unless it is essential, a person should not be submitted to a 'mortification' process upon attaining client status or 'patienthood' (*e.g.* stripped of clothes and possessions, locked up), and that generally he should not be prevented by even nonphysical (*e.g.* social and psychological) means from exercising normal freedom of movement. Furthermore, a person generally should have reasonable control over his physical environment, including freedom to turn lights on and off, to open and close windows, to regulate the temperature in his room, and to decide whether he wants another person to enter or not. A nurse or other manager sweeping abruptly into a resident's room commits an act of denormalization. No person should be deprived of his physical freedom or his freedom of choice because he is housed in a facility with other people who appear incapable of exercising these freedoms.

Residences serving a deviant group must meet at least the same standards as other comparable facilities for nondeviant persons. Imposition of either unnecessarily stringent or indefensibly lax standards would be equally inappropriate; and yet, this is exactly the present situation in North America: community hostels have irrationally stringent health, welfare, and fire regulations imposed upon them, while institutional housing conditions are permitted to descend to the snake-pit level.

It is conceivable that many individuals in various community residential services, especially those for children, will return to their families over the weekend. Thus, for many individuals, residence would consist mostly of five day a week residence. Particularly in areas of high population concentration, it will be possible to specialize residential hostels to such a degree that some units could be placed entirely on a five day a week basis, closing down over the weekend and thereby effecting considerable savings.

Normalization implications to individual placements

In the past, inability to continue normative community functioning independently or within one's family was almost automatically equated with group placement. In most fields, group placement meant institutional placement; in some fields, especially mental retardation, it also meant life-long institutional residence. Often, the life-long total service of the institution was imposed as a solution to a short-term situational family crisis, and while it was difficult to gain admittance to an institution, it was often even more difficult to gain release from it.

Yet, there is an alternative not only to institutional but even to group placement that can not only have powerful normalizing features, but that is often also cheaper. And that is individual placement. Three major forms of individual placement suggest themselves: family boarding, foster, and adoptive placement.

Family boarding placements

The term 'family boarding' can have multiple meanings, some of them equivalent to fostering. I propose to use the term to refer to temporary individual (rather than group) placement of a *child* who has a home which continues to function as the primary and legal residence; and any individual placement of an *adult* into a family setting where he receives room and board, regardless of the likely duration of the arrangement. (Note that this definition excludes the typical community group boarding home.) In both cases, it is assumed that the family providing boarding receives remuneration, and it is obvious that family boarding can be for adults what fostering is for children. The term 'family care' is sometimes used to refer to both foster- and boarding-type arrangements.

Family boarding placements for impaired individuals, especially for adults, were common prior to the advent of institutions. During the alarmist period (*circa* 1890-1925), family boarding was ruled out by attitudes; between 1925 and the recent past, it was ruled out by ignorance and the lack of legal and fiscal frameworks. Today, it is ruled out only by rigidity in our service structures.

Yet, family boarding placement is a creative and very normalizing alternative to the hostel placement of an adult who is in vocational training or in sheltered or competitive work. In rural areas, it is of particular promise regardless of the boarder's age. For instance, in sparsely populated areas, certain services may not be feasible on the local level even in the service system of tomorrow. Day programs in clinics, special classes, workshops, *etc.* may have to be located in regional population centers which are beyond commuting distance of much of the surrounding population. One solution, of course, is the establishment of hostels, including some that operate only five days a week. Such hostels, for example, have been established in many communities in rural Nebraska, and serve severely retarded children who live with houseparents and who attend special public school classes during the day.

However, even more creative than five-day hostels is the provision of five-day boarding arrangements. Again, such boarding situations with individual families have been set up for retarded persons in numerous Nebraska towns. This arrangement has several advantages: a more individualized relationship; a more normalizing atmosphere; economy; reduction of the hostel staffing problem; and a solution to the problems of finding buildings that meet the stringent fire codes for group living.

Once the advantages of boarding arrangements have been recognized, and once resistance to novel service options has been overcome, this provision probably will play a role in reducing demand not only for institutional but also for other types of group residences, at least in some service areas, and especially for children.

Foster and adoptive placements

Foster and adoptive placements constitute additional types of individual residential placement. Again, such placements were often ruled out because of peculiar attitudes and practices that prevailed and largely still prevail in the relevant agencies. Such attitudes often demanded that prospective substitute parents be paragons of parenthood – better even than the typical parent in the community – motivated only by idealism and unmoved by material incentives. Thus, it came about that foster homes were ridiculously underpaid, and that numerous children were placed into no-love high-cost institutions rather than into medium-love medium-cost foster homes, even though a workable legal-fiscal and even administrative structure existed.

In addition, an almost universal agency dogma was that citizens would not accept a handicapped child for foster or adoptive placement. Today, we can only wonder to what degree this agency dogma was an agency myth. What we do know is that prophecies can be self-fulfilling. Obviously, an agency worker who 'knows' that handicapped children cannot be placed is not going to seek such placements and support them with vigor and inspiration, if at all; and he is therefore not likely to make many successful placements, if any. Franklin's (1969a, 1969b, 1969c) documentation of successful adoptive placements of children with even severe medical conditions is highly revealing.

In Omaha (Nebraska), the College of Medicine wanted to find foster homes for seven mongoloid infants who had been transferred from the institution to a ward at the College for a research project. With the agencies emitting the customary pessimism, a young nurse and a social work student were told to go out and do the job. These two people employed unorthodox means such as a mobilization of the news media, and within two months, every child had a foster home. Three years later, six children were still placed; had they been free for adoption, several would have been adopted by their foster parents.

In and near one small town in Nebraska, 36 retarded children live in foster homes. Many of these children are severely retarded, and would otherwise be in institutions. One middle class family fostered a profoundly retarded child who is almost deaf, not toilet-trained, and wears braces on both legs from hip to toe. The placement was mediated by a child-development teacher – not a child placement agency. Had the child been free for adoption, she would have been adopted by the foster parents. Similar reports of the feasibility of foster-placements are beginning to trickle in from other sources.

The realization is slowly growing that removing a handicapped or high-problem child from his home need not be tantamount to institutional or even group placement. Foster, adoptive, and family boarding placements are virtually unmined resources of potentially major proportion. However, to actualize these resources, it may be necessary to provide more vigorous programmatic, and more realistic financial, backup than has been customary in the past. Rearing a handicapped child can be very expensive. Thus, the fees for fostering a high-problem child should be increased substantially – at the same time as certain standards for foster homes are raised and others lowered. Adoption of such children – and perhaps other children as well – should be subsidized (*e.g.* Wheeler, 1969) to facilitate this powerful option. To both foster and adoptive parents, a continuum of services should be made available. Particularly, specific child development guidance and assistance should be offered in order to assist the parent surrogates in surmounting the crises of the family life cycle.

One day these things will be done, and not only institutions but even other group homes will be prevented from admitting any child that can be fostered or adopted. Such developments will not only reduce the demand for group residential places rather directly, but also indirectly: parents who now seek and obtain institutional placement inappropriately will refrain from seeking such placement if they know that another family, probably in the same town, will accept their child as their own.

Concluding statement on individual placement

Obviously, foster and adoptive placements are only normative for children – not for adults. Family boarding can be highly appropriate for adults under select conditions; they are more appropriate for young adults and the aged than for mature adults; and they are more appropriate for young adults in a five-day context in which they attend a program during the week while living with their families on weekends.

Manpower implications of small, dispersed services

A common objection to the dispersal of services is the claim that the professional manpower that is necessary to staff dispersed services cannot be found. This contention is probably partially true and partially false, and must be examined very carefully.

First of all, concentration of services is no guarantee for the solution of manpower problems. For various reasons – not all of these associated with the manpower shortage – agencies even in favored circumstances may have recruiting problems. Thus, dispersed services are not necessarily worse off than concentrated services.

Secondly, in many service fields, dispersal of services consistent with population patterns would actually bring about relocation of previously remote services into population centers, where some manpower problems can be solved more easily. Many large public institutions are located in small communities, and it has been most difficult to attract professional staff to such locations and institutions. In mental retardation, for instance, dispersal would mean the development of many smaller facilities, most of which would be located in cities where professional manpower is easier to obtain, concomitant with the phasing out – or at least the phasing down – of the large institutions.

Thirdly, the majority of residential facilities can be so specialized that they can be opened without a full range of professional disciplines in constant attendance, and those professionals required on the spot could be of lower and intermediate levels of training. In some cases, such as certain sheltered-living hostels, professional personnel is only required on a back-up basis. Fortunately, personnel of intermediate levels of professional training can often be found even in small cities, especially if use is made of married women with appropriate training, and if such women are permitted part-time work (see Cooke, 1969, for relevant analogies in the area of nursing homes).

From the above analysis, it appears that dispersal of residential units, and their specialization around disciplinary rather than multi-disciplinary models, should actually contribute to the easing of the manpower problem.

A system of dispersed and specialized residences works best if it is supported by an adequate back-up system. Such a system would appear to have two major components: a pyramidal continuum of residential options, and a manpower back-up. The pyramidal residential continuum implies that a resident in a more common service that usually requires little specialized manpower can always move back to a more specialized, professionalized, and less common one.

The manpower back-up might be provided out of administrative regional headquarters, and might include the following:

consultants to residential personnel;

counsellors who go to the hostels and other residences to counsel residents on a variety of problems;

recreation specialists who encourage, arrange, or provide recreational activities, mostly for evenings and weekends;

houseparent assistants who can be assigned from day to day to residences where a sudden manpower shortage or need arises;

roving janitorial services.

Conclusion

I can see no reason why small, specialized living units (mostly hostels) cannot accommodate almost all of the persons now in institutions. In turn, I believe that many persons who could be well served in hostels will be served even better in individual placements. Thus, we should bring about not only movement from institutions to other group residences, but also a decline in the demand for any type of group residence.

Furthermore, any feature of a residential service that is normalizing will increase the likelihood that the resident will either return to his family, move to a more advanced form of residence (*e.g.* from hostel to boarding), or be fully habilitated. Therefore, the more normalizing atmosphere and practices of small group residences, the use of community instead of segregated resources, the maintenance of family ties because of close physical proximity, the use of five-day instead of seven-day, and nine-month instead of twelve-month residences, all of these should combine so as to reduce the need for life-long residence, and increase the movement from group to individual residence.

In addition, the open-endedness in the flow into and out of the various types of residences, and the increased availability of residential services specifically geared to genuine short-term crisis relief (*e.g.* 'vacation homes', or 'crisis assistance units' as proposed and described in Governor's Citizens' Study Committee, 1968b) are apt to further reduce the need for long-term or even life-long residences. In sum, there are many features associated with a normalized residential model which will tend to diminish the need for residential places of any kind, while simultaneously being very economical.

8 implications in the field of mental health

As stressed again and again, the principle of normalization has universal relevance to human management. However, for different problems and fields, it usually has at least some implications which are of special salience or timeliness. To date, such implications have only been worked out in a few areas, much determined by historical accident. Thus, the most extensive elaboration exists in mental retardation, for the simple historical reason that here, the normalization principle had its origins and was most readily accepted.

It was for equally accidental reasons that this chapter was written. It was written upon the instigation of Dr. Robert Osborn, former director of Nebraska's mental health and mental retardation services, who wanted to see applied to mental health some of the concepts that had been applied successfully to Nebraska mental retardation services. This chapter is an extensive revision of several earlier position papers developed to that purpose, including one that has since been published (Wolfensberger, 1970c).

Some lessons from mental retardation for the mental health field

For well over one hundred years, the field of mental disorder management had led the trends that eventually governed practices in mental retardation. Suddenly, this is no longer so; indeed, there has come about a partial reversal. The mental health field is struggling with traditionalism and internal confusion in the face of external challenges, and appears to be headed toward a model of service that is likely to be of very limited effectiveness, and to a significant degree at variance with the principle of normalization. In contrast, the field of mental retardation has become more dynamic and innovative than a number of other human management fields, and appears to be gaining at a much faster rate in program development, in popular support, and in public funding.

In miniature, certain events in the State of Nebraska provide a poignant example of the change in the relationship between the fields of mental health and mental retardation. In 1967-68, Nebraska was one of the least progressive of the United States as regards provision and funding of mental retardation services. Yet, by 1971, it had become a national pace-setter in the rate of change, the variety of services, and the innovativeness of these services as well as their associated processes of planning and implementation. Visitors

I very much dislike the term 'mental health', but found it virtually impossible to discard it without losing a great deal of economy in communicating. However, on several occasions, I will use such terms as 'disordered' or 'mental disorder' in lieu of the 'mental illness' concept.

not only from all over North America, but also from overseas came to study what many have called 'the Nebraska phenomenon'.

This change was brought about in good part by the state-wide acceptance of the normalization principle in its official standards and regulations governing community mental retardation services. Thus, by 1971, ideological development in mental retardation was far advanced over ideological development in mental health, where change had been slow and resistance to change high. The difference is particularly striking when one considers how much more manpower and money there had been available for mental health, and the fact that the number of highly-trained mental retardation professionals in Nebraska had always been miniscule in comparison to highly-trained mental health professionals.

The incredible amount of progress in mental retardation was probably the result of a combination of phenomena, reviewed elsewhere (Wolfensberger & Menolascino, 1970a, 1970b). This review holds some valuable lessons for the mental health movement, well beyond the borders of Nebraska, because aside from certain historical differences between the mental health and mental retardation movements in Nebraska, there are several inherent differences between the two fields which make the position of mental health systems a difficult one, and which probably interfere with the innovative process.

Firstly, mental retardation is well along to having overcome the fixation – derived from the medical model – with etiology, and has become management-oriented. This is not to say that etiology is not given adequate consideration in theory and research, but that management on the clinical level is no longer as preoccupied as formerly with etiological diagnosis, and with theories regarding the relationship between etiology and management which, after decades of vast amounts of work and for good theoretical reasons, have proven largely fruitless.

Furthermore, there is a difference in the conceptualization and formulation of management goals. In mental disorder management, goals may be ill-defined or even highly controversial (*e.g.* Hersch, 1968). Often, the goal is stated in idealistic fashion, implying ephemeral states of self-actualization and normality; in some cases, the term 'cure' is actually employed to refer to the return of a client to a marginal social adjustment in the community. Conversely, the goal may be stated in a self-deceptive fashion, as when the manager says 'long-term treatment' when he means warehousing.

In contrast, management in retardation involves generally-attainable and realistic goals which are practical, which are often of an intermediate-term nature, and which are open-ended enough for revision upward or downward. For example, when dealing with a mildly retarded teenager who has adaptation problems, one finds it easy to agree on a management goal of relatively early social and economic independence in the lower socio-economic strata of a community. For a mildly retarded 10-year old, there would be general agreement on an intermediate-range goal of academic advancement and socio-emotional adjustment. In dealing with a severely retarded five-year old, chances are that there would be agreement on an intermediate-term goal of self-help independence, and a long-term goal of partial self-support under sheltered work and sheltered living conditions.

Aside from goals is the issue of what works, *i.e.* to what management actions positive outcomes can be attributed. In mental health, this question is very unclear. Untreated clients may improve as much as treated ones (*e.g.* Schorer, Lowinger, Sullivan & Hartlaub, 1968). Indeed, there is some evidence (Herjanic & LaFave, 1966, cited in Mendel & Rapport, 1969; Mendel, 1966; Pasamanick, Scarpitti, & Dinitz, 1967) that clients receiving a more costly and extensive 'treatment' may actually fare worse than with more limited and less costly efforts.

In contrast, management effects in mental retardation are rather well understood. For example, in order to relieve a mother of stress, it is known that visiting homemaker services or day care for the child are highly useful and effective. Practical training programs are known to improve the self-help skills of virtually any severely retarded children; intensive environmental and social enrichment is known to improve the intellectual functioning of mildly retarded children between the ages of about 3 to 8; work-study programs in high school are known to assist a large proportion of mildly retarded teenagers in developing toward socially and economically independent citizenship; vocational training in sheltered workshops can offer partial economic self-support to severely retarded adults, *etc.* And the relationship between these management forms and outcomes are known to be largely causal, rather than merely correlational, as is often the case in mental disorder management.

If one does not know too well what works in mental disorder management, it is most difficult to match management options meaningfully to management needs. Since improvements due to non-treatment variables are so common that we can rarely be sure of a cause-effect relationship between management and outcome, the needs for individual, group, or other therapies can not really be specified in a rational manner. For instance, Mendel and Rapport (1969) found that recommendations and/or decisions for residential placement by mental health personnel are grossly inconsistent. In a review of a book on residential treatment of adolescents, Miller (1970) summarized a common situation in an uncommon way: '. . . a heterogeneous group of patients was admitted on unspecified criteria, assigned on an unknown basis to multiple social situations, some labelled therapy, some non-therapy, but none with known operations nor measurable impact.' In contrast, in mental retardation, the need for day care, for educational programs, for vocation training, for maintenance-of-life services, for parent guidance, or for family stress relief is usually rather clear-cut; if the service exists it can be fitted to the need; and if it does not exist, the need for and potential contribution of such service can be forcefully presented.

In conclusion, in mental health, goals are imprecise or controversial; clients get better or worse in not very predictable ways; the choice of management techniques is highly subjective and intuitive; and the evidence for even the most widely used techniques, such as psychotherapy, is weak and hotly contested. In consequence, the public has very limited understanding of the field, and views it with mystification. For example, in daily life, there are few analogies to many of the methods of mental health (*e.g.* individual and group therapy) that are readily perceived by most citizens as constituting analogies. That some techniques, such as those involving drugs, are poorly understood is evident, on the one hand, by the difficulty practitioners have in getting clients to adhere to prescribed drug regimens and, on the other hand, by clients' propensity to embark on self-prescribed drug regimens. Indeed, much of management in mental health is still perceived with a bit of awe and fear. The lingering memory of leucotomies ('lobotomies') and electric shock treatment may well contribute to this reaction.

On the other hand, workers in mental retardation can specify less ambiguously what management techniques are effective, and which are relevant to a management goal. Managers can convey good evidence, ideas, and convictions as to what is needed, and strong rationales for methods which can be readily explained to and understood by the laity. As a consequence, they can present the public with more definite, concrete, and *intelligible* guidelines and proposals, such as are of a nature that is known and understood by the typical citizen. For example, the bulk of relevant management is rendered by the schools in the form of special education, and being perceived as slowed-down schooling, it is understood and supported by the typical citizen. By the same token, he can understand vocational training, which he may liken to an apprenticeship; and residential service, which he can liken to providing a home. Every mother can understand visiting homemaker services, or day care.

Although the differences between the two fields are not widely conceptualized or consciously admitted, their existence is problematic to mental health, and has its effects on the mentality and functioning of mental health personnel. It certainly complicates ideologizing in mental health considerably, and has socio-political implications to which I shall return later in this chapter. Adoption of normalization principles will not overcome all of these difficulties. However, it can help by suggesting goals and methods which are more consistent with the cultural value structure, and which the citizen can intelligibly support. For instance, individual and group therapy, and psychoanalytically-derived uncovering techniques have their place, but they are not normal. While we will have to use them selectively, we should forever be alert to apply the most normative techniques that may be both available and effective. Some of these are suggested later in this chapter.

Mental health in turmoil

At present, the mental health field, and especially psychiatry, appears to be in a state of ferment and uncertainty that amounts to a crisis. There exist profound differences between theories and even ideologies in regard to the origins of mental disorders and their dynamics, human management methods, and even human management goals. There is growing dissatisfaction with the traditional human management concepts and terminology, and with the way service delivery systems are organized and structured. Yet both the increasing rejection of old as well as the introduction of new human management concepts have given rise to considerable controversy. Not only is there an increase in the number of publications addressing themselves to the direction and needs of the field, but also the tone of this literature is changing as we note more and more urgency in the concerns expressed. However, while some writers exhort the field to move quickly into new directions, other writers issue dire warnings to adhere to what they consider the tried and proven. Underneath the measured pace of the professional writing styles, and the occasionally grim courtliness of literary jousts, one senses deep anxiety, the profoundest concern, and often an almost now-or-never urgency.

Since day-to-day human management and administrative practices reflect basic management models, the function of mental health agencies can be expected to reflect the confusion of and disagreements among its personnel. Thus, Werkman (quoted in *Frontiers of Hospital Psychiatry*, 1968, *5*, No. 14, p. 1) has recently characterized the current functions of psychiatric clinics as 'compulsive aimlessness'. 'Dr. Whatsisname' (1969), in one of his incisive little essays, has commented on the lack of psychiatric consensus on even rather elemental points. Such lack of consensus has accounted for spectacular disagreements among psychiatric testimonies in court – an event which, to the amusement and bewilderment of the citizenry, is becoming more common or at least more publicized.[2] An extreme form and source of confusion is the appearance of well-publicized psychiatrists who actually reverse the definition of sanity by seeking rebirth ('metanoia') through the experiences of drug use, indulgence in liberated and unorthodox sex practice, and in schizophrenia itself (*e.g.* as by Cooper [1970]) – *i.e.* by a sort of institutionalized insanity. Such an advocacy by prominent figures cannot help but produce utter confusion on the part of the public, not to mention their fellow professionals in the field.

Recently, adequate treatment has been defined as a legal right of court-committed persons – yet obviously, psychiatric managers are deeply split on just what adequate treatment is. In connection with this controversy, Traffert, a state hospital superintendent, has been quoted (in *Frontiers of Hospital Psychiatry*, 1969, *6*, No. 12, p. 2) as referring to 'The vagueness inherent in psychiatric illness and psychiatric treatment, depending on the individual patient, his individual illness and his individual doctor, the confusion between inadequate treatment and ineffective treatment and the lack of knowledge at this point in time regarding specific causality, specific treatment and prognosis. . . .' Judge Bazelon, when requested to define adequate treatment, firmly placed that responsibility upon the shoulders of the mental health professions, and not on those of the courts. However, he stated with some emphasis that while courts and laymen might not be able to define *adequate* treatment, they were certainly quite capable of perceiving *lack* of treatment, even if such lack was *called* treatment. The deceptive/self-deceptive conceptualization of treatment goals has been mentioned earlier. Obviously, such deception no longer works on the public – only on the manager and some of his peers.

Even the market place associated with mental health is beginning to reflect the turmoil of the field. One is startled to read an advertisement (*Contemporary Psychology,* 1969, *14*, 89) claiming that a new book (Braginsky, Braginsky, and Ring, 1969) '. . . makes it irrefutably clear that when attempting to account for even the most mundane activities of mental patients, the dominant psychiatric conception of mental illness is not only inadequate but inappropriate.' A few years ago, an advertiser probably would have judged such wording as more likely to lose than win readers.

Personnel from all strata of the field can be found in the fray: the leaders – as well as followers – of yesterday, today, and tomorrow. For instance, the Group for the Advancement of Psychiatry (1969) – long considered a

[2] One only need recall the public's and the court's confusion in cases involving Ruby, Sirhan, Ray, the Manson group, and Calley.

dynamic leadership group – issued a monograph labelling and condemning as 'bandwagon' and 'slogans' that which substantial other mental health elements view as genuine and urgent 'advancement of psychiatry': community-oriented management that minimizes traditional use of psychiatric residential placements.

Kubie (1968a, 1968b), a consummate clinician, respected leader, and a past-president of the American Psychiatric Association, makes clear that he perceives the traditional clinical interactive model as *the* model for community mental health work, but believing that this would require '. . . *better* training for more men, not quicker, briefer training', he suggests that effective community mental health action is an unattainable ideal because of an insoluble manpower problem. He then cites the American Medical Association, the American Psychiatric Association, and the American Psychoanalytic Association that '. . . no matter how fully schooled and experienced he may be in basic sciences, in experimental and statistical methods, in human biology, in clinical psychology and psychiatric social work, and in the behavioral sciences in general', one who is not a physician should not receive training in psychodiagnosis and psychotherapy (1968a, p. 259-260). He also proposes that any mental health approach that '. . . threatens to limit the maturation of psychiatrists', no matter how apparently beneficial to society, is unacceptable. Settings which aim for rapid turnover of clients are seen as incapable of providing growth experiences to the psychiatrist. The view that mental disorders are to a significant degree related to the structure of our society and its social inequities is dismissed as a 'Russian fantasy'. This latter view is apparently shared – though less floridly expressed – by Kolb (1968), another long-term leader in the field.

To me, an article by Will (1968) provides one of the most poignant illustrations of the distress and partial paralysis of the field. First, Will vividly describes the woes of our present world: 'These are times of change and uncertainty. The increase in populations; the breaking up of colonial empires; the forming of new nations, the conflict of classes, age groups and races; the alteration of sexual standards, child rearing customs, family ties and stability, religious ideas, and of a variety of hitherto seemingly fundamental value systems; the increasing mechanization and urbanization of society; the expansion of communication techniques and accompanying challenge to the cultural barriers of the past; the openly revealed actual and potential violence of man and the threat to his existence posed by today's weaponry – these are just some of the facts of the world in which we live and in which our children must develop and move with determination despite their acceptance of indeterminancy' (p. 448).

But surprisingly, Will then goes on to deplore a 'mass approach to mental health' which, he feels, submerges the individual; instead, Will extols the virtues of one-to-one intensive psychotherapy conducted in residential settings. And this approach is what he calls for – even while acknowledging that it is too expensive for mass application, and of limited effectiveness even at its best. In his article, I can find no suggestion of any viable solution to the woes he recognizes, and to the problems of 'the masses'. Apparently, the possibility of the masses being submerged in mass service engenders more alarm than their being left unserved.

Reading Kubie and Will, I wonder how much clearer a futile, even self-destructive, system can be spelled out: a neurotic process is perceived as universal; the demand for psychiatric services is seen as endless; the meeting of such service demands by traditional means is acknowledged to be impossible; but no viable alternatives are offered – in fact, no alternatives are offered. For instance, alternatives systematically discussed and dismissed (or at least devalued) by Kubie include: treatment at or near home or in general hospitals, shorter hospitalizations, introduction of different and/or more efficient methods, and the training of new types of manpower.

One could almost paraphrase the thinking expressed above by saying that all society really needs is more of that which is done now, and though psychiatry cannot possibly meet this need, it should keep anyone or anything else from meeting it, even a miracle worker if he came along to heal without an MD degree, or if he obviated the need for (more) psychiatrists.

In citing the respected proponents of such views, I had absolutely no intention of attacking them specifically. I have cited them only because they exemplify the current dilemmas of the field so strongly; because they have done so in the recent literature; and because they are acknowledged leaders in the field, thus speaking with no ordinary voices. To me, the fact that these extraordinary voices speak with such confusion and futility means that the field, and our society, is in deep trouble.

The public's perception of the turmoil in mental health

Most of us are under pressures or have commitments which make it difficult to tread an objective course amid the controversies. However, if a qualified and unbiased outsider would suddenly come upon the current scene, he might conclude that management rationales in mental health are peculiarly weak; that clients get better or worse in not-very-predictable ways; that choice of management techniques tends to be subjective and intuitive; that the evidence for even the most widely-used techniques, such as psychotherapy, is weak and hotly contested; and that the public is only receiving a fraction of the mental health services which it needs.

As mentioned earlier in this chapter, lack of public understanding must be expected to have profound implications when it comes to the setting of public policy. At one time, when humanization of the snake pits was a major mental health issue, citizen action found vigorous and effective expression in the mental hygiene movement. Today, this movement lacks the vigor to back progress in the management of mental disorders the way the lay-inspired associations for retarded and certain other handicapped persons back, and often even lead, the professionals. A simple test of this assertion is to count the number of nonprofessional citizens who typically show up at legislative hearings of mental health bills, in comparison to bills in a number of related human management areas.

The blind, the deaf, and even present or former mental clients can speak for themselves. In contrast, the retarded consumer of services is voiceless, and his family or friend must – and does – speak for him. Thus, we see vigorous citizen groups across the country engaged in highly effective action on behalf of the retarded. At one time, such citizen groups consisted mostly of parents of the retarded; today, many nonparents – professional and otherwise – are involved in making the democratic process work for the expansion and improvement of services.

In contrast to the number of citizens 'with voices' who are affected by retardation in their family, there must be at least ten times as many persons 'with voices' who are directly or indirectly affected by mental disorders. Self-sufficient adults who once had been treated for emotional problems and who now live independent lives in the community, they alone may outnumber all the retarded and their families combined. This does not even take into account the families of those who are or were once mentally disordered and under treatment. Where are all these voices calling for more and better mental health services? I propose that the citizen and even consumer apathy in regard to mental disorder management has resulted in good part from lack of understanding, or even partial rejection, of the human management methods in the field as these are perceived by the citizen.

It is quite to be expected that the confusion and dissent within the field, and the public's perception thereof, should have considerable socio-political repercussions; especially now, when a national social crisis is acknowledged to exist, and when, for the first time, serious thought is being given to the setting of national goals and priorities (*e.g.* Gordon, 1969; Kierans, 1972; Lecht, 1966, 1969; Mintzberg, 1972; National Goals Research Staff, 1970; Saltsman, 1972; Science Council for Canada, 1968; Senate Special Committee on Science Policy, 1972; United States Department of Health, Education, & Welfare, 1969) which will be accompanied by the systematic rather than haphazard setting of fiscal priorities, and the increased acceptance of cost-efficiency rationales in human management services (Wolfensberger, 1969a). In the light of recognized needs and greater scientism in approach to them, the public will demand services that are more valid, more efficient, and more comprehensive than they are now. As this happens, a confused field of mental health is not likely to inspire confidence, to be fiscally favored, or to be entrusted with social leadership.

Ideology: both source and solution of turmoil

The turmoil in the field appears to be associated to a significant degree with the following phenomena:

> traditional methods appear incapable of handling the urgent problems that may tear our society apart;
>
> even if methods were adequate, the shortage of traditional mental health manpower would probably be insoluble;
>
> both current methods and manpower structure are based on human management models and socio-scientific ideologies that may have limited utility. For example, there is increasing question as to the degree to which the traditional clinical model is adequate, and whether contemporary problems may not require social and even industrial models for their solution or substantial reduction. A key to understanding the present state of the field may be the fact that mental health personnel have traditionally focused upon intrapsychic and family dynamics, and thus stand impotently *vis-a-vis* the array of problem behaviors which appear to have a major origin in social and economic factors, and which threaten to overpower our social structure (Hersch, 1968).

If – as it appears – current turmoil in the field involves primarily a struggle over and between human management ideologies, and since current service models appear to constitute an inadequate response to societal needs, then perhaps it is time to seek a new, unifying, relevant, and powerful ideology. The normalization principle may be such an ideology. 'When a problem has ideological roots, changes in techniques without the necessary ideological innovations often result in nothing more than old wine in new bottles' (Reiff, 1966, p. 543).

Normalization as an ideological alternative

As mentioned earlier in this text, in mental disorder management as in other problem areas and disciplines, the normalization principle has powerful force *vis-a-vis* competing human management systems. It is simple, parsimonious, and comprehensive. For instance, it requires no assumptions that the client be 'sick' or a 'patient', and yet it can be used to improve and purify the medical model in those instances where it happens to be appropriate, so that it will be applied to disordered, retarded, and handicapped persons at its best rather than at its worst, as sometimes in the past.

Occasionally, mental health orientations have been classified as being somatotherapeutic, psychotherapeutic, or sociotherapeutic. Although the normalization principle transcends the mental health field, it can be viewed as being most consistent with a sociotherapeutic approach in that it uses concepts and constructs rooted primarily in sociology, and does so at a time at which the field appears to be ready to orient itself increasingly toward sociotherapeutic concepts (Sabshin, 1966, 1969). While some management concepts, such as the therapeutic community, have constituted a big step from a medical to a social model, the very word 'therapeutic' still symbolizes medical model thinking. Now we should advance in our thinking from a 'therapeutic community' to a 'normalizing community'.

From the larger viewpoint of how to move society toward effective support of necessary action measures in mental health, the normalization principle has many advantages. While our society has an inadequate understanding of many current management measures in mental health, those that are strongly associated with the normalization principle 'make sense'. Also, at least in intelligible outline, the principle can be explained in a matter of minutes to an average citizen, and usually finds at least partial acceptance. Thus, it would appear that to the degree that the mental health field explicitly embraces this principle and its concrete implications, it may not only become more effective in its management and practices, but will also be able to marshal the necessary societal support for the action that is so urgent.

Mental disorders are unlikely ever to become positively valued. At best, they will elicit tolerance and perhaps pity. More commonly, they elicit fear, rejection, and perhaps even loathing; and they are likely to continue doing so to some degree. In consequence, a person who becomes mentally disordered is also apt to become deviant. Thus, the normalization principle and many of its implications applies strongly to the mentally disordered. Most of the implications are clear to anyone who has understood (or perhaps even merely read) the basic chapters on normalization in this book. Also, many implications to psychiatric residential services are found in the chapters on 'Additional architectural-environmental implications of the normalization principle', and 'Additional implications of the normalization principle to residential services'. However, some implications warrant more specific elaborations, either because of their intrinsic import, or because of their relevance to issues that are currently in the limelight. Most of these implications have to do with the conceptualization of the client role; the conceptualization of the delivery of comprehensive mental health services generally; the structure of residential mental health services in particular; and manpower. Each is discussed below.

THE CONCEPTUALIZATION OF THE CLIENT ROLE

Earlier, extensive treatment, including an entire chapter, was devoted to the role of roles, so to speak. If role expectancy is as powerful as we believe we know it to be, then it should be manipulated *consciously* and/or *systematically*, rather than unconsciously and/or haphazardly, as is typically the case now. Managers with medical backgrounds need to be alert to the temptation to impose the sick role and its concomitant medical model unconsciously, and/or perhaps inappropriately. This, of course, is an issue of particular relevance in mental disorder management: when and why to impose a developmental-normalizing model, and where to impose a detentive or medical one.

There rages, of course, a great deal of controversy today over the application of the medical model. In their efforts to emanicipate themselves from medical dominance, some workers would reduce the medical model to perhaps an extreme degree. Others would convert the world into a hospital. For instance, Kubie (1969a, 1969b) would pattern all of special education upon the medical model. In psychiatry specifically, some writers see the issue as 'medical model or no medical model' (*e.g.* Osmond, 1970), instead of in terms of selective application thereof, or its presence without its predominance.

It is of the greatest importance to understand that normalization principles are not opposed to medical human management models – unless such models are imposed inappropriately. To the contrary, normalization principles demand that the medical model be applied selectively, and be applied at a high level of competency, instead of at a low one as has happened in some fields, such as mental retardation, in the past. However, the criteria for the appropriate application of the medical model need to be carefully explored and specified.

For instance, the Parsons (1951; Parsons & Fox, 1958) sick-role theory suggests the hypotheses that this role might be most adaptive if imposed upon basically strong, self-motivated persons whose mental disorder is of non-chronic nature, and who feel strong guilt in connection with their disorder; persons who have long felt inadequate may fare much better with a developmental-normalization model; *etc.* At any rate, there is a strong body of theory and evidence to suggest alternative courses of action, as well as some very feasible research projects. In this connection, it appears worthwhile to refer once more to an approach developed in the armed forces (Talbot, 1969), where high expectancies for recovery are imposed upon disordered soldiers, and where mental health staff deliberately wear uniforms rather than white coats. In effect, this approach strongly and systematically embodies normalization concepts.

Medically-oriented managers must be alert to the special difficulties that arise when sick role perceptions are imposed upon persons with long-lasting impairments. The laudable medical tradition of seeking cures makes for a predisposition toward intensive treatment activism for 'acute' conditions, with high expectations for early response. If early or massive response does not occur, the manager becomes disappointed and often disillusioned, and it is only too understandable if he feels his talents better invested in more responsive clients. It is probably this type of dynamics which has contributed to the many situations in which medical managers initially imposed medical models upon services to clients with long-term disabilities, have later lost enthusiasm and commitment, then failed to yield management administration to disciplines whose orientation would have given them better ideological protection, and ended up administering services along lines which constituted a perversion of the medical model. Many mental retardation institutions have undergone precisely this type of evolution. The same basic dynamics might explain why psychiatric managers have difficulty in adjusting to a model of management in which the individual may be productive and contributive as a citizen, even though both his domicile and work may be sheltered, and even though he is *neither* a 'patient' *nor* a fully independent member of the community.[3]

THE CONCEPTUALIZATION OF COMPREHENSIVE SERVICES

One issue has to do with the nature of mental health service delivery. At present, such services are delivered primarily via four media: medical and other practitioners in generic community services, mental health personnel in private practice, the new community mental health centers, and the old mental institutions. All of these four media function essentially in a traditional office-centered fashion, in contrast with certain other human services which have been more mobile, and which have been oriented toward taking their services to those in need rather than having those in need come to them.

It is of considerable interest that the laudable desire to provide comprehensive services has led to the exaltation of so-called comprehensive mental health centers which, by their very nature, violate one of the most basic corollaries of the normalization principle: such multi-purpose facilities serve too wide a range of needs and clients. The young, the adult, and the senescent; the mildly disturbed and the severely disturbed; the harmless, the violent, and the self-destructive; they all may be served in the same single-campus center, and perhaps partly by the same personnel. In short, the assumptions are that a wide range of needs can be met well by a single treatment center; that this single treatment center should be on a single campus; and that no alternative is either better or feasible.

One advantage of the multi-purpose single-campus facility is that it is convenient to professionals and administrators. It enables them to function out of stationary offices and to have easy communication with each other, and it facilitates supervisory processes.

[3] Of interest to this and other issues covered in this chapter is a review of studies of the management of long-term residents of mental health facilities (Paul, 1969). Although the term 'normalization' and 'citizen advocacy' (see the relevant chapter later in this book) were not utilized, the concepts were. The power of normalization methods and citizen advocacy functions were strongly brought out by the evidence reviewed.

Disadvantages of the omnibus single-campus facility include the office-centeredness it fosters. Also, human management procedures often have to be aimed at a low common denominator of client characteristics and needs. This is a particularly vexing problem in residential services, and will be discussed in greater detail in the section following. Furthermore, the principle of age separation is violated, and especially so the principle of the separation of domiciliary functions, whereby a client lives in one place, works in another, transacts many functions in yet other ones, *etc.* Combining all these functions on one campus and often even under one roof is not normative. Obviously, some persons will be so disordered that separation of the domiciliary function will not be possible. But the comprehensive mental health center structure generally makes this separation impossible even for those clients for whom it is feasible and desirable. Finally, single-campus service severely restricts the physical and social experiences of many clients at a time when just the opposite may be needed.

Unfortunately, the 1963 US federal mental health act was a 'center' instead of a 'services' act, and in its regulations it demanded that centers be 'comprehensive' in providing that inpatient, partial hospitalization, outpatient, and emergency care must be given, together with community education and consultation. Additional services (diagnosis, rehabilitation, pre- and after-care, training, and research and evaluation) were defined as desirable to 'complete' the comprehensive service system. The same or very similar services have also been defined by other influential bodies and writers as components of the mental health center concept. In consequence, the mental health field has made a major ideological, financial, and architectural commitment to multi-purpose centers. As of this date, there are not too many people in the field who have internalized concepts and language that suggest that they think in terms of service systems rather than centers, and too many important documents in the field keep referring to 'the' mental health center (*e.g.* National Institute of Mental Health, 1968).

THE STRUCTURE OF MENTAL HEALTH RESIDENTIAL SERVICES

General considerations

There are few services in which normalization principles are as readily violated as in residential ones. Thus, in different contexts, this book returns to this problem again and again.

As mentioned above, in mental health as elsewhere, omnibus residential services, almost by definition, violate the normalization principle. One problem is that the less disordered persons in a relatively heterogenous group of residents have to tolerate the possibly gross inconveniences implied in living with the more disordered ones. Because of a small number of clients who have internally- or externally-directed aggressive tendencies, all clients may be deprived of a normal environment and of rights, privileges, and freedoms exercised as a matter of course by other citizens in our society. Even where more individualized management might have been feasible, staff have often used the problems of the more difficult clients as an excuse for regimentation, restriction of freedom, and failure to institute or even experiment with innovations. Because of this common regimentation of the management routine in residential facilities, there has been only modest evolution toward individualization of management, diversification of services, *etc.* Indeed, human management practices of typical psychiatric residential services have been stereotyped and unimaginative. Though less now than formerly, residential service still has an all-or-nothing flavor. Once admitted, a client is likely to receive very expensive, often total, management. If we assume that a perfectly normal person were admitted at the same time as a very disordered one, chances are that in a typical psychiatric residential facility, the *per diem* cost for these two individuals, at least initially, would show relatively little difference. Despite the alleged economic benefits of the traditional management models, the all-or-nothing nature of treatment is highly uneconomical because many individuals need relatively low levels of services which, however, are simply not available under the existing model, or not available in sufficient quantity. Thus, the person who needs the $15 a day residential service may receive either no residential service at all, or the $75 a day service.

At this point, some specific implications will be explored for children and adults respectively. Though of particular relevance to residential services, many implications are also relevant to nonresidential programs.

Children's residences and programs

Among many advanced elements in this country, there is increasing dissatisfaction with the traditional psychoanalytic-, therapeutic-, and uncovering-oriented child treatment approaches. The sentiment is growing that child management should become much more than a translation of traditional and relatively ineffective (or at least inefficient) adult psychiatric principles and techniques to children. It would appear that much of the treatment could be mediated by the security of a warm but structured atmosphere, and by emphasis upon strengthening the self-concept through development of self-help mastery over the environment, and of physical competence. Increasingly, programs incorporating child-development and behavior shaping approaches appear to be showing more promise.

From our understanding of the power of normalization principles, this should not surprise us, since normal (at least in the sense of idealized) child-rearing is perceived as aiming at these goals, and such aims can be pursued with very normative rather than 'odd' means. For instance, derived largely from normalization principles, one could propose a residential model for children that involves at least four types of distinct, separate, and relatively home-like units. Two of these would be based upon the severity of the children's problems; the other two would be based upon considerations of the child's age. Explanations follow.

More severely disordered children could probably be housed in small units, of which no more than a few should be grouped together, with some central facility adjacent for certain services, offices, *etc.* Less disordered children should be housed in ordinary single family houses or apartments in the community, and not in conjunction with central facilities. Younger boys and girls, mostly between ages three and ten, could be grouped together; older children need not necessarily be segregated by sex, but special attention must be paid to the arrangement of the living units, and a few segregated units may be desirable. One can visualize the proposed system in *Table 1*, although in a large service system, as should exist in a metropolitan area, the dimensions would be continuous rather than discrete.

Table 1

		Age		
		Younger	Older	
Degree of Disorder	High	Sex-Integrated Unit Complexes	Sex-Integrated Unit Complexes	Sex-Segregated Unit Complexes
	Low	Sex-Integrated Single Units	Sex-Integrated Single Units	Sex-Integrated Single Units

By developing a variety of facilities as described above, ranging from the typical family-style home in the community to a somewhat more self-contained small treatment complex, a much more effective and useful continuum of options would be available than is typically the case now. The larger the service system is, the more units graded along the age and disorder continuity dimensions can be set up, and the more homogeneously can groups be structured.

As indicated earlier, there are good reasons why the programs of, or associated with these units should focus on those behavior elements that are adaptive in normal children, but that are often disturbed in disordered children. It appears that development of such adaptive behavior can not only facilitate more dynamically oriented therapies; it can also become a vehicle by which a child can compensate for dynamic insults. If this is possible, it would have considerable implications to the manpower problem by strengthening the rationale for increased reliance on education and rehabilitation personnel. More staffing options and probably more personnel would be available, and it would be easier to develop personnel skill in these rather than the more traditional approaches.

What are some of these normal behaviors and processes that could be enhanced – and not merely in association with a residential service? At all levels of childhood, there would be considerable emphasis on 'competence' (*e.g.* Bricker, 1967), and on physical prowess, with activities designed to systematically improve strength, coordination, and specific skills such as running, jumping, climbing, *etc.* Competitive as well as non-competitive methods could be used, as indicated.

In programs for younger children, equipment and activities would also emphasize body awareness and sensory discrimination. Self-help skills would be increased by means of training, equipment, and furnishings. The behavioral structure would be such as to elicit meaningful verbal and other types of communication, and to teach respect for the life-space of others.

For the older children, programming would attempt to strengthen sex roles by means of clearly sex role-related activities and even indoctrination. For example, boys could engage in scout activities and hand crafts; girls in cooking and needlecraft;[4] both could receive formal sex education and in-

[4] I recognize the conflict of this view with the women's liberation movement, but feel that the sex role evolution should not be fought out in disordered children, but in those who have the strength to tolerate the stresses of such a battle.

struction in socialization with peers of the opposite sex, shored up by individual counselling so as to make such education optimally sex role-relevant and least stressful.

In normal society, adolescence is a time of schooling and vocation preparation. Thus, programs for adolescents could have tours and lectures oriented toward career choice facilitation, and a heavy emphasis on academics, although, as in all aspects of programming discussed here, great individualization of needs and approaches would be recognized.[5] Academic work would be conducted *outside* the living units, and by personnel other than those in charge of the residence. Such a measure would avoid a non-formal fusion of the teacher-school and parent-home functions.

As indicated earlier, some of the units, or even unit complexes, could be operated on a disciplinary (*e.g.* child development or educational) model. This, of course, would not mean that only one professional discipline would have access to the residents, but that one discipline would play the key and management-defining role, with other disciplines in consultant capacities.

Adult residences and programs

Like residential services to children, residential services to adults should be based on normalization principles. This means that adult units should be so far and/or effectively removed from children's services that no association between the two is likely to be created in the mind of a typical beholder. Also, units should be so structured, located, staffed, administered, and dispersed as to minimize the deviancy, and maximize the normality, of the residents. Examples of some specific specialized residential service types will be sketched below.

Sheltered living residences One of the greatest needs for specialized residential service is for relatively low-supervision sheltered living. Perhaps the vast majority of long-term residents in our public institutions and 'state hospitals' could live in such residences, and could do so at much lower costs than at present. I envision a large number of hostels for anywhere between 4-12 and sometimes even more residents dispersed across a province or state. The preferred type of building would be family homes and apartment houses in low or middle-class neighborhoods.

In many units, there would be live-in 'houseparents', except that they would not be called that because this term would cast residents into childlike roles. Unit or residential director might be an appropriate term. However, some living units could be operated on a daytime staffing basis only. Yet other units can be completely staffless and run by their residents, although backup by visiting personnel may be desirable or essential in order to render and/or structure recreational activities, personal counselling and counselling in regard to problems of daily living such as transportation, taxes, shopping, *etc.*

[5] One of many options might be *Project Re-Ed*, which is a residential program for disordered children operated on a developmental-academic model (see Bower, Lourie, Strother & Sutherland, 1969, as well as the entire March 1969 issue of *Mind over Matter*). For adolescents or adults, a model described by Albee (1968) might be one of the options. This model resembles a college more than a hospital, with heavy emphasis on occupation, re-education, and rehabilitation.

Most residential units for long-term residents could probably be managed on a group social work model.

Intensive service residences Candidates for this residential service could be individuals who exhibit severely disordered overt behavior; who have a high propensity for self-destruction; or who are in a pre- and/or post-aggressive state, but are not habitually aggressive. Major management techniques for such residents would be individual and group counselling; exposure to community experiences under highly supervised and controlled conditions; and realistic work in hostel and ground maintenance and operations, and in sheltered workshops. Young adults, especially, would be likely to be included in work activities that have a heavy training emphasis.

Residences of this type could be operated on a number of models, including traditional-psychiatric and vocational-rehabilitative ones, but they would not necessarily require on-ground or adjacent central services.

Structured-correctional residences Some adults or young adults have shown aggressive, destructive, anti-social, or similar behavior, and/or appear to require a highly structured and somewhat restricted environment. In present omnibus-type residential facilities, such persons often interfere with the life space and routines of other residents who do not display behavior or needs of this nature. Also, some individuals are committed by court, and there is a need or mandate for very close supervision and perhaps confinement. Often, the needs of this type of person dominate the management atmosphere for other residents. A residential service type could be developed specifically for this population.

At present, we have a situation where individuals who are considered to be 'criminally insane' reside on the same campus with many other kinds of residents. From the normalization viewpoint alone, this is totally inappropriate. By failing to draw appropriate distinctions between various types of disordered clients, one develops or strengthens in the minds of the public the previously discussed role perception of the deviant (mentally disordered) person as a menace or object of dread. When one permits this to happen, one contributes to the 'abnormalizing' or 'dehabilitation' of the majority of the disordered.

It would appear to be desirable to have at least two types of structured-correctional units, one for presumably long-term detention (as may be mandated by court action), and the other for presumably shorter stay and subsequent rehabilitation. The long-term structured-correctional residence is one of the very few in the human management area for which one could advance a strong rationale for isolation and placement some distance from population centers. No such rationale can be advanced for short-term structured-correctional residences where rehabilitation (normalization) back into the community is a reasonable short or intermediate-range aim. Many individuals of this type will be dissocial and other young adults who require intensive and high-supervision socialization under the guidance of 'career models'. About this issue, more will be said in the 'manpower' section following.

I would estimate that the greatest need for habilitational corrective-structured residential services would be for young adults whose instability or sub-cultural socialization mitigate heavily against a college career. Thus, a major potential source of self-esteem for this group will be work competence. Consequently, there should be a strong emphasis on training in specific craft and skill areas, and on remedial functional academic instruction in an adult and industrial atmosphere.

The role of work As mentioned before, there are few activities for adults in our culture which are more normative than work. It follows that for adults under mental disorder management, in or out of special residence, work can be a major means of normalization, and therefore should receive a prominent place in the management scheme. Thus, we should strive to provide meaningful work in as near a meaningful workday as possible. The idleness forced upon many of the consumers of our psychiatric services, especially residential ones, is clearly denormalizing; only slightly less denormalizing is 'occupation' or work that is meaningless. This consideration argues strongly for the establishment of sheltered workshops that can be used by some of the residents of mental health facilities – except that for most such residents, these shops should not be on the grounds of the residential facility, as this would violate the principle of the separation of domiciliary functions.

A related and major implication is that endless 'recreational therapy', as well as the often euphemistically labelled 'occupational therapy' of our mental health residences, are not culturally normative means, and may have an effect opposite to their stated and intended one: they may dehabilitate and denormalize. Even if one were not willing to agree with this interpretation, one might consider whether meaningful work in a typical work routine would not be more culturally normative and therefore more effective than the ambiguously structured, defined, perceived, and valued recreational and occupational 'therapies'.[6] (See also Hauck, 1971).

Although the normalizing nature of work has long been recognized in mental health practice, it has been greatly underutilized (Margolin, 1968). One reason may be that if a client has an episode of severe disorder, the manager may be impressed by the fact that the client's impairment has decreased or even eliminated his ability to carry out his *ordinary* work. The manager may then conclude that the same would be the case with *all* work, overlooking the possibility that the client may be capable of working in, and being normalized by, some other type of work activity. For instance, the certified public accountant, although momentarily too distraught to handle his ordinary job, may be effective in and normalized by the workshop assembly of relay switches.

Another reason for underutilization of work may be that when work was assigned to psychiatric clients, it usually was work associated with the maintenance of the facility, *e.g.* in the laundry or library, on the farm or living unit. Such work has suffered from two aspects that have diminished its normalizing value: it was often exploitive, involving little or no pay and perhaps even leading to 'institutional peonage' (Bartlett, 1964) rather than habilitation; conversely, work was often contrived or viewed with such an indulgent paternalistic ('therapeutic'?) attitude that it lost much of its work nature, thereby its sociocultural meaning, and consequently much of its normalizing effect.

[6] A very subtle devaluation of work occurs when recreational, occupational and vocational activities are placed within the same space or closely adjacent, or when they are administratively under the same department and/or person.

Conclusions regarding residential services

A complete spectrum of specialized mental health residences might have about fifteen components, as summarized in *Table 2*. Such a specialization would offer individualization, dispersal, and better use of manpower, to be discussed in the section following. If the specialization model sketched in *Table 2* appears utopian, then the reader is reminded that an analogous model appeared utopian when first proposed for the field of mental retardation in Nebraska in 1967. Yet as this is being written, the model is being implemented, and the institutional population is experiencing the most rapid decline ever recorded in an institution for the retarded in North America, by means other than the erection of new institutions. Detailed documentation of this model and its effects is available (Governor's Citizens' Committee on Mental Retardation, 1968b; Menolascino, Clark & Wolfensberger, 1968, 1970; Wolfensberger & Menolascino, 1970a, 1970b).

As mentioned earlier, in the chapter on 'Additional implications of the normalization principle to residential services', both the term and concept of the 'half-way' house should be abolished. The term has a de-normalizing perception attached to it – at least in the minds of many citizens. One can too easily think of half-human, half-valued, second-class residents living in houses that are not fully or all of anything. A term such as 'hostel' is neutral and has no such connotation. Also, the concept of 'half-way' contains in it the hidden assumption that the gap between all and nothing can be filled by one residential option. Any conceptualization even close to this one is inimical to the continuum that appears to be consistent with normalization principles.

MANPOWER IMPLICATIONS

Disciplinary services

Psychiatric services are heavily influenced by psychoanalytic theory and traditions. Consequently, the idealized mode of service is a 1:1 relationship between professional and client. However, there is not only room for concern about the validity of traditional modes of thinking about current patterns of psychiatric services, but also about the efficiency and reality of these patterns, even if one could take for granted that they were basically valid.

Reality can be questioned by citing manpower studies and projections which, for years, have indicated that the traditional ideal of highly-skilled face-to-face clinical services is unattainable in the intermediate future; yet even when the manpower situation worsens, administrators keep acting as if the next round of recruiting, of training, or of salary raises would solve their particular local manpower problems.

Efficiency can be questioned by citing evidence that service patterns that have not relied on the idealized sustained personal professional-client relationship have been quite successful – or at least as successful as traditional patterns may or may not be.

If we are to institute atraditional approaches, the disciplinary model that is strongly implied in the dispersed mental health management model would appear to be very promising, at least in the residential service area. A disciplinary model would be one in which the style and competencies of a professional discipline can be actualized to a high degree, and can be expressed

Table 2
A possible specialization of residences for the urban disordered

Type	*Age Group*	*Problem or Severity*	*No. of Resd'ts*	*Location or Context*	*Primary Staffing*	*Management Focus*	*Major profession*
1	Young Children	Mild	4-8	Separate	Houseparents	Developmental	Child Development
2	Young Children	Severe	4-8	Complex?	Houseparents	Developmental	Child Development
3	Older Children	Mild	6-8	Separate	Houseparents	Developmental	Special Education
4	Older Children	Severe	6-8	Complex?	Houseparents	Developmental	Psychiatrists, Psychologists
5	Adolescent	Conduct, Turmoil	6-8	Complex?	Houseparents	Developmental	Psychiatrists, Psychologists
6	Adolescent	Legal Offense	6-8	Complex	Houseparents	Corrective-Detention	Correction
7	Adult	Legal Offense	— 15	Complex	Shifts, Correctional Technicians	Corrective-Detention	Correction
8	Adult	Legal Offense	?	Prison	Shifts, Correctional Technicians	Long Term Detention	Correction
9	Mostly Adult	Neuropsychiatric	— 15	Hospital	Nursing	Medical	Psychiatric
10	Adult	Severe Nondocile	4-12	Complex?	Shifts, Technicians	Structured Socialization	Psychiatrists, Psychologists
11	Adult	Severe Docile	4-12	Complex?	Lay Residents?	Open Socialization	Psychiatrists, Psychologists
12	Adult	Moderate	4-12	Separate	Lay Residents	Socialization	Psychiatrists, Psychologists or Social Workers
13	Adult	Mild	4-12	Separate	Visiting Social Workers	Socio-Administrative	Social Group Work
14	Adult	Mild	4-12	Separate	Visiting Psychologist, Social Worker	Socialization	Psychologists or Social Workers
15	All Ages	Observation, Transition	— 25	Complex	Shifts, Multiple	Diffuse	Multiple

in the location and/or architecture of a facility, its internal appointments, its human management structure, and its staffing and staff training pattern.

Another relevant consideration is that it is quite likely that in a field dominated by the medical model, non-medical personnel can be attracted more readily when there are greater opportunities for professional self-realization. Also, disciplinary management models appear promising settings for the development of more hierarchical manpower structures in top-heavy professions such as psychology, and for the training of sub- and para-professional personnel.

The sections preceding have already identified several residential services which can be structured along highly disciplinary lines. For instance, elderly psychiatric clients might be provided with a nursing model; sheltered group homes for mildly disordered but relatively long-term residents can utilize the social group work model; a behavioral model might be optimal for a behavior modification unit for habit-disordered and compulsive clients; a neuropsychiatric model is indicated for disordered persons with associated acute medical conditions; a child development model appears optimal for most children who are disordered; *etc.*

One embarrassing situation here is the question of the unique competency of the psychiatrist. Most specialists, in any area, have a unique competency, but the specialness of psychiatry appears to lie more in the range of required competency rather than in any extensive uniqueness of skills. Thus, other physicians could carry out most of the medical functions performed by psychiatrists; pediatricians, general practitioners, and other physicians might handle psychopharmacological treatment in many instances, especially if they, in turn, broadened their skills; social workers can perform many liaison roles, initial case assessments, counselling, group work and psychotherapy; psychologists could also do these things, and can often even do better than psychiatrists in psychodynamic assessment and counselling; administration can be done by individuals from many disciplines, especially by trained administrators. Perhaps the most unique psychiatric skill lies in the traditional neuropsychiatric area; yet paradoxically, this is a model from which many psychiatrists have tried to escape, while others have attempted to impose it upon clients whose disorders have not called for this highly specialized management.

The low discipline specificity of psychiatry and other mental health professions may well account for the apparent fact that in this field, there is much more concern with the status of professions. In other words, the less discipline-specific a valued skill or function is, the more a discipline has to resort to role and status definitions if it is to maintain a major or even dominant role. For example, only by building and defending a rigid status system can psychiatry, or medicine generally, maintain dominance in any field where its discipline-specific skills are relatively modest.

The issue of psychiatric competency and role is, of course, controversial. However, it is instructive to go beyond the polemics and look at what psychiatrists are actually doing, and it would appear to be evident that most of what they do, they do not so much do by virtue of *unique* training, but by virtue of traditional role and status definitions; of training and experience neither unique nor even necessarily psychiatric; or by accident. These considerations argue heavily in favor of a disciplinary model of residential services, although the realities of the politics of the field are such that some psychiatrists will continue to play leadership roles in areas in which they are not really *uniquely* qualified to do so. Even as status concerns will continue to be a significant roadblock to innovative action in the mental health field, those in decision-making positions who want to facilitate the innovative process will often have to make decisions which weaken the present status system on the one hand, and which, on the other hand, contribute toward the formation of an alternate status system based on performance, rather than professional identity, degrees, and seniority.

Deviancy juxtaposition

An issue of great importance to manpower development is the one of deviancy juxtaposition. The de-normalizing implications of such juxtaposition of deviant client groups to each other, and/or to deviant personnel, has been discussed in the chapter on 'Societal integration as a corollary of normalization'. Unfortunately, such juxtaposition is very common in almost all human management areas; it has not only been tolerated, but often even been encouraged.

In mental health, the problem may not be larger than elsewhere, but it is large. The field has attracted many individuals who became fascinated with human problems because their own were so prominent. And training institutions have done little to differentially select and retain nondeviant recruits. I have seen individuals with severe overt mental deviancies being passed through the training process, and into the highest professional positions. This problem is serious even in 'glamor' settings such as university clinics and departments. It is calamitous in the backwaters of the field, such as the older institutions, which have become havens for mental health professionals rejected by society.

The effect of such practices upon the image of the field are apparent in the public's mind. There are probably no other human service workers that are as readily derided as are mental health professionals, especially if one considers the high level of training and certification that is characteristic of workers in this field. Almost certainly, this is not merely the result of past attitudes of derision of the disordered person. Today, 'the man on the street' is apt to take his disordered neighbor, friend, or family member much more seriously than he does the professional who treats him. And it seems that the professional is viewed less seriously than the nonprofessional in the field, who is less likely to be seen as deviant himself. After all, the nonprofessional is apt to be a 'four-square' retired farmer or his wife, a student working his way through college the old-fashioned way, or a person of low income toiling to earn an honest living. The nonprofessional may be perceived as overworked, underpaid, and often as under-educated, but not likely as deviant. There are few jokes made about him.

In contrast, it is sobering to assess the image of the mental health professional as expressed by folk humor. To begin with, cartoons, newspaper and magazine picture jokes, as well as popular verbal jokes, depict the mental health professional as deviant, either in appearance and/or in mannerisms. Furthermore, they depict him as being disordered himself. In these media, there appears to be no end to themes suggesting that marriage counsellors have marital problems, that child therapists either do not have children of their own or do not know how to rear them, and that counsellors and therapists in general are rather odd.

Such images could be interpreted away as versions of the type of defensive humor that may ward off anxiety about a self-threatening situation. However, looking at my own experience in the mental health field, I must conclude that there is much truth in the public image, that this image is much of our own making, and that it is not conducive to normalizing action. Thus, we should address ourselves much more consciously and vigorously to the differential recruitment of such kinds of individuals as are apt to be seen by the public and potential consumers as life-style models rather than deviant.

Aside from client-staff deviancy juxtapositions, greater efforts should be made to avoid client-client deviancy juxtaposition. An example would be a public institution which has on its grounds a maximum security unit for disordered criminals and major sex offenders, or a sheltered community workshop where a large number of alcoholics and drug addicts are served together with a small number of persons with relatively minor and temporary disorders.

A common mistake here is to equate deviancy juxtaposition with normalizing generic integration. Juxtaposition mixes groups of deviant persons; it does not necessarily integrate them into the societal mainstream. The type of normalizing generic integration discussed in the chapter on 'Societal integration as a corollary of normalization' emphasizes integration of deviant persons with nondeviant ones.

Career models

The issue of socialization via career modelling has come up repeatedly in this book. Such career modelling can be maladaptive, as it is likely to be when deviancy juxtaposition takes place. We, of course, must be concerned with normalizing career modelling.

Normalizing career modelling is particularly important in services for children (*e.g.* Linton, 1969), adolescents, and young adults, where the manager is very apt to become the model. Unfortunately, typical mental health personnel are not always – or even often – appropriate models for clients, especially not for adolescents, and particularly not for adolescents who are not bound for a higher education. Thus, a special point should be made in developing and training individuals who can act as suitable career models via roles such as trainers, counsellors, and other high-contact personnel. For instance, it is quite conceivable that college students in physical education, athletes (*e.g.* Wright & Mann, 1969), or successful master craftsmen from industry, could be persuaded to take up careers which combine elements of the houseparent, therapist, counsellor, and teacher role.

Conclusion

The reader may recall that the normalization principle suggests action on three levels and in two dimensions. As in most other human management areas, the interaction dimension of the person level has devoured the bulk of efforts in the mental disorder field. But unlike some other fields, movement toward more systemic management has not only been slower and more controversial, but also less successful. Even group and family therapy, and consultation on the agency level, has still concerned itself too much with the management of existing, *ad hoc*, clinical problems, and not enough with the restructuring of the systems involved, especially the type of systems and the type of restructuring which have a strong bearing on prevention. The normalization principle presents a powerful rationale for a redistribution of priorities, so that the systemic and societal levels of action will receive at least as much attention as the clinical (person) level.

Also, while much has been accomplished in the normalizing interpretation of disordered individuals, there is still a great deal of interactive work that will be wasted unless more intensive stress is placed on certain normalizing interpretive practices which have been neglected so far, and which have not been well conceptualized prior to the advent of the normalization principle. The most powerful example here is the issue of juxtaposition of deviancies discussed earlier.

Clinical action can be very satisfying – or merely very convenient. Systemic and societal action can also be most satisfying – though it is rarely convenient. Those who are goal-oriented rather than process-oriented should bear in mind that by such action, as well as by special emphasis on normalizing interpretation, they can often achieve more in a few years than they can in a lifetime of clinical work, if such clinical work takes place within the context of inappropriate and maladaptive systems.

Modern management concepts dictate that when resources available to a service system are limited, priorities must be set. These priorities should be conscious rather than unconscious or chaotic; and they should be consistent with cultural values, societal needs, and national goals. At least, these should all be considered consciously, and programs should not merely be based on tradition, continuity, inertia, or convenience. A number of systemic measures of vast potential come to mind that would appear to implement these concepts.

> The mental health service systems should increasingly reflect the ongoing evolution of civil rights. Thus, both the human management structure and the design of service facilities should maximize clients' privacy, dignity, and freedom.
>
> There should be much more emphasis on prevention rather than on correction. At present, almost the entire mental health effort is devoted to correction only, or to prevention on the secondary rather than primary level. This is tragic, especially considering the billions of dollars and legions of manpower involved. The degree to which the personnel of our mental health system is almost exclusively concerned with conflict resolution rather than conflict prevention is apparent in the following phenomena.
>
>> In most cases, clients enter a service, especially a residential service, *after* a crisis of major proportion has occurred, and the personnel in our service system perceive themselves as successful if the client resolves his major crisis of the moment. Indeed, intermittent residence is increasingly seen as a success, compared to the more common longterm institutionalizations in the past.
>>
>> The bulk of mental health services is rendered to adults (*e.g.* Joint Commission on the Mental Health of Children, 1970; Rosen,

Kramer, Redick, & Willner, 1968), even though it is universally acknowledged that disordered behavior in adulthood generally has its origins in childhood. For example, there are almost half a million persons in average daily residence in US state and county mental hospitals. This service system has a full-time staff of over 200,000, and costs about $1.5 billion a year to operate. Untold other citizens are rendered non-residential services devouring further bulks of money. The great majority of these individuals are adults.[7]

Mental health personnel are only minimally involved in the structuring or restructuring of those societal institutions that play a major role in the causation or potential prevention of disordered behavior. One major societal institution involved here is the school system. Others are social and welfare agencies, civic organizations, and industry.

Preventive efforts would imply a major shift in professional functioning, away from the clinical level, and toward a systemic level. Systemic work would address itself to parent education, classroom structure, school structure, development of early education structures, curricular development, prevention of poverty which is a prime breeder of mental disorder, prevention of ethnic prejudices which result in poverty and disordering in minority groups, *etc.*

Because of the nature of their training and the rigidity of their functioning, I doubt seriously whether most *current* mental health personnel could play highly effective roles on the systemic level. However, dispersal and specialization of services consistent with normalization principles would force such personnel to involve themselves in an entirely new way with the community, a way which is much more meaningful and probably much more constructive than the traditional, usually stereotyped, hospital-type model that often prevails even in non-residential settings.

Although the normalization principle, which may very well become a universal human management ideology, has swept into prominence in Danish and Swedish mental retardation laws and practice, not even in Denmark or Sweden has the principle been accepted by the field of psychiatry. Part of the resistance appears due to the fact that the two 'fathers' of the principle are viewed as amateurs, since one of them had his primary training in law, and the other one in literature.

I expect that in North America, too, the normalization principle will encounter much more resistance in mental health than in mental retardation. Mental health is dominated by a large, highly-trained, and highly 'certified' elite which already has strong commitments to ideologies and administrative patterns which will make implementation of normalization principles difficult. In contrast, in the 1960's and 1970's, the leadership in mental retardation was relatively small, and suffused with persons of modest and often no

[7] Smith and Hobbs (1966) discuss some of the implications of a survey of the eleven supposedly most advanced mental health centers in the United States, which disclosed that these centers were primarily adult-oriented. Unfortunately, comparable data on the allocation of mental health resources to children in Canada are not as readily available (Commission on Emotional and Learning Disorders in Children, 1970, p. 53).

'certification' (academic degrees, boards, *etc.*). Also, the major existing commitment was to an ultimately indefensible model: the dehumanizing institution. If mental health had not made such gratifying progress since the end of World War II, it might be easier to enlist support for normalization measures today. Truly, the good can be the worst enemy of the best.

However, if the normalization principle were adopted in the mental health field, it would probably not only make for adaptive unity, but for a renewed and increased relevance – a relevance all human management areas are now seeking to increase.

On a very personal level, the urgency to adopt and implement an ideology such as conveyed by the normalization principle was forcefully brought home to me by a poignant experience. In the summer of 1969, I attended a meeting of a self-help community action group of which I was a member and which had as its goal the generation and extension of services to unserviced or underserviced mentally and physically handicapped children of the poor and disadvantaged. The meeting had to terminate abruptly, and most of us felt we were fleeing for our lives because rioting and burning had broken out in the immediate neighborhood, touched off by the apparently senseless shooting of a 14-year old Negro girl by a white policeman who was later released on a $500 bond and ultimately pronounced 'not guilty'. Ironically, it turned out that the girl was chronically physically handicapped and thus one of the very children with whom our group was concerned.

This experience impressed upon me even more the futility of past approaches to deal with our urgent social issues. Our society may have very little time left. Ills so eloquently alluded to by Will (1968), such as race hatred, poverty, drug addiction, alcoholism, delinquency and crime, family dissolution, emotional disturbance, national disunity, and other problems combine into such an urgent crisis as to call for different, powerful, and socially captivating human management ideologies; for less bickering over professional role prerogatives; and for more role performance.

In a very profound treatise on the structure and function of what he calls 'settings', Sarason (1969) quotes John Gardner (1965) that '. . . in every case of organization decline that I know anything about, there were ample warning signals long before trouble struck. And I don't mean warning signals that only a Monday-morning quarterback could discern. I mean that before trouble stuck there were observers who had correctly diagnosed the difficulties to come. Now if there are plenty of warning signals, and no organization really wants to go to seed, *why does it happen?* The answer is obvious – eyes that see not, ears that hear not, minds that deny the evidence before them. When organizations are not meeting the challenge of change, it is as a rule not because they can't *solve* their problems but because they won't *see* their problems; not because they don't *know* their faults, but because they *rationalize them as virtues or necessities.*'

Murphy (1969), in a brilliant commentary on mental health and poverty, recently said: '. . . those that speak for the mental health movement need to challenge established ideas and to give some lead to social action, instead of providing painless explanations of our present discontents.' Surely, if we do not adopt radically new measures, if we do not shed our complacency, or if we follow the course advocated by respected but traditionalist spokesmen such as cited earlier in this essay, not merely some of our professions, but our very society may die. I submit that the normalization principle is the means by which both adaptive change and unity can be achieved in the field of mental health, and by which powerful forces can be mobilized to go to work on our societal ills.

9 normalizing activation for the profoundly retarded and/or multiply handicapped

A need for a change orientation

In all fields, frontiers come and go as new frontiers replace old ones. But the rates at which frontiers emerge vary from field to field, and vary within a field from one epoch to another.

In this chapter, I want to write about a frontier in fields concerned with severe physical impairments, especially mental retardation and cerebral palsy. To many readers, it may come as a surprise to hear that mental retardation was a dynamic and change-oriented field between about 1850 and 1920, because thence forward, it lay dormant and stagnant for almost forty years. This stagnation was due to the dissipation of dynamism during the frenzy of the so-called genetic alarm period (*circa* 1890-1920), when it was thought that mental retardation was the mother of all social ills, and could destroy our society.

In the early 1950's, dynamism slowly began to return to the field, and bold leaders began to sketch new frontiers for action. A frontier then, but a commonplace now, is the provision of special education for the mildly retarded. A more recent frontier has been the provision of educational services for the severely retarded, and although the decisive battle here has been won, sizeable mop-up operations remain. One of the most recent frontiers on which the battle has only joined in the last few years is the reform of residential services. Other examples of the expansion of our frontiers may be familiar to the reader.

Most men do not anticipate the future, but yield to it – often grudgingly, belatedly, and inadequately. Yet today, for the first time, we are reaching the point where we can bring the accumulation of a considerable and ever-increasing body of knowledge and understanding about the process of change itself to bear upon our destinies. No longer is it necessary to have change happen to us, or to let it be imposed upon us from without. We can rise up from within to meet new challenges in an anticipatory fashion.

In one's own field, can one not survey the frontiers, articulate the events taking place at its edge, interpret them sensitively, and formulate the challenge posed? Can we not anticipate and lead, instead of procrastinating, and finally being pushed? Of course we can! And in a number of areas, the indicators and omens are rather clear.

I will have the boldness to attempt here to define one of our frontier challenges – but I hasten to state that nothing I am about to say originates from

I am indebted to Rosemary and Gunnar Dybwad, Karl Grunewald, Una Haynes, Elsie Helsel, Robert Kugel, and Robert Perske for substantial critiques of earlier drafts of this paper.

me. It has been said and even done; but it has not been adequately articulated and broadcast, and that will be my goal.

The frontier I speak about is what the Scandinavians have called 'activation'. Activation not only refers to the involvement of persons in meaningful, and hopefully normalizing activities, but to a significant degree, it also implies motor involvement and ambulation, or at least mobility.

The tragedy of the unactivated

Today, in almost all of our traditional mental retardation institutions, and even in some newer residential centers, we can see 'acres of beds' filled with individuals who are not ambulatory, who spend virtually their entire time in bed, and who – for the most part – are profoundly retarded. Sometimes, a superintendent may challenge his staff to 'get them out of bed', but the staff may be so little attuned to the growth potential of the retarded or nonambulatory that little more may be done than to transfer the resident from the bed to the floor. When the next challenge to 'get them off the floors' is issued, the nonambulatory residents may be placed on raised, table-like, platforms. But neither on floor nor platform may the resident be activated any more than in his bed. Even placement in wheelchairs may lose most of its meaning if it is not accompanied by additional measures.

Some interesting data have been provided by a number of studies. Unfortunately, they involve public institutions only in the United States, and I have not been able to locate equivalent studies for Canadian institutions. Thus, in a survey of 22 Western state institutions (Payne, Johnson, & Abelson, 1969), 24% of the 24,257 residents, or an astounding total of 5,943, were found to be nonambulatory. Remarkable also was the fact that the nonambulatory population was reported to be as low as about 2% in one institution, and as high as 96% in another.

In a survey of 26,000 residents of New York state institutions for the retarded (Rosenberg, 1969), 46% were judged to require 'substantial medical or nursing care', 24% had to be bathed or dressed, and 14% could not ambulate independently.

A rather detailed survey (conducted by Craig Affleck, and reported in Governor's Citizens' Committee, 1968b) of 1,908 residents at Nebraska's only and rather typical state institution for the retarded revealed a degree of behavioral inadequacy that is startling (see *Table 1*), especially if one considers that at least 77% of the residents were classified as above the profound level of retardation, and that less than 5% were below five years of age.

Table 1
Behavioral adequacy of residents at a typical midwestern state institution

	Help needed (percent of residents)				
Behavior	Total	Considerable	Some	Little	None
Grooming	32%	6%	7%	14%	42%
Dressing	30%	8%	10%	13%	39%
Eating	13%	2%	3%	9%	73%
Bath-Shower	41%	6%	8%	8%	37%

The report also revealed that 4% of the residents included in the survey could not even sit up, 7% could sit up but not stand, and 3% could stand but not walk. Only 72% could negotiate stairs unsupported. Most tragically, perhaps, was the finding that 48% of the residents never left the 'ward', and only 30% left it regularly, and for at least four hours a day. These percentage figures assume special meaning when one considers the number of individuals involved, and the congregation of these large numbers of individuals into large groups. For instance, most of the individuals who cannot sit up (4%, which translates to 78 persons) were found in two living units.

There has been relatively little or diminishing controversy that much could be accomplished with the mildly, moderately, and even severely retarded residents of our institutions. Especially in recent years, there has also been growing awareness that a much larger percentage of the ambulatory severely and profoundly retarded could be toilet trained. (For purely historical reasons, toilet training has become somewhat of a fixation of behavior shaping approaches). However, when it comes to the nonambulatory retarded, especially the nonambulatory profoundly retarded, there still prevails widespread acquiescence to the inevitability of their helplessness. Also, one encounters the attitude that the normalization principle loses its applicability as one deals with more severely impaired individuals.

Indeed, some well-meaning analyses in recent years have even contributed to this fatalism. For instance, a number of writers in the last few years have documented that institutional admissions have tended toward younger and more seriously impaired individuals.[2] However, rather than sounding a call for extra measures of activation to meet this challenge, most of these projections implied a need to prepare hospital-like wards for permanently invalid and helpless individuals, many of whom were expected to spend their lives hovering near death.

To many, death came swiftly and – in the circumstances – mercifully. The magnitude of the death rate upon admission, though incredibly high, has received very little attention in the field – perhaps because the reality was too unpleasant to contemplate. For instance, in a recent review (Kurtz & Wolfensberger, 1969), it was found that children's mortality in the first year of institutional residence was sometimes near 50%. On the other hand, a time trend study (Tarjan, Brooke, Eyman, Suyeyasu, & Miller, 1968; Tarjan, Eyman, & Miller, 1969) suggested that even when younger and more handicapped persons are admitted, first-year mortality can be reduced sharply, apparently as a result of more aggressive medical treatment policy. Thus, high death rates do not have to be accepted as inevitable concomitants of resident characteristics.

The challenge of the Scandinavian experience

We have so much to learn from Scandinavian services to the retarded that an irrational defensive 'Scandinavian backlash' can sometimes be noted. At some professional and even parent meetings, one merely has to make a reference to the Scandinavian model to feel a wave of resentment, or to note members of the group 'tuning out'. Indeed, this is the kind of chauvinism which Dybwad (1969) discussed as one of the roadblocks to change and

[2] There is reason to believe that this trend has stabilized (Wolfensberger, 1971).

progress. We must be sensitive to the possible existence of such chauvinism within us, and combat it lest it interfere with our quest for self-renewal.

On my visit to Scandinavia in 1969, I experienced some new and profound insights, even though I had seen literally dozens of slide presentations on Scandinavian services, heard Scandinavian leaders talk, and had interacted intensively with them on a personal and collaborative basis (*e.g.* see Bank-Mikkelsen, 1969; Grunewald, 1969; Nirje, 1969a, 1969b). I saw both activation and normalization carried to degrees I had not believed possible, and I can only conclude that for the vast majority of persons professionally 'raised' in North America, no amount of verbal and pictorial communication can equal the learning – almost conversion – impact of a visit to Scandinavia. Some critics who hasten to point to weaknesses in the Scandinavian systems – and I believe some rather obvious weaknesses do exist – fail to recognize the overwhelming reality of the pervasiveness of activation and normalization. Thus, the pictures one sees at the Scandinavian travelogue lectures are not isolated examples and showcases; they are rather typical and actually quite inadequate documentations of the scenes one encounters again and again throughout these service systems.

Activation is merely one of many expressions of the ideology of normalization. But to see the normalization principle implemented, especially via activation, demonstrates that the Scandinavians do not merely have ideas and ideals, but have proven on a broad scale that this state of mind can be converted into concrete external realities.

The fact that profound retardation need not be so extensively equated with immobility was poignantly brought home to me by observing a particular living unit in a Scandinavian institution which was actually rather backward by Scandinavian standards. In this unit, 60 of 68 adult residents were not toilet trained, but only one was chronically bedfast, and about twelve were wheelchair-bound; the rest were ambulatory. A situation such as this would not be particularly remarkable in Canada or the United States – except for the fact that in this institution of 650, these were the most retarded and impaired persons to be found.

When visiting Scandinavian institutions, I made a special point to seek out the living units for the most problematic and retarded pesons – the kind of living units every administrator feels a bit uneasy about. In one modern institution for over 350 residents, visited in mid-afternoon, I searched high and low but found only three persons lying in bed. Even in a larger and more traditional institution of approximately 1,000, there were only about 20 residents in bed, and most of these were sick that day. There were many more who were nonambulatory – but they were up and about in wheelchairs, walkers, sitters, standers, and what have you, doing things and going places. In some living units, it was hard to get about – because of all the wheelchairs and special devices. Acres of full beds replaced by acres of activation equipment!

Also of interest was a policy in some institutions of distributing nonambulatory residents around the various buildings, instead of concentrating them into one unit. The rationale for this is twofold: concentration of the most helpless residents into one area creates an attitude of defeatism and apathy in the staff, as we so well know; and dispersal among ambulatory residents brings the nonambulatory person into a more normalizing atmosphere where he is both expected and apt to participate more, move more, and perhaps become ambulatory or at least mobile, without necessarily affecting the normalization of less handicapped residents.

Another result of both normalization and activation in Scandinavia is noteworthy: one will no longer see the enlarged heads resulting from hydrocephaly. Today, operations are performed in virtually all cases before the head enlarges. What a contrast that is with our attitudes which, to this day, devalue such operations for the retarded or presumed retarded, and with the results of these attitudes: rows of beds with helpless persons, grotesquely enlarged heads, grievous bed sores, and progressive deterioration; all this leading to the creation of major and expensive nursing problems, lack of learning in the child, and deprivation of social acceptance, potential mobility, and often even of life itself.

A North American counter-challenge

I found it remarkable that the Scandinavians could achieve so much ambulation, mobility, and normalization even without the application of operant conditioning which we have come to look upon as our only or major tool in improving the competence of the severely impaired. Furthermore, while much work is done with children, the Scandinavians, like ourselves, have only begun to exploit the plasticity of early childhood for developmental purposes.

These observations have led me to conclude that even the Scandinavians are nowhere near the limit of what can be achieved. Therefore, I have formulated a bold – perhaps foolhardy – challenge to ourselves: to perceive and embrace a concept of activation which includes as a major goal the *virtually total abolition of immobility, and to a large extent also nonambulation, of the profoundly retarded and multiply handicapped.*

Furthermore, I feel that the facts justify the conclusion that the service system which will combine operant shaping techniques, activation, normalization, and intensive emphasis upon the young (age 0-6) impaired child will see successes of a degree beyond our power to conceptualize at this time. Among these successes will also be the prevention of intellectual retardation in many severely cerebral palsied children; and the raising of intellectual functioning of many young retarded children by one, two, and perhaps even more levels (a level having a range of about 15-16 IQ points).

Is this an unreasonable prediction? The Scandinavians with whom I discussed it did not think so, and on the abstract level, most North American workers would probably agree, too. I was amused by the fact that some of my Scandinavian friends, basking in the glory of their programs, seem to be looking over their shoulders with some unease. As one of them put it: 'Once the Americans discover what can be done, and put their energy and money to it, they will not merely catch up with us, but overtake us, and even finally leave us far behind.'

I believe this view has much validity, and that we can bring this state about. However, all of us, and Americans in particular, must divest ourselves of a widespread 'American delusion' that money alone is the solution to all problems. With all the money in the world, we shall achieve nothing unless our ideology tells us what to do. I have seen one attendant sit and stare from behind a glass wall at a vast day room with 50 children milling purposelessly, and I have seen the same scene with seven attendants sitting and staring. Money for 50 attendants would have yielded no additional benefits – because there would have been no ideology to convert the money or the manpower into beneficial action and tangible results.

Perhaps for the first time, we now have some comparative data to support objectively some of the impressions gained by visiting Swedish mental retardation services. The mental retardation office of the Swedish National Board of Health and Welfare has recently conducted a national survey of movement-impaired retarded persons in 161 residences for the retarded all over Sweden (Wallner, 1970), accommodating a total of 12,338 persons. Only 382 persons were defined as 'bed-lyers'. Even among these, 34% got out of bed at least 6 hours a day, 24% got out 7 hours, and 17% got out up to 8 hours. Only 126 (33%) never left the bed. Furthermore, 117 (31%) were below age 10, and only 37 (10%) were above age 60, bearing testimony to the effects of activating programs earlier in their lives.[3] When these figures for a population of 8 million are compared to figures which I happen to have available on Nebraska (with a population of 1.5 million), we find that Nebraska has a rate of approximately 0.00024 bed-fast or bed-near retarded persons, versus 0.000048 for Sweden, *i.e. five times as many* at a comparable point in time. I would not be surprised if more precise comparisons revealed a difference that is even larger.

It seems fairly evident that Scandinavians have virtually solved the problem of non-mobility. Why do we have so many people who see no alternatives to our current practices? Thus, more than money, we shall need an ideology, an attitude, a conviction, a determination!

How is activation to be achieved?

Some approaches to activation have been mentioned above, and obviously, intensive environmental enrichment and systematic developmental programming are the general means of activation. However, seven specific vehicles will be elaborated below. These are physical therapeutics, a movement-oriented curriculum, emphasis on younger children, operant shaping, developmental materials, special developmental environments, and developmental role perceptions.

PHYSICAL THERAPEUTICS

In the last decades, our institutions have usually laid claim to a medical model without being able to deliver either the needed quantity or quality of medical services. An example – if any is really needed – has already been cited: the almost incredibly high mortality rates of those persons newly admitted to institutions, especially of those admitted at an early age (see review by Kurtz & Wolfensberger, 1969). To give another example: in 1962, George A. Andrews conducted a survey determining the availability of various therapies to the multihandicapped residents of our institutions. He concluded that two-thirds of the institutions were providing mainly custodial care for such persons (cited in Stimson, 1967).

Paradoxically, now that we are moving away from medical and toward

[3] Higher mortality in Sweden can almost certainly be ruled out as an explanation for the low number of inactive aged.

adoption of developmental models, we may be able to include in them a medical component of adequate quantity and high quality. Within this medical component, outstanding glory can be earned by what I will loosely call 'physical therapeutics'. By this, I mean primarily orthopedics and physiatry, and related areas such as orthotics and physical therapy.

Orthopedic surgery has been widely withheld from the retarded because of judgments that such surgery was 'wasted', particularly for the severely and profoundly retarded. In part, this was a very dehumanizing value judgment; but in part, it was also an accurate empirical judgment because of the lack of appropriate therapeutic follow-up without which surgery is largely meaningless.

One major aspect of such follow-up consists of the design and supervised use of devices which enable, support, enhance, or encourage sitting, standing, walking, mobility, and other adaptive behaviors. Turning frames prepare for standing and can enhance educational participation of the totally nonambulatory. Corsets, braces, and orthopedic shoes develop erect posture, sitting, and standing, as do various types of chairs such as 'relaxation chairs'. Cut-out, stand-in, and standing tables, as well as standing stabilizers support or develop sustained standing behavior and thereby prepare for walking. Walking aides include suspension devices, skid walkers, infant walkers, C.P. walkers, walkerettes, and diverse types of gliders and crutches. A multitude of wheeled equipment, such as specially designed 'belly-boards', velocipedes, tricycles, and trainer bicycles provide playful mobility as well as excellent activating experiences to children. The ways in which wheelchairs for adults can be modified appear to be limitless.

The list could go on. There is nothing new about any of these devices – except that one does not see them used very much in retardation, and even less so with the young and/or severely damaged retarded person. It is time to introduce to the field of mental retardation the ingenuity practised in the mainstream of orthopedics, orthotics, and physiatry, and to correlate – even integrate – these aspects closely with other medical and behavioral measures.

Another aspect of follow-up is physical therapy. Here, we not only need 'more'; we need a new model. Because of manpower shortage, the physical therapy needs of the retarded may be neither met nor meetable via traditional methods of practice. What is probably needed are large numbers of technicians working under the direction of qualified therapists who themselves rarely engage in direct therapy, except for teaching and demonstration purposes. Also, physical therapists must begin to become effective consultants to educational programs, and thus 'multiply' themselves indirectly.

Young children and the multiply handicapped have the most urgent need of physical therapy. An early investment here will repay itself manifold.

A MOVEMENT-ORIENTED EDUCATIONAL CURRICULUM

Our educational programs must revise their curricula so as to introduce much more movement and rhythmics. I do not mean to imply that we should eliminate present teaching content and methods, but that we should both add to it, as well as revise our methods so that content now taught with little utilization of perceptual-motor processes is taught in more extensive association with them. Many such methods, and even entire systems, exist. However, such methods have often been developed and described in isolation rather than in a systemic context, and the systems themselves have often been idiosyncratic or dogmatic, thereby scaring away many potential users.

For instance, many creative methods have been developed within the Doman-Delacato system, but its quite unnecessary theoretical framework, the questionable nature of this framework, the dogmatic isolation of the system, and its advocacy of certain (actually, a very small number) techniques generally held to be ineffective or possibly even harmful has driven away many potential users. The materials and methods developed within the Kephart system have suffered from unnecessarily close association with the concept of brain injury. One of the more promising approaches appears to be that of Barsch (1967), whose term 'movigenics' I am tempted to apply broadly to what I have called a 'movement-oriented curriculum'. Another term and concept I find useful is Asher's (1969) 'total physical response technique'.

One of the major ways of fusing traditional content with physical activation is via the introduction of music, song, and eurhythmics. Musical rhythmics has the advantage of being not only exceedingly activating, but also very enjoyable. However, it would have to consist of more than the undisciplined movements our teachers tend to accept uncritically in the typical musical action exercises observed in our classrooms. Increased and more systematized use of music is one of the latent, undiscovered giants of North American education.

EMPHASIS ON YOUNGER CHILDREN

The younger the person, the more effective are activating measures likely to be. Virtually everybody agrees to this, but far too little is done about it. We still exclude severely retarded children from programs because they are not toilet trained, or for the supreme absurdity: because they are not old enough. There still lingers the myth that formal programming should wait for some type of 'natural' maturation process to have run its course; and somehow, the largely coincidental legal school entry age of ordinary children is still widely perceived as the minimum age for initiating formal programming for the severely impaired.

Activating programming must begin as early as developmental retardation or impairment is recognized. For many types of learning, there exist sensitive or even critical periods, and a year's intensive activation at age two or three may be worth two or three years at age eight, or a lifetime at age twelve.

Here is where the rapidly developing early childhood education movement in North America could out-perform the Scandinavians who provide relatively little early programming to retarded children outside of institutions. Within these institutions, early programming focuses more on social and physical development; it is not yet deliberately and consciously oriented to the actual shaping of intellect.

However, in order to institute intensive early activation, we shall either need better early case findings, or universal early education, or both. Early case findings will require much reeducation of pediatricians and general practitioners. Fortunately, the prospects for universal early childhood education are excellent, and we shall probably see gradual lowering of public education entry ages down to age three, and perhaps even two.

OPERANT SHAPING

While operant and related principles have usually been present in inarticulated form in all good programming, they are only beginning to be formally recognized in Scandinavian services. Yet, with its pragmatic ideology and methods, operant shaping – and especially the version elaborated by O. R. Lindsley – is an approach of vast potential. We now have adequate foundations in this approach, so that it could be massively injected into our service systems. However, we must address ourselves consciously to using operant principles in a way which minimizes artificial elements and features, and which are not only normalizing but also normalized.

Furthermore, we must be aware of the danger inherent in a merely superficial faddish and ritualistic application of operant principles. Today, many programs pay lip service to operant principles, and purport to apply them, but the staff may lack understanding of and training in such principles, or commitment to them. Thus, their work can only be described as constituting desultory and cavalier dabbling in operant shaping, and can be harmful to the entire system which may be judged and condemned because of the failure of its unskilled application. Also, proponents of operant shaping systems must recognize the limitations as well as the strengths of these techniques, and the need to employ additional means, even if these are not yet (or even ever will be) as operationally specifiable as the parameters which have prominence in operant conditioning.

DEVELOPMENTAL MATERIALS

Many new and good developmental materials have been introduced in just the last few years, but more are needed. Also, their existence and use must be communicated better. Educational material centers in the US must give up their roles as relatively ineffective and passive depositors and exhibitors of materials, and assume the role for which they were largely created, namely that of evaluators and experimenters. Indeed, considering the vast sums of money expended on them, they have the responsibility of becoming innovators!

So far, innovations in educational materials have come largely from overseas. An interesting recent event was an industrial design conference which was held in 1968 in Finland, where students invented, designed, and built toys and equipment intended to enhance the learning of cerebral palsied children. Others invent, and then we copy, manufacture, and market, often ten years later – in the case of Montessori materials, fifty years later. One would think that our vast materials market could also inspire and support more innovation.

Of course, materials should be developed not as an intellectual exercise, but to a purpose. We not only need to invent more devices and gadgetry, but to use what we have.

SPECIAL DEVELOPMENTAL ENVIRONMENTS

Examples of special developmental environments are the prototype playground for the retarded designed by a Canadian (Hayden, 1969) under the auspices of the Kennedy Foundation, the 'model recreational park' depicted in the 1968 report of the President's Committee on Mental Retardation, and Heather's (1970) playground garden. Another example is an experimental residential and learning environment designed by the British architect Bayes, as presented at the 1969 convention of the National Association for Retarded Children. Also, a number of operant living (*e.g.* Roberts & Perry, 1970) and workshop environments (*e.g.* Gardner, 1971) have been designed and described in the literature. Such experimental models need to be extended, made routinely functional, and applied to even the most severely impaired (*e.g.* Ricke, McDaniel, Stallings, & Gatz, 1967).

On the horizon are automated environments which conjoin the potentials of operant shaping, environmental engineering, and computer technology. The 'responsive autotelic environment' ('talking typewriter') developed by O. K. Moore has been an example of a step in this direction, as is the PLAYTEST system developed by B. Friedlander, which automates the shaping of infants' behavior right in their own cribs.

DEVELOPMENTAL ROLE PERCEPTIONS

One of the major facts established by social psychologists is that people generally will play the social role that is assigned to them. Social roles can be demanding, and can motivate individuals to virtually 'rise above themselves'; or they can be degrading or indulgent, and elicit only a fraction of the behavioral potential of a person. Indeed, role expectancies can even reduce a person so that he will function far below a previous level.

In the past, we have imposed extremes of role expectations upon retarded (and often other handicapped) persons. We either demanded normal role performance in all or most aspects of functioning, or we imposed dehumanizing or at least very undemanding expectations, as when we viewed a retarded person as an 'eternal child'. To this day, the vast majority of child development and special education programs for the younger retarded are merely advanced baby-sitting, compared to what could and should be done. All this must change!

To change the unrealistic developmental role perceptions that have been common in our service systems during the last forty years will be most difficult unless we take radical measures. To do this, we must distinguish between *higher* expectancies, and *normal* ones; we must distinguish between various areas of functioning; and then we must impose *realistically high* and *occasionally normal* expectancies on *selected* areas and *selected* individuals. We must endeavor that with the aid of our services, the handicapped attain their potential, and we must formulate roles for them that discourage dependency and encourage growth.

Perhaps one of the major ways of achieving this goal is to integrate the physically handicapped with the physically sound, and the mentally retarded with those of higher functioning. Instead of putting all the nonambulatory together into one sea of beds, we should experiment with dispersal of the nonambulatory among the ambulatory, and impose mobility upon the nonambulatory even if this sometimes means no more than wheelchair mobility. As expectations rise, so will performance, growth, and independence.

We are rather apt to view Scandinavian socialism as leading to pampering, and as imposing low expectations in regard to work and initiative. Yet when it comes to making the retarded ambulatory, the Danes and Swedes turn almost fierce in their determination – but their successes prove that their high expectancies for mobility and ambulation have not been unrealistic.

INTERRELATIONSHIP BETWEEN ACTIVATING MEASURES

An element which is implicit in virtually all of the mechanisms of activation is individualization of approach. Thus, gadgetry and therapeutic appliances may have to be individually designed, fitted, and used; some activities and exercises have to be planned on an individual basis; schedules of activities will have to vary greatly for different persons; *etc.* This need for individualization has certain secondary implications to our residential centers where the majority of the severely multiply handicapped retarded live. One of these implications is the need for small living units, in order to prevent the otherwise virtually unavoidable – almost 'natural' – tendency to regiment large groups, and to manage them according to their lowest common denominator.

Of major importance is the intermeshing of all aspects of activation. These various aspects are not merely additive, but often profoundly interdependent. Thus, orthopedic surgery without physical therapy is largely wasted; physical therapy without orthopedic surgery cannot attain its potential; failure to combine both of these approaches with general environmental enrichment, especially via education (in the broad sense), is grossly inefficient; and so forth.

One issue is particularly timely, and that is the integrated use of physical therapy. Physical therapy practices are still heavily influenced by the polio era, when a major challenge was the strengthening of muscles in individuals who were generally of sound mind. With the passing of this challenge, a new major one today is posed by individuals of severely impaired mentality and with brain injury, who must develop control and coordination of movement, and not merely muscular strength. Even less than for the polio victim, it is not enough to provide physical therapy for them in the typical isolated settings, in special rooms, and at special times. Having a limb 'pumped' or 'cranked' sporadically by a therapist is of little avail to them. If physical therapy is to be fully relevant to them, it must become a part of daily living, and therefore must be practised by all those who work with the handicapped person, particularly teachers. A commitment to such a conceptualization would imply a profound change in the functioning of much of our physical therapy personnel, and many other workers.

By incorporating a heavier movement element and emphasis into our other educational approaches, we are not merely adding content, and not merely adding economy by combining the learning of motor and other elements; we are also reaping the benefits of growth in those perceptual-motor processes which underlie or even constitute what we call intelligence. Many of these processes, though both essential and shapable, have been neglected in our traditional approaches.

Another by-product that can be expected from activation is a strengthening of the body image. In turn, this should result in increased self-confidence and better emotional adjustment.

After reaching its limits, physical therapeutics may still leave the person without having attained full and independent mobility. In such cases, we must strive not merely to maintain the highest level of mobility, but to maximize other kinds of activation and development. For instance, in Scandinavia, I saw many severely retarded nonambulatory children attending school on special beds, in wheelchairs, and in standing tables. In some cases, these devices were intended not so much to be physically therapeutic, but to permit *other* developmental activities to take place. One device was a hoist that could be rolled about, and that could be used to hoist a nonambulatory person from his bed by means of a variety of special-purpose slings, roll him over a bath tub or toilet, and thereby permit him to perform his own toileting or bathing. Such persons we would see in bed with a bedpan, washed with a sponge, or – if 'fortunate' – washed on a slab like a corpse. The hoist and its accessories permitted such persons to gain the dignity of learning to perform these highly personal functions independently and in private.

Much as physical therapeutics can be a means for shaping mentality so that a multiply handicapped child attains his full intellectual potential, so can lack of physical maintenance produce a tragic mental debilitation.

Activation action

Fortunately, there are stirrings on the frontier of activation. Some of these have been mentioned, and a number of others are apparent.

Increasing concern with physical fitness of the retarded: here, an entire new movement had its origin in Canada, especially with Hayden (1964). This movement was taken up by the Kennedy Foundation in the United States, and the Harry E. Foster Foundation in Canada, and has resulted in many developments including the Special Olympics movement. This emphasis has also stimulated the American and Canadian Associations for Health, Physical Education, and Recreation to become very involved in the area, and to issue a series of highly useful publications which are concerned with activating procedures and methods.

A relatively sudden increase in the number of publications concerned with the movement-mediated development of retarded or otherwise handicapped persons: in Europe, perceptual-motor and movement-related approaches to education have been part of the educational mainstream for over a century. These approaches typically involve a great deal of rhythmics and gymnastics – not only to a degree unknown in North America, but also tied to a large number of developmental theories and sub-theories. We are beginning to rediscover the importance of these approaches which previously probably had their most effective proponent in Seguin (*e.g.* Talbot, 1964).

An increased attention to the physical therapy and orthopedic needs of the young and profoundly retarded: unfortunately, advances along these lines often occur in an imbalanced fashion, underlining the lack of understanding that many persons have of the interplay between developmental areas. Thus, I have seen institutional programs where outstanding work was done in corrective and orthopedic surgery – in the virtual absence of a physical therapy and environmental enrichment program which would have brought to fruition the orthopedic investment. Nevertheless, the many fledgling trends on all horizons about us are encouraging harbingers of a whole new vista.

Conclusion

A phrase much-heard in Denmark refers to certain older retarded persons as 'casualities of the pre-1959 era', because it was in that year that the new mental retardation services act went into effect. In analogy, our own unactivated are the victims of the pre-1970 era. At this time, at which we are so apt to introspect about our past, and attempt to fathom the future, will we make commitments to the newly-perceived challenges of activation, or will we some day speak of the casualties of the pre-1980, or pre-1990, or even pre-2000 era?

In concluding, I want to reemphasize one point: the activating measures discussed in this paper *do* cost money, but the reason money has been unavailable has *not* been scarcity of money itself, but poverty of ideology. And we have no right to ask for generous allocations from the public unless we possess powerful and positive ideologies capable of inspiring, supporting, unifying, and directing effective programs.

I could argue that we should embrace activation of the severely damaged merely because it appears that more can be accomplished than we ever dreamed; and/or because reduction of dependency would result in long-range economic benefits. But I would prefer to close with a quotation from an 1847 letter (see Talbot, 1964, p. 67) by the New England reformer and educator George Sumner to Samuel Howe, in regard to Seguin's 'activation' work: 'There is nothing either visionary or impractical in the attempt . . .' and 'for republics, it is an imperative duty, the necessary result of the principle on which they are founded, and by which they are sustained – *the principle of justice,* that accords to everyone, not as a privilege, but as a right, the full development of all his faculties.'

10 reconciling behavior modification procedures with the normalization principle

PHILIP ROOS

Man differs from other life forms in his determination to shape his own destiny. His goal of eliminating culturally unacceptable behavior has been brought closer to fulfillment during recent years by the systematic application of principles of learning.

Definitions

Generally referred to as 'behavior modification', a group of techniques derived from learning theories has been enthusiastically applied to a wide variety of behaviors which violate cultural values. Those behavioral deviations from cultural norms which are subsumed under the heading of 'mental handicaps' have become the prime (though by no means the only) focus of these techniques.

Systematic application of learning principles to deliberately influence all types of human behavior has been labelled 'behavior influence' (Krasner, 1970a). It includes such techniques as formal education, advertising and propaganda. In a more restrictive sense, 'behavior modification' has been used to describe procedures employed in order to alter behavior that has been judged to be undesirable (Gardner, 1970; Krasner, 1970a). Also rather narrowly, 'behavior therapy' is used by some authors to refer to those techniques which derive from Wolpe (1958) which rely on classical conditioning (Krasner, 1970a). Sometimes, a specific type of learning principle – such as 'operant conditioning' – will give its name to a set of procedures that are based upon it.

The term 'behavior modification' is most appropriate since it deals with techniques aimed at altering all forms of deviant behavior, without restriction to specific types of behavior or to specific types of learning principles.

Advantages of behavior modification

Behavior modification's increasing popularity can be attributed in part to its many practical advantages, including the following.

The techniques have been successfully applied to a wide range of individuals, including non-verbal and 'seriously disturbed' ones (*e.g.* Ullmann & Krasner, 1965, Nawas & Braun, 1970).

Using techniques of behavior modification, a broad spectrum of behaviors has been successfully modified, including hallucinations (Bucher & Fabrica-

This chapter is an adaptation of an earlier paper. The reference is Roos, P. *Normalization, de-humanization, and conditioning: Conflict or harmony?* MENTAL RETARDATION, 1970, *8*(4), 12-14.

tore, 1970), self-destructive actions (Tate & Baroff, 1966; Lovaas, 1968a, 1968b), vomiting and anorexia (Bachrach, Erwin & Mohr, 1965), autism (Lovaas, 1968a, 1968b), so-called sexual 'perversions' (Kushner, 1970), and classical psychoneurotic symptoms (Ullmann & Krasner, 1965).

The techniques can be applied by relatively unsophisticated persons, including ward aides, teachers and parents (*e.g.* Wahler, Winkel, Peterson & Morrison, 1965; Conger, 1970).

In general, results are achieved in a relatively short period of time when compared with other procedures.

Procedures have been developed which are suitable for group application, thereby maximizing their efficiency (*e.g.* Schaefer, 1966; Staats, Minke & Butts, 1970).

Contrast with other therapies

Behavior modification differs significantly from the dynamically-oriented – or expressive – forms of counselling and psychotherapy which have been the mainstay for dealing with most forms of socially unacceptable behavior. The following are some of the principle differences.

Whereas the expressive approaches are usually based on an historical analysis of behavior, behavior modification focuses on the present 'here and now' situation.

Traditionally, adherents of analytic approaches have sought the cause of current maladaptive behavior in past experience, and often even in early childhood. Behavior modifiers, on the other hand, interpret behavior primarily in terms of its consequences. Current behavior is analyzed in terms of those aspects of the present environment which maintain it rather than in terms of antecedent conditions.

In order to explain behavior, analytically oriented approaches have typically depended on intrapsychic constructs, such as Freud's concepts of Id, Ego and Super Ego (Sutherland, 1957). Behavior modification, on the other hand, focuses on directly observable interactions with the environment.

Most dynamically oriented approaches have stressed the need for highly trained professionals, often insisting on 'personal analysis' or other intensive 'psychotherapeutic' experience. In contrast, behavior modification has been applied extensively by unsophisticated personnel.

Following Freud's emphasis on 'unconscious motivation' (Sutherland, 1957), psychotherapists have typically resisted dealing directly with observable behavior (often referred to as 'symptoms') in favor of directing their efforts to affecting 'basic personality changes' or 'resolving underlying conflicts'. In fact, therapists were warned against 'removing symptoms' because of the danger of precipitating a 'psychotic break' or generating new symptoms ('symptom substitution') (Glover, 1955; Coleman, 1956). Behavior modifiers have rejected these concepts and do not hesitate to deal directly with manifest behavior.

Contrast with the medical model

Behavior modification can also be contrasted with the so-called 'medical model' of behavior (Ullmann & Krasner, 1965). The medical model has been the most prevalent frame of reference for interpreting culturally deviant behavior during the past decades. Indeed, much emphasis has been placed – even in popular presentations – on interpreting behavior deviancies (psychoneuroses and psychoses), addictions, and even serious learning problems as 'illness'. The medical model attributes such culturally deviant behavior to a 'disease' process which has somehow 'invaded' the organism. This process is responsible for the observable anomalies (usually referred to as 'symptoms') of the disorder. Remediation is understood in terms of 'treating' the 'disease' and 'cure' occurs when the individual is 'freed' of the disease. On the basis of this model, behavior can be dichotomized into 'normal' and 'pathological' – the latter being the product of 'disease'.

This model has been seriously criticized (Szasz, 1961; Ullmann & Krasner, 1965)as being invalid when applied to problems of behavior and as leading to destructive interactions between 'therapist' and 'patient'. Four of the most objectionable characteristics follow.

The relationship between the 'ill' person and the 'healer' is structured so as to foster feelings of helplessness, passivity, and dependency on the part of the former, while generating inappropriate illusions of omnipotence and omniscience on the 'healer's' part. It has been argued, as a matter of fact, that much of the maladaptive behavior noted in institutionalized persons is a function of the staff's 'therapeutic' interaction. 'Patients' are often told that they should conform to the institution's rules and routines and comply with staff instructions. Adherence to this prescription leads to passive, submissive conformity. Observing this behavior in the patient, staff are then likely to label him 'dependent' and to accuse him of 'regressing to 'infantile' levels of adjustment.

Dichotomizing behavior into 'normal' and 'pathological' suggests that different principles apply to the two forms of behavior. It follows that principles which are found effective in dealing with 'normal' behavior may be abandoned in favor of different approaches to the 'pathological'. For example, in contrasting the prevalence of 'paleological' thinking by schizophrenics with the use of Aristotelian logic by normals (Arieti, 1955), there is the implication that totally different approaches are required. Indeed, therapists have evolved systems of 'treatment' based on this very premise (Rosen, 1953; Whitaker & Malone, 1953).

The illness model implies that 'treatment' requires considerable expertise. Advanced graduate training is usually considered prerequisite to assuming the 'healer' role. This premise has led to two unfortunate consequences: the establishment of technocracies based on management monopolies (Roos, 1969c, 1971) whereby a specific profession maintains itself in a position of power; and 'non-professionals', and particularly family members, are excluded from the treatment process and are generally alienated from the 'patient' on the basis that they 'don't understand' and 'might harm' the unfortunate.

To the degree that behavior is attributed to an 'illness', it is perceived as a 'foreign intruder' and the afflicted individual can readily dismiss any personal responsibility for his actions. In this respect, the model is akin to the theory of 'possession' which was popular during past centuries. This interpretation of behavior fosters feelings of helplessness and passivity which tend to further impede adaptation.

In contrast to the medical model, behavior modification is based on the assumption that all behavior manifests the same basic principles, and is the product of the organism's interaction with the environment. Behavior is modified as a result of experience according to the principles of learning – principles which apply to all forms of behavior and to all types of individuals, including 'psychotic' persons, mentally retarded persons, and others who deviate markedly from the cultural norm. Being a result of learning, deviant behavior is qualitatively no different from 'normal' behavior. The concept that 'symptoms' result from 'underlying personality problems' is unacceptable or irrelevant to the behavior modifier. He is concerned only with observable behavior and makes no inferences about 'underlying' causes. Rather than searching for 'unconscious' conflicts or striving to 'cure' a 'mental illness', the behavior modifier attempts to determine relationships between observed behavior and environmental events, and to modify undesirable behavior by manipulating environmental variables.

Criticism of behavior modification

Behavior modification has not been greeted with universal enthusiasm. Serious criticisms have been directed at the approach and, indeed, some of these criticisms are relevant to the concepts of 'normalization' and 'humanization' which are the subject of this book.

A common criticism of behavioral approaches to modification of behavior is that they are superficial and fail to modify the 'basic' aspects of 'personality' (London, 1969; Nawas, 1970). It can be argued, for example, that shaping a child's responses so that he is systematically rewarded for approaching and eventually hugging an adult does not affect the child's feelings toward adults. His 'basic withdrawal' or 'autism' remains unchanged, according to this position, and the observed changes are merely meaningless 'mechanical' actions. Behavior modifiers have countered by citing evidence that 'feelings' and 'personality change' (concepts which would probably be criticized as meaningless by many behavior modifiers) *follow* changed behavior. For example, as a child hugs its mother with increasing frequency, it is rewarded by her reciprocal hugging and other socially rewarding behavior. As these responses become associated with reward and pleasure, the child's feelings toward its mother change and become increasingly positive. Behavior modifiers are able to demonstrate impressive changes in behavior which appear to meet the criteria of 'basic personality change' (Ullmann & Krasner, 1965). An oversimplified summary of this issue would be that the traditional psychotherapist attempts to change personality and incidentally obtains behavioral change, whereas the behavior modifier attempts to change behavior and incidentally changes personality. In fact, behavior modifiers would argue that 'personality' is a meaningless term unless it refers to behavior.

Another common criticism of behavior modification is that it is a mechanistic approach to human problems, devoid of such desirable therapeutic ingredients as empathy, understanding, and warmth. This impression is strengthened by the behavior modifier's use of certain equipment and procedures derived from the laboratory (Schwitzgebel, 1968; Watson, 1968). The use of food, tokens or aversive conditions to modify behavior has also fostered the impression of a mechanistic approach to human problems.

Behavior modifiers do, in fact, rely heavily on social rewards such as praise or hugging. Patterson (1970, p. 10), for example, states: 'In working with human beings a good human relationship, which includes understanding, respect, warmth and genuine interest and concern, is probably the most potent reinforcer.' Behavior modifiers typically work toward replacing food rewards (primary reinforcers) with social rewards (secondary reinforcers). In some cases, however, individuals must be taught to respond positively to social rewards (by classical conditioning procedures). What appears to be seriously 'pathological' behavior is sometimes attributable to failure to establish such social actions as smiling, praising, or hugging as being rewarding.

Roos (1969a) has stressed that mechanical devices and environmental modifications in institutions usually achieve two concrete goals, both of which can be considered humanistic. The first goal is to increase the opportunity for staff to meaningfully interact with residents by relieving personnel of as much routine custodial activities (such as are associated with toileting, housekeeping, food service, replacing soiled clothing, *etc.*) as possible. The second goal is to enhance the resident's control over his environment and to reduce the helplessness which frequently typifies the severely retarded or psychotic person. Referring to profoundly retarded children, Roos (1970, p. 14) comments: '. . . a bedfast, nonverbal, profoundly retarded child typically is completely at the mercy of those around him. If through some simple operant conditioning procedures he learns that rolling to one side of the crib turns lights on, rolling to the other side turns lights off, he suddenly gains control over one segment of his environment; he can now decide when, and for how long, he will be exposed to light. Likewise, he can be conditioned to control sound inputs and to select from among several alternatives. If able to flex individual fingers, for example, flexion of each finger could activate a circuit turning on a different type of music or sound so that the child could select from ten alternatives and determine the length of time he is exposed to each. . . . In a very real sense, the methods offer a medium whereby the nonverbal retardate can communicate his needs and preferences without use of language.'

Yet another criticism of behavior modification is that it is a 'controlling' procedure which robs the subject of self-determination and human dignity (London, 1969). Patterson (1970, p. 4) recognizes the issue when he states: 'With the increasing development and use of effective methods of control of behavior, the ethical problem must be faced. We must be concerned about who controls whom, when, to what extent, and for what purposes or toward what goals.' Behavior modifiers are in danger of being perceived as omnipotently manipulating their helpless clients. The apparent potency of the procedures tends to add to this critical appraisal of behavior modification.

Behavior modification is not, of course, the only form of intervention which is vulnerable to this criticism. As pointed out by Ullmann & Krasner (1965), many of the traditional forms of psychotherapy incorporate potentially highly controlling techniques, including hypnosis, 'manipulation of the transference', 'direct interpretation', 'attack of ego defenses', and so forth. Even the so-called client-centered approaches have been shown to subtly 'control' the client's behavior by selectively reinforcing certain types of verbal behavior (Murray, 1956, 1962; Truax, 1966). The criticism is even more applicable to shock-therapy and neurosurgery, and especially to the various forms of chemotherapy which have enjoyed considerable popularity in recent years.

Behavior modification may be more vulnerable to criticisms of 'controlling' than other approaches because of its generally greater effectiveness in altering behavior into specified channels. For example, a procedure designed to eliminate self-destructive behavior in an autistic child, but failing to do so, would hardly be criticized as being 'controlling'. A highly successful technique, on the other hand, which rapidly eliminates the problem behavior, would be much more vulnerable to being perceived as a 'controlling' force. It may well be that behavior modification's often dramatic success has earned it the reputation of being 'controlling'.

Another important consideration is that behavior modification typically entails stipulation of specific target behaviors, so that 'success' can be concretely documented. Other approaches, on the other hand, tend to focus on ill-defined goals (such as 'decreasing repression' or 'fostering self-actualization'), and often rely on equally vague constructs to reach these goals. Adherents of such approaches may deny they 'control' their clients, in spite of evidence suggesting 'control' is exerted by differential responsiveness to clients' verbalization (Murray, 1956, 1962). Others have openly advocated 'directing' and/or manipulating clients as a desirable strategy (*e.g.* Thorne, 1950).

'Controlling' behavior is obviously not confined to behavior modification. Behavior modifiers seem to differ from some of their colleagues not in that they attempt to control behavior while others do not, but rather in that they are often successful in achieving control, they are more aware of their attempt to control, and they are less hesitant to admit their intent to control.

Control need not, however, be an inherent part of behavior modification. The procedures are, as a matter of fact, well-suited to vesting the locus of control in the client rather than in the behavioral manager (Krasner, 1970a). Behavior modifiers have, for example, accepted requests for 'symptom' alleviation as a legitimate therapeutic goal, and they have candidly discussed with their clients the therapeutic process as a cooperative effort to reach the client's goals (Wolpe, 1958; Ullmann & Krasner, 1965; Kushner, 1970). Adherents of 'dynamic' personality theories, quite on the contrary, typically reject requests for 'symptom removal' and insist on directing their efforts to achieving goals which may be of little interest to their clients (*e.g.* 'personality reorganization', 'development of insight', or 'exploration of conflicts'). Also, the behavior modifier typically explains to his client the rationale for procedures used, and may even train him to use the procedures himself. For instance, behavior modifiers have tried to involve their clients in selecting target behaviors, establishing reward systems, and developing program goals (Krasner, 1970b; Kanfer, 1970). In contrast, a 'dynamically-oriented' colleague is likely to issue dogmatic orders which are likely to leave the client confused or puzzled (*e.g.* 'tell me everything that comes into your mind' or 'let's just chat together three hours a week for the next few months').

It could be argued, then, that behavior modification, as such, is no more 'controlling' than other forms of intervention. The manner in which the procedures are used, rather than the procedures themselves, determines the degree to which manipulation or control is involved.

De-humanization and normalization

The concept that environmental conditions can aggravate deviancy is now generally accepted. Particular attention has been directed to the adverse effects of institutional placement (Goldfarb, 1945; Spitz, 1945, 1949; Provence & Lipton, 1962; Shotwell & Shipe, 1964; Stedman & Eichorn, 1964). Vail (1967), for example, has outlined the impact of life in psychiatric institutions in terms of 'de-humanization'. He examines the consequences of mass-living, lack of privacy, loss of personal property and other results of attempting to manage large groups, often with inadequate resources.

The 'principle of normalization' parallels Vail's concern over dehumanization and has likewise developed largely as a reaction to institutional patterns. It has recently gained considerable support by workers in the field of mental retardation, and is having a major impact on the design of programs as well as facilities for retarded persons (Bank-Mikkelsen, 1969; Gunzburg, 1970; Nirje, 1970; Roos, 1970; Zarfas, 1970). The widespread acceptance of this principle in the field of mental retardation is reflected by the conclusion of a recent symposium of the International League of Societies for the Mentally Handicapped (Roos, 1969b, p. 24): 'The principle of normalization is applicable to a wide variety of residential settings, and it should serve as the basic guideline for the design of facilities and programs. Normalization techniques which have proven very successful with most retarded children and adults may be modified to the degree that such modifications are more successful in developing normalized behavior in individual retardates.'

In designing residential facilities, the prototype is that of 'homelike' settings; small, cottage-like residences; and small groupings of residents (Gangnes, 1970). Private or semi-private rooms are replacing the 'dormitories' or 'wards' of the traditional institution. The actual size or style of the residence is less important, however, than having it blend harmoniously into its neighborhood. Although the Scandinavian architectural features have been lauded, the basic principle is that the living conditions in the facility approximate those found in relatively typical homes in the culture. Hence in large urban centers such as New York City, facilities are being designed to blend with the surrounding apartment buildings.

One of the basic premises of normalization is that behavioral deviancy can be reduced by minimizing the degree to which persons are treated differently from 'normal' persons. Conversely, deviancy is enhanced by treating persons as if they were deviant (Wolfensberger, 1969b). To the degree that they are grouped together and segregated from the mainstream of society, individuals will be perceived as different from others and will tend to behave differently. Likewise, facilities which differ from culturally normative living arrangements will generate behavior which deviates from the cultural norm.

Behavior modification has been criticized as de-humanizing and as violating the principle of normalization, partly because of the perceptions of behavior modification as being 'controlling' and 'mechanistic', as already discussed. Below, an attempt will be made to demonstrate that behavior modification can be quite consistent with normalization principles.

Behavior modification and normalization

Review of the extensive literature on behavior modification leads to the conclusion that behavior modification, including selective use of aversive conditioning, is not necessarily de-humanizing. Specific behavior modification techniques could be used to achieve de-humanizing results, but so could most other techniques in current use. Behavior modification is not inherently more de-humanizing than other approaches, and it is probably less de-humanizing than some, such as certain forms of somatotherapy and neurosurgery.

Although behavior modification may, in specific instances, seem to conflict with the principle of normalization, the conflict is often more apparent than real. For example, child-rearing practices in most contemporary cultures rely heavily on selective reward and punishment. Parents react to those of their child's actions which they hope will be repeated with approval, while they punish or disregard behavior which they hope will not be repeated. Formal schooling, and even advanced education, incorporate systems of contingent rewards. Our whole vocational structure has likewise been based on 'reward for performance', one of the basic principles of operant conditioning. In short, most of the normative cultural means for developing, maintaining and eliminating behavior really embody some of the basic principles of behavior modification.

It can likewise be demonstrated that behavior is continually modified as a result of daily interaction with the environment. Although most people may remain quite unaware of it, careful observation reveals that responses occurring with high frequency have been regularly followed by environmental events which maintain the behavior (*i.e.* which are rewarding). Hence, both in structured learning situations and in everyday life, the principles of behavior modification are continually in operation. From this standpoint, these principles are certainly 'normative'.

Behavior modification, as a technique for altering specific behaviors, differs from other applications of learning principles in that it is more structured, more systematized, and explicitly delineates the relevant variables. The usually haphazard use of praise and punishment is replaced by clearly structured reinforcement schedules related to defined target behaviors, which are themselves systematically altered to gradually bring behavior more and more in line with the desired behavior – a procedure generally referred to as successive approximations. Specific behavior modification procedures have been discussed in detail elsewhere (*e.g.* Ullmann & Krasner, 1965; Rubin & Franks, 1969; Neuringer & Michael, 1970), and it is not the purpose here to present the methodology of behavior modification. The point to note, however, is that its application differs only in the degree of specificity and objectivity from what occurs in our everyday life. As such, behavior modification is compatible with the principle of normalization.

Even so, there are instances when the actual procedures used by behavior modifiers are different enough from 'normative' procedures to present at least superficial disparity with the normalization principle as defined by Nirje (1969b). Extinction procedures, for example, which rely on *not* responding in the 'normal' (*i.e.* culturally common or acceptable) manner could be interpreted as non-normative. Hence, when a teacher systematically ignores some specific highly disturbing classroom behavior of one of his pupils, it could be argued that he is violating – at least to some degree – the normalization principle. His 'normal' pattern of responding would probably be to attend to the behavior in some obvious manner.

More serious objections could be raised to the use of specially designed equipment which differs significantly from that found in our 'normal' environment. It could be argued that to the degree that equipment differs from that found in the person's normal environment, the 'patterns and conditions of everyday life' are not 'as close as possible to the norms and patterns of the mainstream of society' (Nirje, 1969b). It is difficult to ascertain at what point adherents of normalization and behavior modifiers would part ways with regard to this issue, or if, indeed, there would be any real conflict at all. Advocates of normalization certainly endorse extensive use of prosthetic devices to minimize the effects of physical limitations. Likewise, there is no argument with use of devices to enhance sensory functions (hearing aids, glasses, *etc.*). As a matter of fact, such prosthetic devices are used so extensively in our culture that they would be considered 'normative'.

On the other hand, the use of devices designed to cope with intellectual or emotional factors may be questioned. To the degree that training incorporates such devices which are not in common use with 'normal' persons, it differs significantly from the normative cultural patterns. Clothing designed to facilitate the teaching of dressing skills, eating utensils modified to enhance self-feeding training, or specially designed furniture to foster training (rather than to minimize the limitations of physical handicaps) (Roos, 1965; Kimbrell, Luckey, Barbuto & Love, 1966) may differ significantly from what is used in everyday life, and hence might be considered as incompatible with normalization. Use of highly specialized equipment, such as remote shocking devices (Schwitzgebel, 1968) or automated toilets (Watson, 1968) would be more extreme examples of deviations from normative patterns.

Modification of the total physical environment so that it departs from the 'normative' homelike situation advocated by adherents of normalization obviously violates the principle of '. . . making available to the mentally retarded patterns and conditions of everyday life which are as close as possible to the norms and patterns of the mainstream of society' (Nirje, 1969b). Although homelike settings have been widely advocated for residential facilities for retarded and emotionally disturbed residents, it has been suggested that non-normative environments specially designed to meet the unique needs of some profoundly retarded or otherwise seriously handicapped persons might be more desirable (Bensberg, Colwell, Ellis, Roos, & Watson, 1969). Advocates of this position contend that homelike environments have not proven conducive to either training or optimal functioning of persons with serious cognitive impairment, and they suggest that settings which are human-engineered to the special needs of such persons might prove more beneficial. These same authors suggest that normative patterns of life – such as the 'normal rhythm of life' (three daily meals, approximately eight hours of sleep at night, *etc.*) – may not be as desirable for some seriously impaired individuals as alternative patterns.

Deviation from normative environments has been justified if it proves more successful in achieving training goals, in increasing the individual's control over his environment, or in releasing staff from time-consuming routine functions which interfere with meaningful interaction with trainees (Roos, 1970). Using Watson's automated toilets as an example (Watson, 1968), Roos (1970) has argued that this equipment may be more effective than human trainers in that it is better suited to detect the desired response and to furnish immediate reinforcement. In addition, staff would be relieved of the tedious task of monitoring toilet behavior, thus allowing more time for social interaction with the trainees. Roos (1970) has likewise suggested how even profoundly retarded multi-handicapped individuals could develop some control over their environment by application of relatively simple human engineering.

The use of aversive conditioning, particularly punishment, has been especially criticized as a dehumanizing practice. Behavior modifiers themselves have been divided in their endorsement of aversive practices (Bucher, 1969; Watson, 1970). Some insist on using only positive reward, claiming that punishment (and avoidance and escape conditioning as well) is less effective and has potentially destructive consequences (Colwell, 1966). Punishment only suppresses responses, they assert, whereas use of rewards develops desirable responses. Aggression and/or avoidance responses are likely to be evoked toward the person responsible for punishment (Azrin & Holz, 1966; Powell & Azrin, 1968). Concern has also been expressed that aversive conditioning will implicitly sanction cruel or punitive treatment, particularly by ward attendants or similar personnel.

Advocates of aversive conditioning, on the other hand, feel these risks can be minimized, and that they are greatly outweighed by the benefits of the techniques (Hamilton, Stephens, & Allen, 1967; Kushner, 1970). Aversive conditioning has been used primarily to eliminate (or decelerate) behavior which is highly debilitating to the individual and/or his environment. There is now considerable evidence that judicious application of aversive conditioning can be dramatically successful in suppressing long-standing highly incapacitating behaviors (Wolf, Risley, & Mees, 1964; Lovaas, Freitag, Gold, & Kassorla, 1965; Tate & Baroff, 1966; Bucher & Lovaas, 1968). It can be argued, therefore, that selective application of aversive conditioning can be a highly humanitarian procedure. It can free individuals from crippling behavior, enabling them to interact more meaningfully with their environment and thereby enhancing their opportunities to develop their human qualities. In short, while deviating from the principle of normalization in its procedures, aversive conditioning has been successful in yielding more normative behavior.

Some therapists insist on consent by their clients as a necessary prerequisite to aversive conditioning. For instance, Rachman & Teasdale (1969, p. 74) conclude that: 'Aversion therapy should only be offered if other treatment methods are inapplicable or unsuccessful *and* if the patient gives his permission after a consideration of all the information which his therapist can honestly supply.' It is not surprising that individuals may elect the brief discomfort of aversive conditioning if it offers possible relief of chronic behaviors which are a constant source of frustration and misery.

Means and ends

It is essential to recognize that the principle of normalization, as defined by Wolfensberger in chapter 3, refers both to a means and to an end, or as Wolfensberger states: '. . . both a process and a goal'. In contrast, Nirje's (1969b) definition was strictly in terms of means and, indeed, until recently emphasis has been placed on the process of normalization rather than on normalization as an outcome. Adherents of normalization may have *inferred* that normative procedures would yield normative outcomes, but this assumption does not necessarily follow logically nor has it been fully established empirically.

As a process, normalization and behavior modification are both techniques or procedures for accomplishing specific goals. The enthusiasm generated by these procedures can lead to the unfortunate tendency to view the application of the procedures as a goal. Programs or facilities then are evaluated in terms of the degree to which they embody these particular approaches. The danger of basing evaluation on such a premise is that it begs the question by assuming that a given approach is by its very nature the most desirable approach possible. Action based on this assumption would be based on faith rather than on empirical evidence.

Outcome measures, rather than the degree to which procedures conform to a given model, are the appropriate basis for evaluation. That is, the effectiveness of a program or facility should be judged by the degree to which it succeeds in accomplishing its goals, not by the degree to which it incorporates behavior modification principles or by the extent to which it adheres to the normative practices. It thus becomes possible to compare the effectiveness of normalizing and behavior modification procedures in terms of the degree to which they succeed in accomplishing specific goals.

Program goals are selected on the basis of value judgments. Until recently, for example, institutional programs often aimed at the reduction of behavior considered to be a nuisance to the staff (fighting, cursing, demands for attention, *etc.*). Procedures successful in reducing such forms of behavior were judged to be effective and were incorporated in the institutional armamentarium. Other goals have now been deemed more desirable, such as increasing the number of discharges from institutions and increasing the economic productiveness of institutional residents. Roos, McCann and Patterson (1970) recently suggested that programs for mentally retarded individuals be judged effective to the degree that they enhance human qualities (as culturally defined), increase complexity of behavior, and foster the ability to cope with the environment.

Normalization, *as a goal*, does not refer to the use of specific procedures or settings, but rather it defines desirable program outcomes as the establishment and/or maintenance of '. . . personal behaviors and characteristics which are as culturally normative as possible' (Wolfensberger, chapter 3).

The appropriateness of goals selected for judging programs is a matter of *values*, whereas the degree to which programs succeed in reaching the goals is an *empirical* issue resolvable by application of research methodology. For example, the goal of normalization for retarded persons can be accepted or rejected, depending on what is considered to be desirable for such individuals. Having once decided on specific goals, however, the degree to which individual procedures are successful in reaching the goals is determined by empirical investigation.

More specifically, it can be argued that it is desirable for individuals whose behavior varies significantly from culturally-sanctioned patterns to alter their behavior so as to minimize its deviancy. Another way of stating this goal is that mentally retarded or disordered persons should behave as 'normally' as possible. The adoption of such a goal is a value judgment. By defining the principle of normalization as referring both to a goal and to a process, Wolfensberger suggests we are dealing with a dual concept. The appropriateness of normalization as a goal is not an issue open to investigation – it is strictly a matter of values. On the other hand, the effectiveness of normative procedures in reaching this goal is very much an empirical matter, open to empirical investigation.

Most behavior modifiers adopt the goal of developing behavior which is as normal as possible. In this respect they accept normalization as their goal. They may contend, however, that with certain individuals (such as profoundly retarded persons, procedures which vary quite markedly from normative approaches are the most effective means for reaching this goal. This contention could, of course, be tested empirically. It would be relatively simple, for example, to compare the effectiveness of homelike environments and normative procedures with conditioning procedures (including aversive conditioning) and human-engineered environments on decreasing the frequency of self-destructive behavior. In such comparative studies, the possible long range consequences of using non-normative procedures must be evaluated. Of course, included in a study of such long-range consequences must not only be the changes brought about in a person by the direct interaction of the methods used upon him, but also the indirect effects created by the interpretation of him in the minds of others – an interpretation which may affect the way they respond to him and others like him in the long run.

The assumption that normative approaches are the most effective strategy for generating normal behavior is still largely untested. Empirical studies, using a wide spectrum of subjects and conditions, are needed before this assumption can be accepted as scientifically valid. The conclusion of a recent symposium of the International League of Societies for the Mentally Handicapped (Roos, 1969b, p. 24) seems to be a reasonable operational principle, 'The principle of normalization . . . should serve as the basic guideline for the design of facilities and programs. Normalization techniques which have proven very successful with most retarded children and adults may be modified to the degree that such modifications are more successful in developing normalized behavior in individual retardates.'

Conclusion

In summary, normalization as a goal is generally accepted by behavior modifiers, as it is by those who apply normative procedures. Behavior modification procedures and the use of normative procedures are rapidly gaining support as effective approaches to altering deviant behavior. Although specific techniques derived from the two approaches may differ, they are usually compatible and directed at the same ultimate goal. Assuming that fostering normative behavior is a desirable goal, departure from normative procedures seems justified only in those cases where alternative procedures prove to be more effective in reaching this goal.

11 changing vocational behavior through normalization

'. . . When we take a man as he is, we make him worse; but when we take a man as if he were already what he should be, we promote him to what he can be . . .'

GOETHE

SIMON OLSHANSKY

Introduction

All service agencies and institutions, unless committed to custodialism, and unless content to function as a human warehouse, intend to change behavior as far as possible, so that the person served can function better, *i.e.* fulfill whatever potential he may have. Very often, this intent is not achieved to the extent hoped for. There are many reasons for this failure. One, which we are concerned with here, is that those providing the leadership and service are guided frequently by clinical theories which focus their attention on the abnormal, rather than on the normal. Finding what they are looking for, they find so much abnormality in the client as to limit their effectiveness in improving his behavior, as well as to justify their own ineffectiveness. Since the principle of normalization has already been explained, the author will proceed to review some of his assumptions which guide him in implementing this principle.

Some assumptions about behavior and its modifications

Whitehead has noted that in all arguments, the premises one holds are more fundamental than the conclusions one reaches. Since each of us makes certain assumptions about behavior, some stated and some tacit, it is necessary to examine them. The tacit ones are generally the more vicious, since they remain hidden, beyond criticism, and therefore beyond correction. My assumptions are simple and I shall state them.

First, each person seeking help has some capacity and need for self-direction and self-determination.

Second, the amount of self-direction and self-determination possible for any person depends not only on factors within a person, but on opportunities outside a person. What any person is capable of achieving is not determinable on the basis of 'inside factors' alone, for so much depends on the quality and frequency of opportunity. The opportunity, say, of attending school is not enough unless the schooling is of such quality as to give meaning to the opportunity. The tendency and practice have been to provide opportunity with little or no regard to quality. We build institutions for the mentally retarded which house the bodies while destroying the 'souls'. We provide special classes to meet the legal school requirements of the city, but fail to provide enriching experiences within the special classes. Formal compliance often becomes informal defiance!

Third, raised expectations tend to raise performance. If one expects little, one achieves little. If one is certain a person cannot learn, the outcome that he will not learn is almost inevitable. While undue optimism can become unrealistic and depressing, without an appropriate sense and amount of optimism, failure is inescapable. To tell a child he is doing poorly, while true, is likely to discourage effort. To tell him that he can do better is more likely to stimulate greater exertion.

Fourth, any process of labelling and segregation tends to lower expectations. When one labels and segregates the 'dumb' kids and 'smart' kids, one sets limits to exertion and thereby predetermines outcome. It is not always clear which group of kids suffer the most by labelling and segregation. While some segregation may be inescapable, any segregation which can be avoided should be. The obvious existence of differences in ability and the administrative convenience derived from segregation do not justify the cruelty of the process, even if it could be demonstrated that the smart kids gained in the process. There are human values to be learned while learning to learn, not achievable when children are labelled and segregated. To the degree that a person is defined as normal, and treated as normal, to that degree may he become capable of more normal functioning. While classification of children for any reason may be an administrative convenience, it often becomes a psychological calamity. Vulnerable people, uncertain of themselves, are easily influenced by labels which define them and the (usually low) expectations held for them. They need encouragement and increased confidence in their potential, not the discouragement implicit in most special labels.

Fifth, growth and development occur best and most within natural settings. Few institutions – no matter how good – can equal a home. Few sheltered workshops can provide or equal the reality of a regular place of work. While it is not always possible to avoid use of institutions and workshops, we should be aware of their inevitable limitations as 'unnatural' settings which tend to hinder growth and development. However, we also should be aware that some natural settings are defective and that, in some instances, an unnatural setting may be profitable and necessary. Though the current ideological preference for keeping disabled children at home is a valid one, an examination of some particular homes may lead to its abandonment in some instances.

Sixth, persons are more likely to change through practice than through 'talking therapies'. Practice may not always or ever, precede and produce insight and understanding, but neither does it foreclose these outcomes. To deny persons opportunities for education, or jobs, or mental hospital release, until they demonstrate insight and understanding is often to foredoom their ever achieving them. Moreover, insight and understanding do not necessarily, or always, or often, produce behavior change. If one wants to become a swimmer, one has to swim (Wheelis, 1969). Without access to a pool, one cannot become a swimmer. Too long we have been telling people how to become swimmers while failing to build many pools and failing to provide competent and concerned instructors. If practice does not always make perfect, improvement can be achieved in no other way.

Seventh, implicit in the preceding assumption is the assumption that nothing motivates a person as much as opportunity. If we want people to like school, schools should become likeable. If we want people to leave institutions, we need to develop numerous exits and places of destination. Putting it another way, we can say that if we want persons to achieve certain goals, then we have to provide the concrete means of achieving those goals. Too long, the practice has been to talk abstractly of goals while revealing our true feelings and values by neglecting the means of reaching these goals. The charge of hypocrisy may be too strong to describe this neglect of means, but this failure suggests indifference to the plight of those persons for whom we have accepted responsibility. Sacred ends become profaned when we fail to provide the concrete means to their achievement.

Finally, it is assumed that each person from the moment of birth, whatever his limitations, has a natural drive toward independence and normality. He seeks to manage himself and his life as far as possible. This natural drive can be destroyed in varying degrees when opportunities are not available to develop it.

Professional resistance to the normalization principle

Professionals, despite their denials and protestations of their concern for the person needing care, generally see their own needs better than they see the needs of the people coming to them for help. While, as has been noted, professionals continue to proclaim lofty goals, they continue to neglect the means of achieving these goals. Step ever so lightly on any professional toe, and obstreperous exclamations of assault are quickly expressed. In contrast, chronically and consciously deny quality services to those for whom professionals are or should feel responsible, and barely audible whispers of protest are heard. There is little evidence of a genuine concern and commitment for those who need help to survive and prosper.

More specifically, what are some factors which account for the resistance of many professionals to the acceptance of the principle of normalization?

First, professionals, by training, are committed to treating pathology and abnormality. One might say they always see pathology and abnormality even where none exists. Mothers showing understandable difficulty in managing and living with a mentally retarded child are quickly seen as psychiatric cases. Children showing understandable problems in 'growing up' are quickly defined as emotionally disturbed, as are college students who vigorously protest societal ills. One sees that the professionals' obsession with pathology and abnormality have destroyed their sense of normality. The throbbing disorder and disequilibrium which characterize most lives are not very well understood by them and are quickly redefined and treated as abnormal.

Second, professionals too often develop a sense of superiority to the people they help. Enjoying feelings of superiority, they somehow lose interest and faith in the capacity of their 'inferiors' to change, to grow. Moreover, they expect less from these 'inferior' persons.

Third, professionals tend to see, in Rabkin's (1970) terms, only the 'inner space', the intrapsychic. Despite the long labors of John Dewey and his lifelong concern with experience, professionals tend to place a low value on experience. The only experiences they value are the clinical ones, where they are in control and their contacts are brief. The experiences outside the clinic seem to them to be of little value.

Fourth, professionals are imprisoned by their habits. They prefer to do what they have done. It is easier and more comfortable to treat pathology as they have been doing and as they have been trained to do. The principle of normalization is a challenge to change their focus and habits. For anyone, a challenge to change is very hard and very painful. How many professionals can or will change remains to be seen. The process of change can be made easier if more professionals would make the imaginative leap: to see the persons seeking help as human beings struggling for fulfillment; without such a leap, the tendency is to see these persons as objects, to be searched and researched.

Other factors can be stated to account for professional resistance to the principle of normalization. But these are the most important.

Focus on experience

Before proceeding to describe some strategies or models for implementing the principles of normalization, it is necessary to emphasize that this principle rests on the central importance of experience as a way of learning, day by day, hour by hour. The more the available opportunities for experience approach the normal, the more the capacity for normal behavior can be actualized. While the history of a person can not be overlooked, such history should be seen more as a beginning than as an end. History too often forecloses efforts for change. We surrender so easily and quickly to histories of failure and neglect, despite the fact that our efforts and investment in planning and effecting change have been so limited, so sporadic, and so biased by Freudian ideology and pessimism.[1]

Essentially, then, the principle of normalization rests on the notion of experience as the great teacher, on presentness as against pastness, and on optimistic confidence in man's plasticity as against pessimistic views of man's rigidity. The best assurance for future fulfillment is an enriching present. Looking too far ahead, besides being distracting, tends to diminish concern for day by day experiences, which inescapably shape the future.[2]

We are not suggesting by any means that the task and challenge are easy; far from it. We are suggesting that they are not impossible. To help each person develop whatever potential he may have deserves our total commitment and best efforts. We cannot be satisfied with less if we are to live for – not off – the people for whom we have accepted responsibility as caretakers.

A workshop model

Although moving from principle to practice is always difficult, we shall attempt to suggest how it might be done in reference to the organization of a workshop. Through the process of implementation, we can see better the

[1] W. M. Cruickshank (1970), in his presidential address presented at the Division 22 meeting of the American Psychological Association, said: '. . . mental retardation, the result of deprivation can be created, and its reversibility under later conditions of social stimulation is negligible.' How can he claim negligible reversibility, since so little effort has been invested in attempting reversibility?

[2] John Dewey's observation 'What, then, is the true meaning of preparation in the educational scheme? In the first place, it means that a person, young or old, gets out of his present experience all that there is in it for him at the time in which he has it. When preparation is made the controlling end, then the potentialities of the present are sacrificed to a suppositious future. When this happens, the actual preparation for the future is missed or distorted. The ideal of using the present simply to get ready for the future contradicts itself. It omits, and even shuts out, the very conditions by which a person can be prepared for his future. We always live at the time we live and not at some other time, and only by extracting at each present time the full meaning of each present experience are we prepared for doing the same thing in the future. This is the only preparation which in the long run amounts to anything.' John Dewey. *Experience and Education.* London: Collier-Macmillan, 1969, p. 49.

meaning and significance of the principle of normalization. We should remember that the intent of a workshop is to enable the person coming to it to experience himself as a normal person. Thus, we first have to be concerned with how a person comes to the shop. He can be instructed by a 'powerful' professional to enter a workshop as a client; or he can be consulted about attending a workshop and be invited to visit all available workshops in the area to make his own choice. Thus, he is asked to make two decisions: one, if he wants to go to a workshop; two, which one he wants to select based on this experience. Once having started at a workshop, he should have the opportunity to make two further decisions: one, if he wants to continue; two, if he wants to switch to another on the belief that perhaps he has made a poor choice.

Many professionals will object strenuously to surrendering decision making of this kind to a person perceived to be less knowledgeable and less wise. Even if we grant (without necessarily accepting) that the professional may be more knowledgeable and more wise, the issue is still unchanged. Each person, as far as possible, should have the opportunity, as part of his process of growth, to make certain decisions regarding his career. Should he make a poor decision, it still is much to be preferred to a wise decision imposed by another person. Moreover, a poor decision may become a source of growth and maturity. Only as a decision maker can a person develop the kind of self-respect necessary to gain the image of a normal person. In any case, the process of admission to a shop becomes a matter of importance to a workshop modelled on the principle of normalziation.

A second issue is what name or label one attaches to the person entering the workshop, since names can be as hurtful (perhaps more hurtful) as sticks and stones. The trauma from sticks and stones may pass into recesses of faded memories, but names somehow endure and shape expectations. If we are to help the person at the shop develop a more normal image of himself, we should call him a worker, and hopefully, treat him as a worker and expect that he behave as a worker. In contrast if we call him a client, the appeal is to his weaknesses and to his inadequacies, to his sense of helplessness and dependence. As a worker, the appeal is to his strength, his self-respect, and to his hoped-for independence. If he is to practise the role of worker, then he should be given the name of worker, and the clues and expectancies implicit in that name.

Relatedly, if the person is to be called a worker and treated as a worker, and persuaded that he is a worker, the workshops should resemble a work place rather than a clinic. A clinic tends to focus on the abnormal. Though clinics may protest their interest in normalizing behavior, they paradoxically give a client an investment in maintaining, defending and justifying his abnormality.

Organized as a place of work, the workshop establishes the policies, practices, and expectancies of a place of work. The concern is with work and work role. The relationships are those that characterize any place of work. The worker is expected to dress as a worker and carry himself as a worker. As a worker he is paid for what he produces, and increased rewards are based on increased production. The work is made as interesting and challenging as possible in order to stimulate maximum exertion. In many shops with a clinical orientation, little concern is given as to the type of work tasks available, since the feeling is that the work experience is of little account compared to the clinical experience – whether in the form of counselling or casework. Professional insensitivity to the work experience, which in terms of time alone is the major activity of an adult, suggests an incapacity to understand behavior and modes of behavior change. Wheelis has pointed out that if one wants to become a thief, one has to practise stealing. If one wants to become a worker one has to practise working.[3] A man is, as he suggests, what he does (Wheelis, 1969). Moreover, if we expect the workshop experience to prepare the worker for regular work, the best way is to give him practice in the role of worker.

Industry has little interest in hiring clients; it wants workers who can function as workers. It has little patience for and tolerance of workers sliding into the role of clients. And even though some large employers are beginning to offer some clinical services, many workers interpret them as a public relations deception.

If the workers are to have enriching experiences as workers, the workshop should be located within an adequate business building shared by other companies with normal workers. Workshop workers will have frequent opportunities of interacting with normal workers, discovering that normal workers are not as normal as they have have thought, and that workers at the workshop are not so abnormal as they have always feared. It is encouraging to see that differences are not so marked as one has believed when one is isolated and segregated from normal populations. A person employed at a workshop returned to it after working for two weeks at an insurance company, saying that she had learned two things; first, she is not as crazy as everyone has said she was; secondly, normal girls are not as sane as she expected them to be.

Again, professionals within many workshops fail to see the impact of isolation and segregation because they fail to value the experience of working. Some workshops visited by the author remind him of workhouses described by Dickens. Professionals somehow feel that the impact of shabby work situations is softened in the vapors of 'talking therapies'. That workers within workshops do not protest their foul working conditions demonstrates the extent to which we have emasculated them. But we deceive ourselves if we think that workers do not resent the degradation to which they are subjected in a workplace which combines so many of the horrors of the 19th century workhouses. And then to have them spend much of their work time sorting rags (coyly called 'textile selection') adds insult upon insult. And so many professionals, so tolerant of other people's miseries, are willing to call this kind of experience a work experience. And rehabilitation agencies, often co-sponsored by federal, state and provincial governments, are willing to continue to refer their clients to these isolated and degrading work places and are satisfied because the reports coming back are written in acceptable professional jargon. Ironically, many professionals employed by governmental rehabilitation offices insist that workshops be run as clinics, and that persons seeking help be treated not as workers but as clients. To a considerable extent, professionals with these governmental rehabilitation offices are

[3] A Chinese proverb states it well: 'I hear and I forget; I see and I remember; I do and I understand.'

responsible for blocking workshop changes so that these function less as places to work and more as clinics.

That some workers in clinically oriented workshops do succeed and go to work demonstrates the capacity and stamina of some persons to cope with insufferable obstacles and to overcome the barriers established by their professional caretakers. Nothing impresses the author so much as the capacity of disabled persons to function as normal workers, if given a chance.

Of course, the danger exists of romanticizing disabled persons and making them appear better and stronger than they are. It is recognized that some will not succeed, despite our most creative efforts. However, the danger is greater that we continue to undersell disabled persons, persuading them of their inadequacies by continually treating them as inadequate. As suggested at an earlier point, we still know very little about the process of changing behavior, and we still have very little firm knowledge which would justify an attitude of pessimism. The bulk of professional efforts has been spent and is being spent in defining, diagnosing, and exploiting pathology:[4] only minor efforts, and not always creative or consistent ones, have been spent in encouraging and developing growth and improvement.

WORK AND ITS MEANING WITHIN A WORKSHOP

The professionalization of workshops' staffs has had at least two negative effects as seen from the point of view of those practising normalization. First, it has tended to distort the workshop's functions, giving it a clinical quality, and defeating or diminishing the value of work as a normalizing experience. Second, it has deflected attention from the importance of work and the need for providing work which is diversified by complexity and kind. More often than not, workshops provide work which is dull, deadening and demoralizing.

In a sense, the workshop, without so intending, may be giving the client an improper message, that is, the work he does is secondary to how he feels and thinks. The person is being prepared to function more as a client than as a worker. How else can he interpret the fact that so much of the work made available to him is so inconsequential?

If a workshop is to function as a workshop, with the work experience serving as an opportunity for normalization, then considerable thought has to be given to the kind of work made available. A workshop should consider the following factors.

First, the work should be *real*, intended for the market. 'Make' work, 'sample' work, 'handicraft' work – all have a quality of unreality about them, inviting more a response of playfulness than of real exertion. The best way to test work capacity is over time in real work situations involving real work in relationship to other workers.

Second, the work should vary in kind and complexity so as to meet the varying interests, skills, and needs of the heterogeneous population of workers. Some workers, for example, may need masculine tasks to enable them to develop a sense of manliness. Others may need opportunities to use power-

[4] Clinicians often mistake and/or equate the diagnosis of a problem with its solution. Their ability to solve problems lags far behind their ability to explain them. This disparity in skills seems to be much less of a source of stress and much less of a stimulus to reconsideration of their underlying assumptions than one would expect.

driven machinery to develop the discipline necessary to respond to externally imposed rhythms. Still others may require complex tasks, challenging them to a higher level of performance. Too often, workshops test a person's capacity to be bored, giving each person the same dull work day after day.

Third, to provide normal incentives, workers should be paid wage rates prevailing in regular industry, with increments based on increased production. Money may not be everything, but in the labor market it is a measure of one's worth.

Fourth, work involving rags or objects sold as charity should be avoided since it tends to diminish a person's self-respect and pride. How can a person feel good about himself when he is engaged in rag picking or the manufacture of articles sold in appeals to the buyer's feelings of pity. Labelling items as 'manufactured by the handicapped' can only serve to abnormalize the disabled, making them feel *special* and sorry for themselves. They may begin to see themselves as 'objects of charity', much like the products they make, and thus exempt themselves from the rigors of regular work.

Every theory opens some possibilities and forecloses others. The clinical theory assumes that the work experience is of limited consequence until intrapsychic clarity is achieved, and therefore, a 'good' workshop is clinically oriented and provides more time and effort in helping clients achieve such necessary clarity than in developing work skills. The theory of normalization, by way of contrast, assumes that a person is capable of functioning at a level higher than his present one and that a person's capacity can best be tested and developed in real work situations.

PERSONNEL SELECTION

If a workshop is to function as described, it is necessary to give substantial consideration to the hiring of staff to carry out the workshop's ideology.

The staff to be hired have to accept the principle of normalization. They have to believe with faith, confidence and reason that persons with limitations can grow and develop, if given a chance. They have to believe that the informal processes are generally more effective in producing normal responses than the formal processes. They have to feel confidence in themselves, so they can have confidence in others. They have to respect themselves, so that they can respect others.

Staff workers have to be capable of growth, so that they can enjoy growth in others.[5] They have to be flexible, experimental, and open-minded as they recognize as the air they breathe that error is ever possible and correction is ever necessary. They have to appreciate that yesterday's truth may become tomorrow's falsehood, and that every idea, practice and policy should be subject to continuing criticism and review.

They have to like people and derive pleasure in seeing them grow to their maximum independence. Staff members have to be tough enough to endure unavoidable defeats and failures, without the need to disguise them as victories and successes.

They have to be committed to the philosophy that means and ends are part of the continuum of experience: the end is self-fulfillment as far as possible, and the means are those steps which lead to self-fulfillment. Decision

[5] For evidence of the importance of this point, see Goldenberg (1971).

making, as an example, belongs to the person who comes for help. Imposing decisions on someone violates the continuum of means and ends, increasing a person's feeling of helplessness.

Finally, the staff should have sufficient discipline to avoid sentimentalities and indulgences of self and others. They have to behave as models for others, since their behavior in relation to themselves and others is the major message communicated to the observing workers.

The kind and amount of professional training for a workshop staff can be debated without end. Whatever kind and amount of training are agreed upon, such training is of little account unless the staff have some of the qualities described, or the capacity to achieve these qualities. No amount of training can ever be a substitute for *menschlichkeit*, though, too often, training is offered and accepted in place of it.

WORK AS A ROAD TO NORMALIZATION

While intellectuals may debate the passing of the protestant ethic, and while for them, work may not be as meaningful as in past decades, the fact is that for many disabled persons suffering intellectual, physical or emotional limitations, work continues as one of the central facts of their lives. Without work they feel as if they are nothing. They feel useless, abnormal, childish, and wasted. They agree with Flaubert that 'one must establish onself . . . one must be useful . . . one must work.'

The routine and rhythm of work, the work tasks, the socializing associated with work, all these become part of the pattern of normalization. Leaving the house each morning, boarding the bus, punching in, coffee break, arguing with friends or foes, lunch, back to work, and then returning home, another day passed and another dollar earned are parts of the work process needed to give and sustain a person's image of himself as normal.

Paradoxically, while our society fears and condemns dependency, while it continues to condemn public welfare as an alternative to work, it offers only limited opportunities for work. Its chronic toleration of large amounts of unemployment of able-bodied and disabled-bodied workers suggests an unwillingness to face reality and to deal with its fears. It wants to solve the problem of unemployment and dependency by surrendering to the natural force of the marketplace, or by indulging in rhetorical rages. If people are to become independent, jobs must be made available at wage rates which do not diminish a person's sense of dignity. If industry cannot provide enough jobs, and it is clear (in 1971) that it cannot, then government must provide jobs for those able and willing to work. For unless work becomes available after the rehabilitation and educational processes are completed, it would appear to both professionals and persons seeking work that the rehabilitation and educational processes were dead end roads, consuming time, money, and energy toward an outcome which can only be called a hoax. The rehabilitation and educational process might produce more successes if all participants knew that some kind of employment was likely after its completion.

PASSING AS A TECHNIQUE OF JOB FINDING

Every minority group uses various devices to cope with prejudice and discrimination (Goffman, 1963). Within the labor market, one of the accepted devices is that of passing. A black person may pass as white if nature gave him the necessary complexion. An ex-mental hospital patient or mentally retarded person may pass if he is sophisticated enough to see its need and value and capable of carrying it out. Experience in looking for work soon teaches many of them both the need and the value. For there is little question that employers – like many professionals – have low confidence in the capacity of the mentally handicapped to achieve normal work performance. As a result, they prefer not to hire these persons or, if they do, not to promote them, since they judge their work performance in terms different from those they use to judge other workers. From the point of view of the worker, the value of passing is that it enables him to be judged as other workers and, therefore, to be able to achieve more normal performance and acceptance, with the result that he will not be continually watched or treated with kid gloves. By passing, he will be treated like anyone else, no better or no worse.

Many agency personnel tend to view passing as a form of deception, an immoral practice, and one to be avoided. First, it is not up to agency workers to decide whether a worker entering the labor market should pass or disclose his history. This is a decision to be made by the worker. While a discussion with the worker of the relevant issues is in order, the decision should remain his.

Second, is it immoral? To act in one's own interest in dealing with the widespread practice of employer discrimination is not, in my view, immoral. What is clearly immoral is the practice of discrimination! Moreover, it is the tradition of the labor market to stress one's assets and to play down one's liabilities. If there were less discrimination, and if fellow workers were more enlightened and more tolerant, then the practice of passing would be less frequent, because less necessary.

One other question often arises regarding passing: is it anxiety-producing? The whole process of seeking employment is anxiety-producing, with the degree of anxiety varying worker by worker, situation by situation, at different points of time. But for many workers, it is probably less anxiety-producing than the identification of oneself as an ex-mental hospital patient or as a mentally retarded person. Finally, it should be repeated that to pass successfully requires a certain level of sophistication and discipline, a certain skill to play the game of a normal worker. While many may attempt to pass, some do not succeed because they lack the skill to play the game. Others may not want to play, preferring the role of patient to that of worker.

OTHER IMPLICATIONS OF THE NORMALIZATION PRINCIPLE FOR WORKSHOP PRACTICE

We have suggested that what a person is capable of doing or becoming depends less on what he was, or what his history may disclose, or what level IQ he may have, or how he has been labelled. His potential for normal behavior will depend more on the kind and quality of opportunity he may be offered. To repeat: *how little we really know about the capacity of many persons to improve, for the obvious reason that we have never invested enough of our resources and talents in creating appropriate and timely opportunities.* We are more concerned with the defence of our theories and dogmas than the consequences of our acts upon the people coming to us for help. We are more interested in labelling than in helping.

THE INTAKE PROCESS AND HISTORY TAKING

Given these assumptions, applicants would be admitted into workshops with relatively little background information. Enough to avoid injury to the person, but beyond such information, little else is necessary that would not be prejudicial to the applicant and limit his opportunity to develop. For example, the workshop should know of a worker's history of epilepsy in order that he avoid certain tasks and in order that better care be given in the event of a seizure. But should the workshop know an applicant's IQ? Knowledge of it may lower expectations and therefore lower his chances for improvement. Should the workshop know how many years an applicant spent in an institution? Again, a long history of institutionalization may reduce confidence and reduce the likelihood of his improving.

Some workshops spend considerable time determining who should be admitted for service, basing their judgment to admit or reject on the applicant's history. The workshop should admit anyone who applies, and the applicant should be given an adequate opportunity to see if the workshop can help him to develop. *A priori* decisions based on histories are generally prejudiced against acceptance of the seemingly more difficult case. And how good are professionals as prophets? Who can predict the outcome if creative and appropriate efforts are exerted in behalf of the applicant? If an applicant is rejected without a trial, we can be quite sure what the outcome will be! The professional too often acts out the role of undertaker, burying someone else's hopes and possibilities. Such a role is hardly a creditable one!

INTERPRETATION OF FAILURE

Let us assume that a person is admitted to a workshop and fails. How should one interpret such failure? Traditionally, failure is attributed to the inadequacies of the worker. While in some instances, such attribution is probably correct, it would appear to be more useful for the professional to attribute failure to the workshop. By so doing, he can become more sensitive to the shop's management of the work and more alert to different or better approaches to achieve a more positive outcome. Or he might suggest that the worker be given a chance at another workshop, or if none is available, to be permitted to return to the same one at a later time. By accepting some or all of the responsibility for the failure, the professional often can keep alive the hope and possibility of improvement for the worker who failed. By accepting little or no responsibility for failure, he in a sense writes the worker off and forecloses future opportunities.

MANAGING A WORKER WITHIN A WORKSHOP

The principle of normalization carries with it some implications for the management of a worker within a workshop. If the intent is to help him become a normal worker, then he has to learn to act as a normal worker. The process of managing him within the workshop will either help or hinder his achieving this goal. Two aspects of the kind of process designated as helpful will be stated.

First, the worker will be called a worker and not a client. The name declares the role and communicates the message: you are a worker and are expected to dress and behave as a worker. While the workshop may not always be successful, the expectation will provide the lift the worker may require.

Second, behavior will become of more concern than attitudes and feelings. If a worker steps on my foot, I will respond by asking him to get off. I will not ask him why he is angry with me. The point is that he has to learn to control his feelings so that he can behave in an acceptable way. While discussions of his feelings may be helpful from time to time, in the work setting such a discussion tends to divert his attention from the immediate issue of acceptable behavior. Employers want and expect acceptable behavior, not discussions of feelings and attitudes. The chance exists that learning to live by the rules of acceptable behavior may reduce the worker's feelings of anger and reduce the need to act out this anger. But the danger also exists that a discussion of anger within a place of work may exacerbate the anger since the angry person knows that such feelings and discussion of them are inappropriate within a work place. In the event that the person persists on stepping on my foot, then it is clear that he is more interested in expressing his anger than in becoming a worker. His referral to a clinic, along with his temporary exclusion from the workshop, might be considered. The worker would be confronted with the options: to work and to control his feelings, or to be excluded.

Other aspects of the managing process need not be elaborated, since it should be clear that the intent is to normalize behavior by dealing with the worker in as normal (non-clinical) a way as possible, always making clear the rules of expected behavior. Such management helps the worker feel better about himself and gives him more encouragement to accept responsibility for improved behavior.

JOB PLACEMENT: WHOSE RESPONSIBILITY?

When a worker in a workshop is considered ready for work, the tradition is that he is generally *placed* into a job. This is abnormal and is not always, or often, helpful to the worker, though it may be more efficient, at least in the short run.

It should be recalled that work is an adult activity and work capacity implies that one can function as an adult. In addition, if the worker is to develop an image of himself as a normal worker with appropriate and necessary feelings of self-respect and self-esteem, then he should be allowed and encouraged to negotiate his own entry into the labor market. While the job applicant should be given whatever orientation and assurance he may require from time to time, he should make contact with the employer without professional intervention. In practical terms, the worker values what he does for himself. And he should experience the difficulties of looking for and securing work, so that he can more realistically measure and value any job secured. Too often, a person who is 'given' a job places small value on it, since it came to him with little or no effort. By securing his own job and negotiating directly with the employer, he will – in the process – diminish the employer's suspicion and skepticism of his readiness for work. Most employers feel that if a person is ready for work, he should be capable of representing himself as a job applicant. By normalizing the placement process, we in effect enhance the applicant's chances of employment and help him develop the confidence and stamina necessary to survive in the world of work.

Obviously, there is a small number of applicants who may be ready for work, but who, for any number of reasons, cannot find their own jobs. This group should be given whatever help is necessary to effect their placement. While such efforts are abnormal, they constitute an unavoidable cost the applicant must pay if he is to work.

Summary

The central fact is that by and large, the helping professions have imprisoned themselves within an ideology of pathology which limits their effectiveness. Their concern has been with the abnormal aspects of experience, and with ways of reducing the abnormal. While their efforts have only been moderately successful, they have not been very willing to change and to consider the principle of normalization. While they see failures all around them, they attribute these failures to lack of time to practise their skills, lack of manpower, or to the persistent pathology of the persons helped. They are still convinced that to build a better future for a client they have to reconstruct his past. Given their biases, they have tended to disregard the experience of the people they serve. They have functioned as archeologists.

If helping professionals were to accept the principle of normalization, their focus would shift from the past to the present. Attention would be on the experiencing and its many interconnections. They would become more concerned with 'outer' aspects of experience, and less with the 'inner' aspects. Essentially, the principle of normalization is based on man's tendency to be normal, *i.e.* as self-sufficient as possible. *Man wants to manage his own affairs as far as is possible*, and the principle of normalization utilizes this natural and normal tendency.

Because experience is central, those applying the principle of normalization attend to all aspects of experience, such as the setting in which it occurs, the labels attached to persons, the quality of opportunities for doing, and the quality of relationships among the population served.

The application of the principle of normalization makes the person served the major actor in the helping transaction. The professional helper, as a consequence, takes on a minor and supporting role.

12 meeting the socio-sexual needs of severely impaired adults

A Scandinavian experience

In the spring of 1969, I visited Denmark and Sweden. I had very much looked forward to this visit as an opportunity to become better acquainted with these countries, to study their mental retardation service systems, and to commune with leading thinkers in the field, such as Bank-Mikkelsen, Grunewald, and Nirje, to all of whom we owe so much.

Some of the things I learned on this study tour are documented elsewhere in this book. In this chapter, I want to discuss a topic we often associate with Scandinavia with a good deal of awe, indignation, and/or merriment: sex. To be specific: sex for impaired and retarded individuals, and even those who are severely impaired or severely retarded.

It is generally well-known that in Denmark and Sweden, unmarried couples who are fond of each other readily engage in sexual relations. They will not make a secret of this fact, and everybody takes the practice for granted. While in many cases, these relationships eventuate in marriage, in that culture, sexual relationships between unmarried consenting adults who are attracted to each other is culturally normative behavior. It may come as a surprise to us to learn that sexual permissiveness prior to marriage is accompanied – at least in Sweden – by relatively strict standards in regard to marital conduct, and by a divorce rate that is only about half our own.

However, knowledge of what some have called the 'dedramatization of sex' did not prepare me for the Scandinavian attitudes I encountered regarding the sexuality of the retarded. Early during my trip, in Copenhagen, I visited one of the finest hostels for mildly to moderately retarded young adult women that I have ever seen. There I learned that as the 14 residents in this hostel are socialized into the culture and into adulthood, they are also socialized into 'normal' *i.e.* culturally normative, sexual patterns.

For instance, as these young women learn to date and relate to male peers, they may become very attached to a young man; in time, the young couple may decide to have sexual relations, and the girl may ask the housemother for contraceptive guidance. The housemother sees to it that the girl will be counselled, and if her intent is confirmed, she may be given a choice such as between the pill, an intrauterine device, or voluntary sterilization. In time, she may go to live with the young man, and the national mental retardation service system may provide the couple with an apartment. Eventually, she may marry. The woman might not have children, but the fact that she is married, or lives with a man, or engages in a socio-sexual relationship, does

For helpful criticisms, I am especially indebted to Gunnar and Rosemary Dybwad, Karl Grunewald, and Robert Perske.

not faze the retardation service system, which continues to provide services to her. In other words, where a Canadian or American housemother might admonish one of her date-bound retarded girls to 'be good', the Scandinavian housemother is more apt to remind her to 'be safe', to know her own mind, and to make her decisions strong ones.

In an institution in Sweden, the canteen sold girlie magazines on the rationale that the magazines were available on every community newsstand, and if one did not accustom institution residents to this phenomenon, they would then react maladaptively during later community habilitation. In some hostels, men residents were not discouraged from posting provocative pin-up pictures, because it was felt better that this be out in the open, supervised, and worked through rather than hidden. In some institutions, resident couples were permitted to live together, and perhaps even furnished with their own small apartments. In time, such couples might be permitted to marry.

I freely admit that these discoveries (in early 1969), as well as the matter-of-fact way in which they were viewed and communicated to me, shook me up. But aside from my personal moralistic attitudes (call them hang-ups if you wish), I could see a logic and consistency in this approach.

Many people have stereotyped misconceptions about sex in Scandinavia, and may dismiss Scandinavian management of sexuality of the retarded as merely reflecting poor moral standards. This would be missing some very important points. Firstly, Scandinavian sexual practices are perhaps different than ours, but there is probably less difference in what is done than in what is said, claimed, admitted, and pretended. Secondly, the management of sexuality in the retarded reflects not merely cultural attitudes toward sex, but is part of a much more comprehensive human management system that subscribes to the ideology of normalization, and in which normalizing sex management is only a minor aspect.

Especially this last fact has crucial implications for the management of the severely impaired, since normalization ideology prescribes that culturally normative means be employed in order to enable a person to emit culturally normative behavior. This applies not only to sex, but to innumerable other aspects of living. Most of these other aspects do not have overtones of moral controversy to us, although some may stir up controversy on historical and programmatic grounds, as has the issue of normalized residences versus traditional institutions. But there may be aspects which are nearly as controversial to us as sex. An example here is alcohol consumption by the retarded, which the Scandinavians are also handling in a way which, to them, has become largely noncontroversial because of their acceptance of the normalization principle.

In most of Europe, drinking, *per se*, is not attached with the many conflictful symbolisms of our Puritan past.[2] Therefore, no one thought much of it when a mental retardation service system in Uppsala, Sweden, operated a bar in order to initiate retarded adults to drinking in socially accepted ways

[2] Surprisingly, however, drunkenness is much less sanctioned in Scandinavia than in North America, and a number of indices of alcoholism suggest lower rates for Scandinavian countries than for the United States. A manifestation of this difference in sanction is found in drunk-driving laws. These laws are extremely strict in Sweden, as in many European countries, while in North America, they are not only lax, but it is even difficult to obtain a jury conviction when the evidence is overwhelming.

and manageable quantities. The rationale is nearly unassailable: either you teach the retarded adaptive ways of using alcohol, or many of these men and women who will live partially or fully on their own in society will come in contact with alcohol in maladaptive and potentially disastrous ways.[3]

To return now to sex, it is clear that to the Scandinavians, the normalization principle very logically dictates that steps should be taken to make available to the handicapped – as much as possible – those sexual and socio-sexual privileges and benefits which are considered normative in the general culture. Since regular Danes and Swedes are relatively free in regard to sex, and since the principle of normalization is universally accepted, their attitude to normative sex practices by the handicapped is: 'So what is the problem?'

Why does the sexuality of the retarded and impaired make us uncomfortable?

Why did this shock me? Why would so many of my fellow North Americans have been shocked – at least in 1969? I suspect that aside from a general cultural Puritanism, there are many and varied reasons, but that among these, five are prominent.

The first two reasons imply a historical but now invalid perception of the equivalence of sex and procreation. Thus, reason No. 1 is that many of the impaired should not engage in sex because this might result in impaired offspring. Reason No. 2 concerns the more severely impaired specifically, and implies that they would be inadequate parents.

Reasons three to five concern primarily severely and multiply handicapped persons, and/or severely retarded ones. Thus, reason No. 3 is that such individuals are not fully human, and though perhaps capable of mating like animals, they cannot 'marry'. The fourth reason is similar, in rejecting any socio-sexual or marriage relationship other than one we can imagine for ourselves. The fifth reason is largely religious, in questioning whether severely retarded and other severely impaired individuals can meet certain marriage criteria which have their origins largely in theological considerations. These five reasons will be elaborated below.

EUGENIC TRADITIONS

Ever since the 'alarmist period' and the 'genetic scare' (*circa* 1890-1920), there has prevailed a general attitude in this country that it would be better if retarded (and certain other deviant) persons did not procreate. During the eugenic alarm period itself, the major rationale for this view was that the deviant would beget the deviant – and perhaps do so in large numbers, outbreeding the rest of the population. Today, a major rationale is that the retarded and other limited persons could adjust better if they do not have to raise children; that they would make inadequate parents; and/or that their children – though perhaps endowed with good developmental potential – would be socialized into mental retardation, poverty, *etc.*

During the alarmist period, wholesale and involuntary sterilization of deviant groups (especially the retarded, epileptic, and legal offenders) was widely advocated, but was only selectively implemented because broad strata of the population had social, political, moral, and religious objections to this measure. However, the idea that many such persons should live a life

[3] I am told that the training bar has been discontinued, and that training now takes place in regular, integrated bars.

of celibacy and chastity was readily accepted. As has been documented elsewhere (Wolfensberger, 1969b), most of our residential institutions for the retarded owe their location, isolation, size, and design to attempts to impose celibacy upon the residents by segregating them from the community and from members of the opposite sex.

We now need to reflect upon the fact that while segregation was accepted, and sterilization rejected, the alternative of contraception was for a long time not available or feasible, and after it became available and feasible, it was long impractical for the retarded. Also, until very recently, it was morally unacceptable to almost as many persons as once was sterilization.

Today, however, we are undergoing three revolutions: one has to do with the methods of contraception; the second with attitudes toward it and toward sexuality generally; and the third involves a reassessment of the institution of marriage itself. The time has come to examine the relevance of these revolutions, taking place in the mainstream of our culture, as they relate to the sexual needs of deviant subgroups within this culture, such as the mentally retarded.

FEAR OF INADEQUATE PARENTHOOD

In regard to the mildly retarded, it is known and generally accepted that many or most of them will marry; that they will have children; and that they will be much less successful parents than most citizens, but also much better parents than had once been thought. To a degree, their adjustment will depend on the services they receive, and on the number of children they have. In regard to the latter, it appears that many of the married mildly retarded increasingly follow the pattern of the general population in adopting contraceptive methods, and in using them effectively.

It is also widely accepted that in regard to socio-sexual practice, such as premarital and extramarital sexual relationships, divorce, and remarriage, the mildly retarded can be expected to do approximately the same things which are typical and/or legal in the mainstream culture – even if these typical and legal practices may not always be considered moral or desirable.

Thus, while there is appreciable cultural acceptance of normative socio-sexual behavior in the mildly retarded person, most of us still experience unease or outright disapprobation at the thought of more severely impaired persons becoming married, or worse, engaging in extramarital sexual activity. These feelings of ours are probably derived from a chain of conscious or unconscious thinking that goes somewhat like this: the more severely impaired will not be suitable parents; if they cannot be suitable parents, they should not get married; if they are not married, they should not engage in sexual relations; ergo, the severely impaired should lead lives of chastity and celibacy. Yet, we must now ask the question: if the more severely impaired are willing to practise contraception, and if this contraception can be made effective, can we continue to deny them the privilege and benefits of those socio-sexual relationships and arrangements available to other citizens?

Obviously, a heterosexual relationship unencumbered by childbearing and child rearing is apt to bestow many advantages upon an impaired person. Not only are urgent and near-universal bio-sexual needs fulfilled, but very important affectional, social, and socio-sexual needs as well. This point is so self-evident that it scarcely requires discussion. But what does require discussion is our reluctance to enable the more severely impaired to enjoy these benefits.

In this context, one thing in particular disturbs me about our attitude toward sexuality in severely impaired persons. In effect, what we have been saying is: 'You are not capable of rearing children, and *therefore* you should control your sex impulses.' As long as our society offered considerable cultural support for celibacy, this may have been a tenable view. Today, when it is almost impossible to escape the cultural demands for and encouragements of sexuality, this view has lost its validity. If even priests and bishops, nuns and monks can no longer bear celibacy for the sake of God and Church, can we ask the weaker members of our society to remain celibate?

PERCEPTIONS OF THE RETARDED AS NONHUMAN

Earlier, I referred to the history of mental retardation, and how it predisposed toward an attitude of rejection of marriage for the retarded via an attitude of rejection of reproduction by the retarded. Closely related and very relevant is another historical view, namely, that of the retarded as nonhuman. In two other chapters in this book, I have attempted to document that this view is widely prevalent (although it is often held without explicit awareness), and that it may find expression in subtle and indirect ways. One such subtle expression may involve opposition to marriage for the retarded. After all, while animals mate to reproduce, they do not marry in the human sense; therefore, the (nonhuman) retarded should not or cannot marry, either.

EGOCENTRIC CONCEPTS OF SOCIO-SEXUAL RELATIONSHIPS AND MARRIAGE

Aside from the historical reasons mentioned, the idea of socio-sexual and marriage relationships for the more severely impaired may be rejected by the nonimpaired because such relationships might be different from the type that they can picture for themselves. True, love and sex involving severely and/or multiply handicapped persons may be quite different than it would be for the nonimpaired; but then, this does not mean that important and very human functions would not be served.

I am here reminded of the now almost classical description by MacAndrew and Edgerton (1966) of the symbiotic friendship between two men, one of whom was moderately retarded and blind, and the other one severely retarded, epileptic, partially paralyzed, and nearly speechless. Here, between these two very impaired and grossly deviant persons, a touching long-term and very symbiotic and functional relationship developed which, if it had involved a man and a woman instead of two men, would have had many of the features of a marriage.

Thus, we must strive to become aware of our prejudices and our 'normatimorphic'[4] interpretations of the world. Perhaps there *can* be socio-sexual

[4] A neologism, analogous to 'anthropomorphic', and referring to a tendency to perceive only that as correct, proper, and true which is statistically normative in a society at a given time. Here, we must be careful in our interpretation of the principle of normalization. This principle encourages normative behavior and argues that what is normatively accessible to members of a culture should be accessible to a culture's deviant members. However, the principle of normalization does not imply a judgment that those things which are culturally normative are also moral, true, correct, *etc.*

relationships and marriages quite different from the ones most persons would choose to engage in, and we must extend tolerance to relationships that we cannot even imagine for ourselves.

RELIGIOUS-THEOLOGICAL OBJECTIONS

Obviously, a fifth major reason for reluctance to support the idea of marriage for many of the severely impaired has its origins in religious-theological grounds. Here, it is even possible that by habit, some people will hold on to religiously-founded objections while no longer identifying themselves with the religion that once inspired these objections.

The issue of contraception is likely to disappear very soon as a major stumbling block here, but the one regarding a person's physical capacity for sexual relations, or of his intellectual understanding of marriage or of a marriage-type relationship remains. Thus, it may be argued that a severely retarded person cannot give an intelligent, meaningful consent to a marriage-type contract, and therefore a union between two such persons would be 'mere' (and normally illicit) cohabitation.

However, moral-religious-ethical views such as these are undergoing change. A very relevant parallel is the Catholic attitude toward the sacrament of communion. This sacrament is supposed to be administered only to those capable of appropriate understanding, and at one time, it was denied to young children and even to the retarded. Today, it is administered to very young children, and even to severely retarded youngsters. In other words, there has been a change in the interpretation of what appropriate understanding is, and/or who is capable of such understanding. We are all familiar with other recent changes in religious views, in theological interpretations, and in traditional practices in our major faiths. Further changes are almost certainly in the offing.

In regard to the specific charge that unions between severely retarded persons would be mere cohabitation, it may be sobering to recall that we legally sanction many unions which are no more than serial cohabitations – as long as the partners are not retarded!

Also, we must distinguish between religious objections on the one hand, and socio-legal issues on the other. There are many things a religious system may command from or deny to its adherents, and there may not always be a state of harmony between what religion commands or proscribes, and what secular law sanctions or forbids. A religious command may call for behavior forbidden by secular law which, in turn, may demand behavior forbidden by religion. Thus, certain culturally normative and legally sanctioned sexual behaviors may well be contrary to the moral-religious precepts of private individuals; but in a *secular* and *pluralistic* democracy such as ours, we must practise our moral-religious beliefs in such a fashion as to let others act in accordance with their own precepts – as long as these are harmonious with secular law.

In consequence, from a socio-political viewpoint, it would be wrong to let private moral-religious views about the legitimacy of marital unions of the severely impaired stand in the way of providing a retarded adult with access to socio-sexual privileges that are accessible by law and custom to other citizens. Article 1 of the recently promulgated Declaration of General and Special Rights of the Mentally Retarded (International League of Societies for the Mentally Handicapped, 1969) states: 'The mentally retarded person has the same basic rights as other citizens of the same country and same age.' The Declaration is reprinted in the 1969 President's Committee Report, which adds: 'The retarded are due the same inalienable rights to life, protection of the laws, dignity of person and opportunity as all other Americans' (p. 27). One would think that these rights would include the opportunity for socio-sexual fulfillment.

A new orientation, and its implications

What does all this mean in terms of specific management implications in mental retardation, cerebral palsy, *etc.*, and in regard to the implementation of the normalization principle in our culture today?

First, we need to recall that normalization is culture-specific. Both the human management tools employed, as well as the behavior outcome desired, should be normative to the specific culture involved. Nonmarital sex may be no more common in Sweden than in North America, but what does differ is the overtness of these practices, and public expression of approval thereof. Thus, in our society, it is doubtful whether at present, we can gain widespread public approval for the advocacy and support of nonmarital heterosexual activity on the part of the retarded (and probably other handicapped groups as well), no matter how rightful we may judge such support to be.

However, what this society does approve is the marital state of adults. In fact, our society values the marital state so much that it is almost impossible to resist social pressures to enter matrimony. Unlike in many other societies, in ours, unmarried older adults are viewed almost as deviant and freaks. Thus, it would appear that advocacy of a childless married state for more of the retarded, and some of the severely retarded and impaired, can be successful at this time. I stipulate 'childless', because the North American public will not now approve, and probably never will, childbearing by those unlikely to be capable of child rearing. The same stipulation would probably apply to most other societies.

Perhaps our ideologizing will be facilitated if we distinguish between three types of socio-sexual unions: those perceived in a traditional religious – one could say sacramental – fashion; those more along recent lines of thought about close relationships, which may not necessarily be legitimized by either law or organized religion; and those which are legal in nature, but do not necessarily involve either a close relationship or a religious element.

Many mildly retarded persons, and some who are more severely impaired, could probably meet the requirements of what would be perceived by many in our society as sacramental marriage. Additional impaired persons could form close relationships. Yet others are capable of benefitting from sexual relationships in which the interpersonal element is of an immature nature. However, some observers would accord a more severely impaired person the right to a legal marriage only if he were perceived able to make a meaningful choice, to love, to be faithful, to be considerate, and perhaps to assume community responsibilities. As noble as these things are, I am compelled to view such a stance as discriminatory. While we idealize these qualities, we do not make their absence impediments to legal marriage in the nonimpaired.

There are many nonretarded, physically healthy people who are sex-driven, shallow, incompetent, unstable, and incapable of deep and perhaps even of sustained relationships; yet our political system accords them the constitutional right to enter a legal marriage. In our society, a citizen has the right to treat sex on the 'itch-and-scratch' level, and to enter a legal marriage that does not rise above this level. Therefore, we should either apply more stringent criteria to *all* citizens, or cease applying them to the handicapped. Actually, we should look upon *legal* marriage as a political, rather than sacramental or emotionally meaningful act; if it is an act available to citizens who are not impaired, it should also be available to those who are impaired. One might say that just as in a spiritual sense, human dignity implies the freedom to sin, so does dignity in the socio-political-constitutional sense imply the freedom to perform those unwise, immoral, and even destructive things which the law does not define as illegal.

One could even argue that whether a couple is likely to have offspring which it cannot or will not raise is irrelevant. There are nonretarded persons whom the law permits to marry even though their chances for begetting normal children, or for raising or supporting them, are quite low. For instance, we permit couples to reproduce even though genetic examinations may reveal that the probability of their having a normal child is nil; even though one or both partners may be so grossly unstable as to make it exceedingly unlikely that they will rear the child, or rear it to be normal; or even though both parents may already have been living on public support. In other words, our society has not as yet established as an impediment to marriage or reproduction either the likelihood of having an impaired child, or of rearing him competently, or of supporting him adequately. Yet strangely, when a person is retarded or physically impaired, these factors suddenly become impediments. This underlines that the above factors are not the real criteria, but that attitudes toward the impairment – usually mental retardation – are. This, clearly, is bound to be unconstitutional, in being discriminatory. If unfitness for parenthood becomes a criterion, then it should be applied both to the retarded and nonretarded alike – and many bright, well-educated persons are unfit parents!

However, in our service development, we must deal not only with constitutional issues, but also with socio-political realities, and one such reality is – and may remain – that when a person is impaired *and* unlikely to be able to rear his own offspring, his fellow citizens will not accord him the right to reproduce. Therefore, in order to assure such persons access to socio-sexual benefits, we must also assure that they remain childless. Furthermore, as long as society will not permit socio-sexual unions of impaired persons without legal marriage, then we must use legal marriage as the vehicle for enabling and supporting such socio-sexual unions.

Thus, it appears that if a potential union is very unlikely to result in offspring, we should accept the concept of marriage for those adults, regardless of their intellectual or physical impairment, who: can derive emotional, social, and/or sexual benefits from a heterosexual relationship; can relate to a potential mate in a constructive manner; and who, when in public, can relate in a relatively normative decorous fashion to a potential mate.

Sterility of such a union can be assured either by sterilization or contraception. Sterilization, unlike in the past, should be voluntary, and it should be assumed that any adult who can act decorously in public and relate constructively to a person of the opposite sex will be capable of giving a meaningful consent to such voluntary sterilization. Other means of contraception should also be feasible with many couples, even if one or both partners are severely retarded. Of greatest relevance here will be the almost certain advent of long-acting contraceptive drugs, the development of subcutaneously implanted continuous-action capsules, and similar means that do not require frequent and conscious attention. Finally, impotence and sterility are more common among severely impaired persons, and in the future, more effective and less expensive techniques may be developed which will reveal whether a person is sterile, thus obviating the need for contraceptive measures for them.

It is often argued that sexual impulses in the severely impaired are neither as strong nor as common as among other persons, and that therefore the issues I raise are irrelevant or premature. I submit that we must confront the issue regardless of the number of the severely impaired to whom it applies. Within a given service system, there may be 10 such persons, 100, or 1000; whatever their number, they have, in my opinion, a constitutional right to the sexual and socio-sexual privileges available to their fellow citizens.

While there is reason to be concerned with the stability of marriages of the severely impaired, the same is true for the marriages of the presumedly unimpaired. Even among those opposed to serial marriages, few would advocate that civil law prohibit divorce and remarriage. Should such serial marriages then be the civil right of only the unimpaired, or of those who can pay the costs of divorce proceedings?

If we are to accept marriage of even severely retarded persons, then we must reorient ourselves to providing services which not only take into account but also support such marriages. Some such needed services (*e.g.* citizen advocacy, described in a later chapter, and intensive and sustained contraceptive guidance or supervision) are self-evident; others we will not fully conceptualize until we have had more experience working with couples in which one or both partners are rather retarded.

Obviously, one service implication is that in the development of the future residential service system, which at least in mental retardation will consist primarily of dispersed, small, specialized, community-integrated residences (Dunn, 1969; Dybwad, 1969; Wolfensberger, 1969c), we should begin to think about residences for impaired married couples. One possibility here would be hostels with live-in houseparents, and several kitchen-less small suites for married couples; meals might be cooked for such a hostel as a whole, and taken in a joint dining room. Another alternative is apartment houses for impaired couples, with separate kitchen facilities and some supervision, perhaps by houseparents living in the same building. A third alternative is the placement of one or more impaired couples into larger apartment houses for the general public, with itinerant staff personnel dropping in for a minimal type of supervision every few days. Each of these alternatives could be modified so as to apply to both married couples and unmarried persons. For instance, once could think of an apartment house in which ten retarded adults live, of which some may be married to each other, while others are single. Regardless of the alternative, for maximal normalization, all of the adults will be expected to work during week days, either in community workshops or in competitive employment.

Conclusion

Earlier, I stated that our culture today will probably not sanction nonmarital heterosexual relationships for the more severely retarded and perhaps otherwise severely impaired. This may change as cultural views toward sexuality generally undergo further changes, and in consequence, some years hence we may have to reassess what sexual normalization for the severely impaired means.

Also, throughout this article, I have referred to the sexual needs of impaired adults as if these needs exclusively involved 'typical' forms of heterosexual activity. There are, of course, those (*e.g.* Albert Ellis) who interpret this view as being very old-fashioned. Yes – we are our own prisoners; I feel accomplished to be able to accept a new view of an adult sexuality for the impaired that would have been totally unacceptable to me a few years ago, and others undoubtedly share my own change experience. Maybe tomorrow, I can write of not only another but even a different sexual frontier for the impaired, but today I can see it no more than I could see the present one some years back.

13 the right to self-determination

Action by the unimpaired on behalf of the impaired

Self-assertion by the impaired

Social training for self-assertion

- Social training for equality through special community experience courses
- Social training for independence through social clubs
- Social training through parliamentary procedures

An historic step toward self-determination: the Malmö congress of the retarded

Are self-directing groups of the handicapped segregating?

Various frameworks for self-directing groups of the handicapped

Self-determination for the retarded as a test case for other devalued groups

Appendix

- Summary of the proceedings of the National Conference of retarded, young adults – in Malmö, Sweden, May 8-10, 1970

BENGT NIRJE

Action by the unimpaired on behalf of the impaired

One major facet of the normalization principle is to create conditions through which a handicapped person experiences the normal respect to which any human being is entitled. Thus the choices, wishes, desires, and aspirations of a handicapped person have to be taken into consideration as much as possible in actions affecting him. To assert oneself with one's family, friends, neighbors, co-workers, other people, or *vis-à-vis* an agency is difficult for many persons. It is especially difficult for someone who has a disability or is otherwise perceived as devalued. But in the end, even the impaired person has to manage as a distinct individual, and thus has his identity defined to himself and to others through the circumstances and conditions of his existence. Thus, the road to self-determination is indeed both difficult and all-important for a person who is impaired.

In society, one common and accepted way to assert oneself and the endeavors one feels identified with is through cooperation within social bodies of common interests and goals, such as political parties, labor unions, teatotaler clubs, social and recreational organizations, *etc*. Through these bodies, common feelings and needs can be shared and expressed, and common demands formulated. If bodies suitable to one's own important goals do not already exist, they may be created as needed.

Overt and especially collective expression of thoughts and feelings is not only a traditional therapeutic device to relieve tension, but is also the way of cultural exchange and politics. It provides modes of identification with one's self, helps define a 'cause', and serves as a medium for establishing meaningful and functional social relationships.

While voicing one's striving for self-determination and recognition through deliberations within a peer group – however small – might be the accepted way in society, it has taken a long time for certain handicapped, disadvantaged, and devalued groups to gain an adequate voice and representation in society, and to be recognized in their demands to participate in decisions involving their interests. Thus, we have seen the formation of self-help action groups not merely in behalf of, but also by, the blind, the deaf, the physically handicapped, the poor, *etc*.

Regardless of how much encouragement and understanding the handicapped might have received during their youth and their training periods as adolescents, it is to be expected that as adults, their weak ego-images and their feelings of insecurity in their relations to their social environment will

Special thanks and inspiration are acknowledged to Ann and Mogens Bakk without whom the subject matter of this chapter would have remained but a vision.

express themselves through descriptive statements of feelings of dependence and degradation, inferiority and injustice, humiliation and aggression. Such statements are never comfortable to hear, and therefore one must anticipate that various bodies in society will react with equal discomfort when confronted with very normal expressions of and demands for a very normal self-determination on the part of persons who have previously been viewed paternalistically, and as incapable of and unentitled to speaking for themselves.

Self-assertion by the impaired

Let us assume for the moment that we were dealing with a self-interest organization of handicapped (young) persons. From such a group, one would fear, expect, or welcome platform statements such as the following.

'We want to chose our vocations ourselves and have influence over our education.'

'We demand that our capacity for work should not be underestimated.'

'We demand more information about our handicap and our job prospects.'

'We want to have leisure time together with other (young) adults of the same age.'

'We wish to have an apartment of our own, and not be infantilized.'

'We think that we should be present when our situation is discussed by doctors, teachers, welfare workers, foremen, *etc.*'

To gain a voice and a power presence when one is blind, deaf, physically handicapped, poor, of a despised minority group, *etc.* is difficult enough. But when it comes to the mentally retarded – where part of the basic handicap is an impairment in clear expression, and in adjusting to social demands and realities – such aspirations are not yet commonly accepted as feasible or even desired. This is why the interests of the retarded to date have been represented primarily by their parents who have taken steps to unite in bodies capable of formulating common policy and expressing strong demands. While this is taken for granted in North America, an even more radical step has been taken in Denmark and Sweden where the parents of the retarded succeeded in having laws and regulations enacted which prescribe that the responsible authorities *must* have regular contact and discussions with the associations for the retarded.

If this path toward assertion could be trod also by the mentally retarded themselves who, by the very nature of their handicap, are less capable of speaking on their own behalf, and who are thus among the most handicapped of the handicapped, then a much-neglected facet of the normalization principle would be implemented. Not only the involved professionals, the retarded, and their parents would be affected by such developments, but many other groups in society as well, because this enhancement of the voice of the most voiceless of all would point the way to the strengthening of the voice of other devalued and impaired groups.

Much as the voice of the parents of the retarded has an almost unique force given to it in Denmark and Sweden by legal mandate, so have similar steps been taken to break new ground in strengthening the voice of the retarded themselves. As a matter of fact, the self-assertive platform statements listed a few paragraphs back as expectable from handicapped young adults were not hypothetical in nature, but were actual outcomes of an historic first move by the retarded to gain meaningful control over their own destinies.

Statements such as those listed were made in Malmö, Sweden, during May of 1970, by 50 adult retarded delegates to a three-day conference representing 24 of the 25 counties of Sweden, and two Danish guests.[2] The participants were moderately and mildly retarded men and women, 20 to 35 years old, who had in their backgrounds the experiences from classes for the retarded, vocational schools, institutional boarding schools, small institutions, hostels, independent apartments, adult education courses, unemployment, sheltered workshops, independent employment, club activities, earlier and smaller conferences, *etc.* By means of committee work at the conference, they could not only experience that they had a role to play and to fill, but they were also able to redefine by and through themselves their roles as mentally retarded persons. By giving a voice to their common experiences, aspirations, and right to self-determination, they appear to have made the first organized attempts to break through our communication barrier, thus reaching toward a more direct relationship between themselves and the mainstream of society.

In an earlier chapter of this book it was pointed out that normalization is both a goal and a process, both a means and an end. The conference of the retarded in Sweden thus points to the formation of self-interest groups of the handicapped as a major normalizing measure, and the desirability of teaching group processes to the handicapped by which such self-interest groups can be attained and made effective. The formation of self-governing social bodies consisting of student councils, independent clubs for handicapped youths or adults, committees on various levels for various programs, and smaller or larger conferences where their experiences, desires, and recommendations could be identified, surveyed, expressed and summarized, could serve both as a means and an end of normalizing their conditions of life.

In Denmark and Sweden, much of this has already been accomplished in the field of mental retardation where national authorities in 1969 and 1970 recommended that whenever possible, councils of the retarded should be established within institutions, special schools, vocational schools, residential centers, group homes, boarding homes, sheltered workshops, *etc.* For instance, a few years ago, the student council of the vocational school for the mentally retarded in Stockholm was unhappy with some of the regulations of the school. They held a meeting where they wrote their own suggestions, and most of these were later implemented by the school authorities. To prepare pupils for such tasks should be looked upon as part of the social training component of the curriculum, so that in the future, handicapped graduates will have had more experiences of this kind as part of their background than most of the handicapped young adults of today.

Social training for self-assertion

A major means of enhancing the capability for self-determination is through various forms of social training, in some cases through means which are different from or more vigorous than those employed in the past. In the fol-

[2] See the appendix to this chapter for a full rendition of the demands formulated by the conference delegates.

lowing, I will outline various prerequisites and numerous steps that can be taken in this direction.

While still in childhood, many of the handicapped will receive some form of special (but hopefully not always segregated) education .The goal of such special education or of the training component of a residential facility is to provide an education that enables the student to become a socially competent and adjusted adult, and to make him as personally independent as possible.

Growth to adulthood is difficult for anyone, and adaptive social interactions and communications are necessary means for such growth. When young people leave the schools and go out into the labor market, or into higher studies, new relationships are formed to support the orientation in the new contexts and conditions. New friends or new 'career models' are sought or discovered to assist in finding the direction for the development to independence in the adult world. This process is both frustrating and exciting, but generally also rewarding.

For a handicapped (especially retarded) adolescent, growth into adulthood is an even more difficult and uncertain process. He is very much aware of and sensitive in regard to his handicap, and lacks confidence in dealing with social situations in an adult way. His longings to have friends and to share the common experiences of his peer group are not easily satisfied. Thus, the loneliness of the handicapped is often vast even though most of them live in so-called integrated circumstances.

In order to build up self-confidence, facilitate a handicapped person's growth into adulthood, and combat alienation from life and his nonhandicapped peer group, social training programs which provide varied and repeated constructive experiences in authentic situations in the community are indispensible. In Scandinavia, one of the major means emphasized with the retarded are various forms of adult education which draw from the simple insight that being treated in as adult a fashion as possible is even more important to a maturing handicapped person than to a nonhandicapped one.

If, after having left special education, a handicapped young adult either has no work, or after work has no meaningful leisure activities and contacts, he will tend to 'shrink' and regress, thus increasing the fears of his parents in regard to his future. Natural tendencies to overprotection will reinforce the vicious circle originally created by societal prejudice towards the handicapped person's differentness. The risks for family breakdown in such a situation are not to be ignored, and the handicapped person is usually well aware of these implications and his role in them. Programs which provide the positive experience of feeling that he is meeting the same situations as are other adults, that he is being recognized as an adult, and that he is accorded attitudes that are the same as those expressed towards other adults – with the same expectations, demands, liberties, and responsibilities – assist not only in the development of his maturity, but are also critically important to his parents. Through the results of these programs, they can gain new insights into the extent of independence that their son or daughter can achieve. As normal as it is for children to grow up within their families, so it is just as normal for adults to become emancipated from their family. Ultimately, all families dissolve, but in a relationship between parents and their impaired adult child, the process of dissolution is especially difficult.

Swedish experience has shown, however, that when a retarded adult son or daughter has taken part in adult education programs, in club activities which provide more advanced social training, and in representative work in councils or committees for the retarded, families can gradually redefine their parent-child relationship in such a way that their relations are closer to the normal patterns of development, emancipation, and change in the relationships between parents and unimpaired adult children.

In their previous schooling, the handicapped have been used to the vertical teacher-pupil relationship where the teacher, however encouraging, almost invariably has related in no other way than that of a teacher talking down to the pupil. In adult education, this approach is not feasible with adults generally, is damaging if used with handicapped adults, and can be particularly damaging to retarded adults. In their self-concept and their growing awareness of being adult, they have to be fortified by being treated and met and talked to as adults, and on the level of adults in a horizontal relationship. Thus, the nonimpaired dealing with retarded adults have to play a double role: while having to be aware of the specific demands of the handicap of retardation, they should avoid showing those concerns openly, but must fortify the retarded by meeting them as regular adults.

Major means in Sweden and Denmark to transmit adult education have been the sheltered workshop, programs of independence training in hostels and boarding homes, and specific adult educational programs which have included advanced forms of social training. To experience a normal rhythm of the week (which for most people consists of having one place to live, another place to work, and having leisure time at a variety of places) provides the handicapped adult with the range of conditions and experiences of life that will support his self-confidence and feeling of adulthood. Being able to work in the open market or at least the sheltered workshop, and making some money, strengthen motivations for further learning. Living in hostels and apartments adds motivations for adult education in budgeting, cooking, sex education, *etc.* In boarding homes and sheltered workshops, the residents are confronted with the necessity of reaching agreements on rules, regulations, and cooperation, and on the means of establishing such rules.

The subjects of the adult education courses do not only include further work in reading and arithmetic, but also in foreign languages, contemporary society, and political elections and how to take part in them. The trainees have also had increasing practical training in how to handle themselves when out in town: how to use cafeterias, restaurants, movies, theaters, libraries, concert halls, amusement parks, public transit, taxis, sports centers and swimming pools, *etc.* In order to be able to freely choose among and utilize such facilities for cultural and leisure time activities in their communities, the trainees have to acquire self-confidence by experiencing themselves as capable of passing over various thresholds of challenge and growth. From lack of social experiences and previous practical training, they have often acquired handicaps on top of the original impairment, but generally, they are highly responsive to encouragement to pass successive thresholds. One of the major motivations is being able to do what the peer group of the same age is doing.

SOCIAL TRAINING FOR EQUALITY THROUGH SPECIAL COMMUNITY EXPERIENCE COURSES

One type of social training for the retarded developed in Sweden has sometimes been structured as a three-day course given on a weekend, with the aim of teaching the retarded to overcome various barriers or thresholds in their social functioning which had previously increased their feelings of being alienated, and of not being able to take part fully in the social and leisure time of their community. The result of this alienation is a feeling of being a tourist in one's own city, without the pleasure associated with tourist experiences. Therefore, these courses have had the theme of 'being a tourist in a new city'.

The retarded and the nonretarded volunteers travel from their home communities to meet in a first-class hotel of a larger city. The nonretarded often arrive with the thought that they are to be the teachers, and the retarded will be their pupils. However, soon after arrival, all participants discover that they are taking part in a course common for all. As tourists, they are all going to learn and be enriched through new experiences and meeting new people. All are given the same amount of money for budgeting their weekend needs and activities, such as meals, shopping, sightseeing, and entertainment. When they are exploring the city in small mixed groups of three or four persons (which are changed at certain intervals), they gradually learn not only about the life and the assets of this new city, but they also learn from being together. They find out about public transit, price levels of various restaurants, the amusement possibilities for their Saturday night, and the interesting sightseeing places for the Sunday morning walk.

Through these experiences, occasional lectures, and comparative reports and discussions, the nonretarded gradually learn more and more about the proper ways of being together with the mentally retarded, as well as vice versa; and when they later listen to the report from the retarded, and to their reactions to the attitudes of the nonretarded they have met, the nonretarded commonly experience that they were the pupils and the retarded the teachers. They have also learned about the loneliness of the retarded; their hunger for age-typical experiences; and something about the methodology which enables them to assist in program developments whereby the wishes and desires of the retarded and their self-determination can be strengthened, encouraged, and respected. The retarded have found that they can express and expect respect for their wishes for more social activities of the same kind that they have just experienced and in which they can participate in their own home town. Returning home to their cities, both the retarded and the nonretarded have higher incentives and motivations for carrying on leisure time programs, involving more and more people – retarded as well as nonretarded – all working together with a definite attitude of 'here we are all adults', and of respect for the wishes and desires of the retarded.

SOCIAL TRAINING FOR INDEPENDENCE THROUGH SOCIAL CLUBS

The term 'leisure time activities' refers to things done at one's own leisure, initiative, and according to one's own personal rhythm, interests, and wishes, free from external pressures. It is a time for relaxing or for expression of other parts of one's self than are being expressed or used at work. It is a period of freedom, of privacy or communication with others. For very many handicapped adults, however, leisure time is grey, monotonous, and confined, without much sense of freedom. Actually, they are often relegated to themselves with a feeling of being outsiders, having their handicap awareness increased. Thus, they have strong motivations for participating in different types of leisure time activities. In recent years, this has been increasingly provided for them, but often without freedom to choose alternatives. Rarely have handicapped adults had much influence over the direction of these programs, their carrying out, or the introduction of different types of programs. They have had little influence on their own leisure time situation and options, or opportunity to relate to nonhandicapped persons of the same age with a feeling of peer group relationships, or an expression of peer group independence.

In contrast, participants in the above-mentioned social training courses have mostly gone ahead and formed clubs consisting of not more than 30-40 members. These clubs have carried on leisure time activities which provide more varied social experiences and exposure to different types of cultural resources in their communities. Even if mentally retarded, members have formed part of the executive body of the clubs, such as president, secretary, treasurer, *etc.*, with the nonretarded assisting as vice-president, *etc.*, and gradually withdrawing. Generally, the retarded have been over 18 years of age, and the nonretarded volunteers over 22 or 23, as it was imperative that the nonretarded have enough maturity and experience at being adult to be able to provide fortifying 'career models', and to have the ability to deal with confidential problems.

Through the meetings, the retarded were not only assisted in influencing their leisure time, but even planning it was, itself, part of leisure. Through the clubs, they also had the opportunity to meet new peers and form friendships. In this way, they gradually gained the confidence in themselves and others to dare express themselves about their own problems on the job, in the home, or when venturing about the city. Their nonretarded friends could give support and sometimes also quietly intervene as advocates.

In time, different clubs began to arrange visits to each other as part of their programs, thus widening their options and increasing and deepening friendships. Growing confidence was one of the results of the practical experiences gained. Also, the realization that they were sharing problems and interests with others helped the members in redefining to themselves their situation as retarded, as well as experiencing their awareness of being retarded in a new and dignified way. Through these clubs, the retarded were able to contact other organizations, other groups of young adults, and key social bodies dealing with leisure time activities in the community. They were also able to express and make known publicly their problems and endeavors, in newspapers and on television.

SOCIAL TRAINING THROUGH PARLIAMENTARY PROCEDURES

The growing number of clubs created a demand for courses in parliamentary techniques. Through weekend courses, the retarded were provided orientation to the procedures of decision-making, the basic rules of discussions and vote-taking, the functions of a committee, election of a board, the roles of the board members, and means of financing and budgetary control. The main element of the course was most practical: the participants elected a chairman and a board, then formed the necessary committees to decide upon a full program for social evenings, and to carry it out after having presented the budgetary requests. The social evenings resulting from these decisions, the work and preparations in which the nonretarded were only observers, were always highly successful. Afterwards, the participants realized that they had done everything by themselves, taking on both the responsibilities and the consequences. The final part of the course was devoted to technical advice regarding club affairs, and to discussions of general club issues. Increasingly, the specific problems of the retarded in the community were aired as they realized that others in other places were sharing the same experiences and problems.

These experiences suggest that in order to provide realistic steps to higher and more secure platforms of social interaction, and for the formation of clubs, committees, conferences, *etc.*, schools should increasingly utilize parliamentary procedure and decision-making as a training device. Discussions and vote-taking are not only good pedagogic tools, but they also assist in building up motivation. Class conferences can be held as proper preparations for taking part in the school's student council where rules and regulations, leisure time programs, and other matters are discussed.

An historic step toward self-determination: the Malmö congress of the retarded

With the increase in adult education and leisure time programs for the retarded, the growing number of clubs run by retarded adults, the more frequent contacts through weekend courses, exchange visits between clubs, and regional conferences, there developed a need in Sweden for a national conference of retarded adults. In 1968, the first one was held, with 20 participants, in order to discuss leisure time activities. The second one, in 1970, was a full-scale three-day conference attended by two elected representatives from all but one of Sweden's 25 counties, with two Danish guests attending as observers. This conference was called in order to discuss problems within the areas of leisure time activities, residential living, vocational training, and work. Work was carried on through small committees of 6-8 persons, and when each problem area had been discussed, the groups reported their points of view to the whole conference. The nonretarded observers were not allowed to influence the deliberations of the committees, other than occasionally moving discussion from one issue to the next, and making supporting notes.

The group reports were sent to the conference as a whole, and the resulting comments and reactions established a consensus on the main points. These were then immediately edited into a final report by a joint committee of the retarded with some nonretarded observers, and presented by three representatives elected by the group to the national conference of the Swedish parents' organization which was taking place at the same time, each representative reading part of the report. The full report is given as an appendix to this chapter, and the reader is advised to study it before proceeding further.

As mentioned in the introduction to this chapter, when a handicapped person expresses himself, one should expect certain demands and statements of frustration. However, the retarded delegates expressed some things which not only may come as a surprise to most people, but which can give us new insight into appropriate behavior toward and programs for the handicapped in general. I will selectively discuss some of these expressions found in the appendix.

Wanting to be in small groups during leisure time activities, and not to be seen in large groups in public, reflects the retarded persons' wish for individuality, and for not being unnecessarily stigmatized. They are objecting to the mass management procedures to which they have so often been exposed in programs arranged especially for them and/or in public. Experiences of this kind have increased their already high frustrations and their awareness of their handicap.

The desire to have more opportunities to relate to persons of their own age in their leisure time expresses their need to be brought out of their isolation and loneliness, and their need to establish real friendships and ties with model peer groups. It is also a demand for recognition.

The strong opinions held by the retarded on their right to take part in decisions regarding their own leisure time activities reflect their dissatisfaction with situations they have so often experienced when things have been arranged *for* them and not *with* them, thus increasing their feeling of dependency, and depriving them of a part of the pleasure of motivation.

The extremely negative sentiments expressed toward summer camps have their explanation in the fact that the retarded are typically sent to camps with retarded children. This makes the adults feel that they are being equated with children, segregated as a special group, and excluded from activities with and enjoyed by their age peers. This kind of experience is inimical to their growth into adulthood. Summer programs for handicapped young adults should be structured in such a fashion as to meet recreational needs in a manner that is as culturally comparable as possible to summer activities and recreational endeavors of nonhandicapped (young) adults. Also, the handicapped adults should be included in the planning and the carrying out of these programs.

With regard to the points of view on residential circumstances, the drive towards more independent living is obvious. There is awareness of the need for a continuum of residences and programs providing an evolution toward decreased dependence. Demands for respect of privacy are reflected not only in the descriptions of humiliating routines, but also with regard to an age-appropriate sharing of privacy with a member of the opposite sex. This has also to be understood in terms of the insights of the delegates that in a partnership with another person, they are more able to have a competent social and independent life.

With regard to vocational training and work, increased demands for more varied and demanding jobs are to be expected from the participants. Compared to other issues, the stereotypical underestimation which is so frequently experienced by the retarded elicited the strongest emotions and reactions.

If some of the work-related expressions were relatively expectable, others might come as a greater surprise. When asked why they wanted their fellow workers to be informed of their handicap, the delegates' reaction was 'They are not stupid; sooner or later they will find out.' It had been their experience that it was better to deal with this problem straightforwardly. Their handicap is no secret to themselves, and they are often far less hypocritical about it than other persons. This same insight and stamina was also reflected in their demand to have more information about their own handicap and their opportunities in the open market. It was realistic that they wanted to know how their impairment reflects on their opportunities, and thus how to handle their limitations. They wanted to be dealt with honestly and on the level. This same concern was also expressed when they described their feelings of humiliation when other peolpe meet in team conferences, *etc.* to deal with their situation and prospects. Since those deliberations and decisions are concerned with their existence and their future, they have a strong feeling of their right to take part in a nonhumiliating way.[3]

Are self-directing groups of the handicapped segregating?

The question might be raised whether the formation of self-directing groups consisting entirely or substantially of the handicapped will not tend to set them apart and encourage segregation. There is no doubt that segregation is a danger, but this danger must be balanced against the important functions these groups perform.

First of all, such groups can provide an opportunity for social interaction and self-expression which otherwise may not be available in the same quantity or quality. For instance, it could be that some handicapped young adults will find it easier to mix with the nonhandicapped, but that the older handicapped will have much greater difficulties in meeting their social needs in an integrated fashion. Many of them may wish to join a self-directed group in order to state this hunger.

Secondly, these groups can serve as essential media for bringing about greater integration, by providing occasions of sharing in the social life of the community. By being more experienced, and having increased their competencies, the handicapped have multiplied their options to join other organizations, clubs, and social groups.

Thirdly, to persons who previously had no alternatives available, these groups open yet another option. Here, it is important to realize that a person may participate in the group even as he simultaneously engages in other totally integrated or even yet more segregated activities elsewhere. Some handicapped persons will have no need for special groups, and should not belong to them. Yet others can benefit from short-term membership. Perhaps most important is the fact that the group does provide a new option, and that the handicapped person gains the freedom to determine for himself whether and how much to utilize it.

Finally, there will be handicapped persons who will want to belong only to a self-directed group which has a highly specific goal. For example, many persons may wish to belong to a body that provides them with an opportunity to speak for their own interests and to exercise power on behalf of these, but not to a body concerned with leisure time activities.

Various frameworks for self-directing groups of the handicapped

Questions may also be raised concerning the frameworks within which creation of self-directing groups of the handicapped could or should take

[3] Informal discussions, not recorded in the conference report, revealed that while the retarded wanted to be present in the deliberation of their case, they did not want to be confronted with a large team, but a small group of two or three others.

place. Here, three major options can be defined. One is for groups *of* the handicapped to function as a part of the groups *for* the handicapped, such as parent organizations working for the interests of the retarded. However, it would be essential for parents to have confidence in the development of groups of handicapped adults, and to be able to support these developments even as they become increasingly aware that their relationship with their adult children is gradually undergoing a change. As an organization advocating the interests of the impaired, they will also learn realistically about the actual and changing needs of the handicapped adults, and thus will be better able to provide supportive social action.

As a second option, organized bodies of residents and clients might also be established, in order to exercise self-determination within the framework of institutions and agencies. Developments of this kind have taken place not only in Denmark and Sweden, but also in other parts of the world, *e.g.* Canada and the United States.

Finally, it is also possible that the growth of groups and clubs and local organizations for handicapped adults might be developed independently in special organizations, cooperating with other handicapped groups or other social bodies.

Self-determination for the retarded as a test case for other devalued groups

In concluding, it is important to confront a major issue often raised specifically in regard to the mentally retarded. Thus, it is sometimes argued that the described techniques of giving the retarded support on their road to participation in decisions concerning their own situation are feasible and desirable; that they can provide social enrichment in a satisfactory way; that these steps allow for a more positive way of dealing with the stigmatization and the retarded persons' awareness thereof; and that they might give them a social role commensurate with their abilities. However, the argument might go, this still does not mean that they are really able to render meaningful judgment about the things they are dealing with, and that consequently their expressions should not be taken seriously or as having real social validity.

It might be argued that training in parliamentary procedures, learning how to make decisions and carry them out, taking the consequences, and learning from the experience is merely a good pedagogic and social training tool. It is useful in many situations, and leads to desired behavior modifications, an increased social realism on the part of the retarded, and thus in a nice way offers them a confrontation with their limitations – but that is all there is to it. When the retarded start dealing with all but minor decisions, they are out of their own realm.

There is, however, more to it than this.

It might also be argued that all these programs for enabling the retarded to express themselves, to express their own wishes to participate in the forming of their leisure time, to express themselves concerning rules and regulations in institutions where they are living, and even to express themselves as a political body is a very good therapeutic device. These devices enable the retarded to give vent to their frustrations, and to readjust to their situation in a more satisfied frame of mind. And that is all there is to it. The expressions of their frustrations and their hopes can not be taken seriously as to their specific content, and as to the actions that consequently should be taken, as this would not assist the retarded to adjust to their real situation and limitations.

There is, however, more to it than this.

It might even be argued that these procedures are more than pedagogic, behavioral, and therapeutic devices, and that the content of what the retarded say is interesting and worth listening to, but that it still only confirms that they are retarded. The arguments presented, and the wishes, anger, and dissatisfaction that the retarded adults express, are only to be seen as a delayed youth revolt, which means that after all, as adults, they still remain children. Therefore, in an adult society, what they have to say should only be expected to be received with the relative respect shown to enterprising young people who may some day be adult and mature enough to adjust their demands and expectations. And that is all there is to it.

There is, however, more to it than this.

There are admittedly some pedagogic and behavior-modifying values in the programs described, even in the experiences of the councils and conferences. In the same way, all people benefit from good pedagogic methods, from learning by experience, and from taking part in conferences of the nature described. There are also admittedly important therapeutic values to be gained from participatory experiences in decision-making, and in the public expression of personal or shared experiences. These participatory experiences are the same self-supporting instrumentalities used by many people when they gain more satisfaction in their lives by taking part in minor or major social activities which fulfill needs for expression, which support feelings of importance, and which provide recognition of the respect due to a regular citizen. Experiences of this kind serve to reconcile all people with the terms of their existence, and to derive identity from the role they are playing. Thus, the therapeutic values experienced by the retarded in these matters are the same as those experienced by others in comparable contexts – nothing less, nothing more.

There is, however, as said repeatedly above, more to the issue of self-determination than pedagogic and therapeutic benefits. And this is the realistic content of what is being said. That is what counts, in the same way as it does for others. The persons affected most intimately – the mentally retarded themselves – have added the voices of their real experiences.

Admittedly, in the expressions quoted from a conference such as at Malmö, and in the trend of the views there presented, there are elements remindful of experiences of youth. This is to be expected, since the process of growth into adulthood takes a longer time for retarded adults. They are, however, in their daily lives dealing with experiences and attitudes of those who are delaying their adjustment as adults; and as they have a need to identify themselves as adults, these real frustrations have to be expressed and recognized.

Also, retarded adults such as those who attended the Malmö conference are not only talking out of this kind of real experience, but are also able to describe in detail conditions of life with which they are familiar, and in which they have deep-going concerns and interests. Their experiences have not only a sufficient personal experience base, but are also shared by many others whom they know. They can express not only their own concerns, but those of their retarded friends who are less capable, and perhaps even incapable, of expressing themselves. They know what they are talking about, and they know that they are describing the realities of their existence. They realize as well that they have or should have the right to express those concerns. They are acting as citizens with the same right to be respected as others.

If this right is not acknowledged and respected, if the retarded are not treated and met on that level, then the procedures described might become harmful and dangerous. If the problems and the aspirations presented by the retarded adults are not dealt with realistically and with respect, but manipulated and essentially disregarded, then the persons treated this way will become injured and will experience the rejection and devaluation they have so often confronted. If, however, their representation and aspirations are dealt with in regular democratic ways, leading to whatever decisions and actions, then the procedures remain meaningful, strengthening, and are able to lead to further developments.

Whatever the organizational framework in which the right to self-determination of the retarded is being expressed, this respect has to be shown openly. If only lip-service to the benefits of the right to self-determination is given by the parent associations, the institutions, the agency bodies, or by other organizations, then damage will be done, developments will be frustrated, and the role of the retarded will diminish. If the right to self-determination is not respected, it is not there.

And here follows a point which I consider to be among the most important ones of this chapter: by resolving the issue of self-determination with the retarded who are among the most voiceless and devalued of those considered deviant by society, then we can reach new heights in achieving a meaningful and culturally common self-determination for other devalued and impaired groups, thus normalizing their conditions of life and increasing its quality. But if the right of self-determination is not taken seriously for the retarded, it will not be taken seriously for many other groups.

Where and how far the self-determining developments with retarded adults will lead, only local enterprise and initiatives will completely reveal. But when mentally retarded adults express their right to self-determination in public and in action, and thus gain and experience due citizen respect, they also have something to teach, not only to other and obviously more capable minority groups, but also to society in general; something about the deeper importance of democratic opportunities, the respect due to everyone in a democratic society – and that otherwise, democracy is not complete.

APPENDIX

Summary of the proceedings of the national conference of retarded young adults in Malmö, Sweden, May 8-10, 1970

Below follow the translated and slightly edited conclusions and demands formulated by 50 retarded delegates who attended what appears to have been the first national conference in the world of retarded young adults. Explanatory comments are included in brackets.

Leisure time activities

We found that:

We want to be together in small groups during our leisure time.

Dance evenings ought not to be for more than 14-16 persons.

Under no circumstances do we want to walk in large groups in town.

There should be more evening courses in, among other things, alcohol and narcotics.

The counties and the communities should give more money and assist in getting locations for leisure time activities.

We want to have leisure time together with other youngsters of the same ages.

We think, further, that the financial situation of the handicapped today is such that he cannot afford the leisure time activities or organizations he wants to take part in.

To have better contact with leisure time leaders, we think they should be of the same age as we.

We all agree that we want more rights to participate in decisions, especially in planning and carrying out our leisure time activities.

Vacations

We all think one should decide oneself what to do during vacations.

We think travel abroad is good, but one should travel with other non-retarded young adults of the same age.

Travel should be prepared with courses in the language, manners, and habits of the countries we visit.

We have all agreed that summer camps for adults should be banished. (This refers to segregated camps for both retarded adults and children).

Living conditions

We found that:

We wish to have an apartment of our own and not be coddled by personnel; therefore we want courses in cooking, budgeting, *etc.*

We want to have a right to our own apartment but without priority in the waiting list. (In Sweden, one may have to sign up for an apartment well in advance).

We want the right to move together with members of the opposite sex when we feel ready for it, and we also want the right to marry when we ourselves find the time is right.

We who live in institutions and boarding homes have found that:

The homes should be small.

We want to choose our own furniture, and have our own furniture in the room.

We will absolutely not have specific hours to follow in terms of going out, returning, *etc.*

We want to have more personal freedom, and not as it is now in certain institutions and boarding homes where you have to ask for permission to shop for fruit, newspapers, tobacco, *etc.*

We want the right to invite other youngsters to our hostels.

One should not have food coupons in institutions and hostels, even if it has practical advantages; but we want to pay with our own money.

When we are living in institutions, we want social training so as to be able to move out into society and manage on our own.

Even in institutions, we want to be able to go steady and live together with members of the opposite sex without having the personnel meddle in our private lives.

We who live at home have found that:

It is largely good, but one ought to move out when the time is right to a sheltered apartment or small hostel, because one cannot for one's whole life be dependent on one's parents.

We want, however, to have our own key when we live at home.

Education

Separate (special) schooling

We think ten years of separate (special) schooling is good enough, but there should be more courses in languages, math, contemporary events, social orientation, handwriting, social training, *etc.*

We think that the name 'separate school' is degrading. (The objection here was to the term 'separate school', which specifically connotes mental retardation in Sweden, and not to 'special school' which refers to special education more broadly).

There should be student councils which can take part in decisions about the curriculum, the choice of books, leisure time activities in school, *etc.* The same goes, of course, for vocational schools.

Vocational schools

We think that one should attend the vocational school for three years, but that the possibility for an extra year should be available. (This was already available according to Swedish law).

We demand more training in a wider range of vocational fields so that we can have a larger freedom of choice in determining our vocations.

We want to choose our vocations ourselves, and have influence over our education.

We demand that longer periods of real work experience than at present should be provided to vocational students, and that higher salaries be given during these practicum periods. At the same time, we want to have study grants (stipends) during our vocational education.

Adult education

We ask for adult education in the daytime, either in study circles a few days a week, or during a longer continuous period.

To compensate the salary one loses during the study period, we ask for study grants (stipends).

Work

We demand more interesting jobs.

We do not want to be used (exploited) on our jobs by being given the worst and the most boring tasks, as at present.

We demand that our capacity for work should not be underestimated.

We want that when we are working in the open job market, our fellow workers should be informed about our handicap.

We want employee councils at our place of work (sheltered workshops).

We think that we should be present when our situation is discussed by doctors, teachers, welfare workers, foremen, *etc.* Now it feels as if they talk behind our backs.

We demand to have more information about our handicap, and the possibilities we have of entering the open market.

To have a better atmosphere in the work setting, we demand the following:
A smoking room, with machines for pop and coffee; toilets with doors that lock; doctors and sick rooms available; our own closets with locks; and a lesser number of study group visits.

We demand a salary high enough so that we do not need to depend on the pension which we think is denigrating when one is so young. (Most pensions are given to the aged).

At the same time, we think that savings accounts should be voluntary (instead of mandatory).

We think that piecework pay is tiring and stressful, and instead we want higher pay per hour or per month.

Last day of the conference

Today we have talked about what to do to improve the bad conditions we have found during the discussions Friday and Saturday.

We demand that continuous information about the prevailing bad conditions should be given to the counties and communities, schools, sheltered workshops, and other institutions for our handicapped group.

We demand also that much stronger information be given to people in general through newspapers, radio, and television.

We have today elected a committee of six members and two alternates with the following tasks:

The committee shall continuously receive reports about the decisions of the National Board of the (Swedish) Association for Retarded Children.

The committee shall work for the general public and pressure the authorities.

At the same time, the youth conference demands that the committee shall participate in decision-making when the national board of the ARC is dealing with youth questions.

We think it fair that the National Association pays the cost in connection with work with the committee.

The conference today elected the following: Bo Carlsson, Uppsala; Lars-Rune Larsson, Stockholm; Lena Ljungkvist, Borås; Göran Ivarsson, Östersund; Anders Lindström, Eskilstuna; Lars Thomsen, Göteborg. Alternates: Maj Ahlkvist, Uppsala; Jörgen Jonsson, Uppsala.

We think it fair of the National Board to take the demands we have presented into consideration, and through the support of the National Association we hope for a rapid change of the unsatisfactory conditions that exist today.

14 the dignity of risk

ROBERT PERSKE

Many who work with the handicapped, impaired, disadvantaged, and aged tend to be overzealous in their attempts to 'protect', 'comfort', 'keep safe', 'take care', and 'watch'. Acting on these impulses, at the right time, can be benevolent, helpful, and developmental. But, if they are acted upon exclusively or excessively, without allowing for each client's individuality and growth potential, they will overprotect and emotionally smother the intended beneficiary. In fact, such overprotection endangers the client's human dignity, and tends to keep him from experiencing the risk-taking of ordinary life which is necessary for normal human growth and development.

We often say that the aged person, the spastic person, or the mentally retarded are 'courageous' when it comes to struggling against whatever it is that limits their functioning. On the other hand, we make it almost unthinkable that these people could be seen as courageous in the sense of taking personal risk. In 1966, a ten-year-old severely retarded boy named Billy wandered away from the institution where he lived, and became lost in the woods that skirted the institution grounds. The temperature was below freezing. All off-duty personnel were called back to the institution to form emergency parties to search for the boy. Two moderately retarded teenagers, Ray and Elmer, asked a staff member if they could search for Billy, too. The staff member 'moved through channels', and, after some time, received approval for the boys to join in the search, and *they* found the lost boy! At a later program, the superintendent gave Ray and Elmer special recognition and letters of commendation. By this time, many of the staff were haunted by the fact that there were 35 adolescent boys and 40 girls in the institution who functioned every bit as well as Elmer and Ray. Since the wooded area involved is not very large, they might have been mobilized more efficiently and quickly than the staff.

All this helps one to see the many ways in which the handicapped can be denied their fair and prudent share of risk-taking. Many who have worked in the field for any length of time can be aware of the clever ways in which all of us have built the avoidance of risk into the lives of many of our clients (especially the retarded, disordered, and aged) by limiting their spheres of behavior and interactions in the community, jobs, recreation, relationships with the opposite sex, *etc.* Even buildings constructed for the benefit of the handicapped are filled with things designed to help the residents avoid risk. Fortunately, there is a growing awareness and many beginning efforts in

A version of this chapter has previously been published. The reference is Perske, R. *The dignity of risk and the mentally retarded.* MENTAL RETARDATION, 1972, *10*(1), 24-26.

North America to allow the impaired to assume a fair and prudent share of risk commensurate with their functioning.

New attitudes toward risk and the handicapped in Scandinavia

With the backing of a Rosemary Dybwad International Award from the National Association for Retarded Children, I had the opportunity to travel to Scandinavia and study the ways in which Swedish and Danish people have given human dignity to their retarded, multihandicapped, and aged citizens. During this study, one of the most exciting things I observed was the many new and different ways these people are attempting to put reasonable risk back in the life of these limited persons in their midst. Though these attempts are still rather new and somewhat isolated, sound principles underlying what is being done seem to be developing.

The beauty of it all is that new attitudes toward risk seem to be one of the quite unforeseen by-products of Denmark's and Sweden's crash programs for the mentally retarded. It is my hunch that neither the Danes nor the Swedes completely planned or predicted this new and fresh attitude when Denmark passed the 'Act of 1959' (Bank-Mikkelsen, 1969), and Sweden enacted the 'Normalization Law' in 1968 (Nirje, 1969b).

In this chapter, I will present first-hand observations of incidents where workers in these two countries allowed their handicapped to experience a reasonable amount of risk. Since we, in North America, are beginning to struggle with this problem as well, it is hoped that these incidents will illuminate and clarify the directions and attitudes we may choose to take in the future.

Programming risk-taking experiences in Scandinavia

Some Scandinavian workers with the retarded are developing innovative ideas to literally 'push the retarded out of the nest' as a means of finding new growth. Such experiences in a number of areas of living are illustrated below. At the other end, extraordinary means are being used to keep the aged from moving into an overprotective nest.

NORMAL RISK IN COMMUNITY EXPERIENCES

Bengt Nirje, former secretary general (executive director) of the Swedish Association for Retarded Children, has developed a special interest in the formation of youth clubs in Stockholm, where both ordinary young people in business or still in school, as well as mentally retarded youths, serve as co-members. In four years, the first such *Flamslattsklub* has grown into 24 clubs. Kept to approximately 20 members each, these clubs plan a wide range of recreational and educational activities. To be a member in full standing, a retarded person must first learn to find his own way from his home to the clubroom in the center of downtown Stockholm.

Nirje has attempted to build into each club something he calls 'hidden social training'. Members are required to do for themselves what they have never done before. For example, a group may travel for a special program to a section of Stockholm where they have never been before. When the program is over, they are expected to find their way home alone, even though this involves the struggle of asking questions of strangers, getting one's own direction, finding the right bus or subway, *etc.* At another time, a day's outing at a particular amusement area may be planned, and then the leaders may be 'called away', leaving the retarded persons to entertain themselves.

There are a variety of experiments where mentally retarded persons are allowed to live in apartments in the city. The degree of supervision while living alone in these apartments ranges from intensive to none. In a boarding school outside Vingåker, this period of self-reliance may amount to a weekend after which the mentally retarded return to the school to evaluate their experiences. In Flen (also in Sweden), institutionalized persons move into a rented hostel for a period of training and supervision. Later, they move into apartments and live alone.

The different plans for programming experiences of being left alone in a city, or of being placed in a strange apartment, varies with the region and the agency, but I was amazed at the great number of such programmed risks that had been developed.

NORMAL RISK IN INDUSTRY

Workshop personnel anywhere can be very imaginative in designing jigs and fixtures or in modifying industrial equipment, either to simplify an operation, or to make it safe. In either case, such ingenuity may be the critical element in opening up many tasks to severely impaired persons. However, in our good intentions, we may go too far and once more lose sight of individual differences in the capabilities of the handicapped. To reshape a task that might be performed by an ordinary industrial worker solely because a limited person is to perform it is dehumanizing if the limited worker is capable of performing the same task on the same equipment as safely and/or as well as the industrial worker.

The general movement from basket weaving, ceramics, potholder making and other occupations of a handicraft variety, to productive manufacture of useful and marketable items has served to expose many handicapped Scandinavian persons to the normal risks found in any industry. For example, in the Örebro district in Sweden, I saw a nineteen-year-old mongoloid man sitting at a large punch press with all its mechanical shafting and mechanisms standing ten to twelve feet high. He pushed a button and a mass of metal came hurtling down on the press plate with a thud. There would not be much left of his hand if it got in the way. This type of operation was also observed in Gothenburg, Uppsala, and in a Danish workshop in Farum.

Throughout these two countries, one can see retarded persons operating heavy-duty punch presses, drills, and saws while they do simple repetitive operations on a Volvo automobile fender, on brass fittings, or on Danish modern furniture, to name only a few. I noticed that the risks these persons took were normal for industry in these countries.

In Örebro, the Frykstagarden workshop contains a work force of 15 deaf adolescents and young men who turn out routine machined items on heavy-duty lathes. Their foreman felt the need to tell me: 'That's not easy, you know. A regular worker can hear when the machinery is going to break and fly in his face. These people can't hear. So, I teach them to watch things with an alert eye.'

There was danger here! In fact, there was enough danger to put great fear in the heart of any worker with the deaf who tended to be overprotective.

But, the remarkable thing about these workshops was that their foremen expected their workers to be safe. For the most part, these persons lived up to the expectations of the leaders. It could be conjectured that there would have been tragic consequences if the foremen expected the deaf workers to get hurt.

NORMAL RISK IN HETEROSEXUAL RELATIONSHIPS

In healthy human beings' attempts to build close, creative human relationships, there is always a risk and a chance for failure and pain. We have yet to completely evaluate what we do to the human dignity of a person when such relationships are denied.

Bö works in an assembly line for TV terminal strips at the Frykstagarden workshop in Örebro. Approximately 26 years of age, he suffers from spastic paralysis, but has an ingenious way of putting metal pieces into plastic parts using a vice (others can do the same operation much more readily with a hammer). Marie, age 21, works elsewhere in the line; she is spastic also. Bö and Marie look forward to being together in the lunch room. Their social worker pointed them out to me, saying, 'they're in love'. Slowly these two persons, with professional help, were working out plans for the day when they could live together and make a closer relationship. Because of the spasticity of both of these persons, sex could hardly be a very large issue, but there seemed to be so many other creative possibilities between them. It was obvious that everyone respected these two and their attempts to find one another.

Older men and women with many years of institutionalization behind them are given the chance to attempt a life together when the chance for success is reasonable, though in any close human relationship there must be some risk. Many human beings choose to live out their lives keeping distance between themselves and others, a fact also true of many of the handicapped. But there are some who would not choose isolation. Throughout Denmark and Sweden, there seems to be a movement away from dormitories for men and dormitories for women, with a 'never-never land' in between. Instead, the tender, patient, sensitive building of closer human relationships under supervision was observed in many areas of both countries. The healthy, carefully evolved decisions of these persons were honored and regarded by the helping professionals as being within the limits of normal human risk.

NORMAL RISK IN BUILDING DESIGN

For years, in both Scandinavia and North America, when architects were contracted to build a facility for the mentally retarded, they automatically drew up plans for a 'heavy-duty' and 'super-safe' facility. In both countries, the building codes have reinforced this attitude. For example, if a small 'family' of handicapped persons are to be housed in a two-storey home, some local governments will demand an outside fire escape, special exits, expensive fire detection systems, and special electrical wiring and plumbing, to name only a few restrictions. If a professional attempts to move his own family of the same size into the same two-storey home, these 'special' standards do not apply.

Sweden and Denmark are now struggling to break this tradition, and have already made much progress in this direction. New residential facilities are being constructed more and more the way homes for normal human beings are constructed. They are being designed with plenty of glass, many doors to the outside, and lots of brightly colored fixtures and furniture. Beautiful hanging lamps can be seen everywhere, and nobody seems to swing from them – because it is expected that no one will. This new architecture is saying some powerfully hopeful things to and about human beings who happen to be handicapped.

Sweden has a penchant for spiral staircases. They are rather beautiful but dangerous. One can stand at the top of one of these staircases and look down at the inner pole, and see nothing but a spiral of space curling around and around. Walk down on the wrong side of one of these staircases, and you can be maimed or killed! Yet, such staircases can now be seen time and again where the mentally retarded as well as the physically handicapped may live.

We are now beginning to learn that there is such a thing as the 'language of a building' (see chapter 6). We do 'say something' to the person who lives in the building that we build for them. We can say: 'We will protect you and comfort you – and watch you like a hawk!' Or we can say: 'You are a human being and so you have the right to live as other humans live, even to the point where we will not take all dangers of human life from you.'

The new Scandinavian attitude toward risk: is it applicable to the North American scene?

What is it that we in North America who work with the handicapped can learn from Sweden's and Denmark's attitude of allowing these people to experience normal risk? Before an answer is attempted, it might be well to recall how much they have learned from us. In an endless range of situations, they can quote North American experts – even to the point where a Swedish man was able to inform me that Henry Ford called his first automobile the Model 'T', because it was the first 'tempo' manufactured car. These people seem to be the skilled implementers and appliers of a wide range of knowledge from other lands. They seem to do it in the same way that they gather raw materials from all over the world and then design and manufacture some of the most excellent products on the face of the earth. Most of these ideas about risk-taking were not new with the Scandinavians. We have theorized about such things for years and years, but in many cases, they implemented what we often only felt or talked about.

It would be spurious to try to make Swedes and Danes out of Canadians and Americans. We gave up such 'missionary' action years ago. But, it would be expedient to watch the hopeful struggle in which the Scandinavians are involved, focus on their attitudes, and see which would be compatible with healthy life here and which would not. God knows, we cannot continue the type of overprotection we have usually given the handicapped.

The world in which we live is not always safe, secure, and predictable. It does not always say 'please' or 'excuse me'. Every day that we wake up and live in the hours of that day, there is a possibility of being thrown up against a situation where we may have to risk everything, even our lives. This is the way the *real* world is. We must work to develop every human resource within us in order to prepare for these days. To deny any person their fair share of risk experiences is to further cripple them for healthy living.

A book published in German not long ago could haunt us all (Teufel,

1960). It graphically describes the human responses of retarded and spastic children and adults in a 700-place institution at Stetten (Germany) when, in 1940, two gray buses with windows painted gray drove up to the institution for the first of many trips. The driver presented a list of residents who were to be 'transferred', and then drove them off after saying to a worker: 'Soon there will be seventy-five less idiots in the world.' During an extended period of time, 322 of the 700 were driven off to be gassed and cremated. But, the most interesting thing in this account is that it makes one aware of the fully human reactions of these people in the face of this risk.

The ambulatory persons became deeply concerned for the nonambulatory, knowing they had little chance to fend for themselves. Many used their best wits to scout and plan special hiding places to which they fled every time they saw the buses coming up the road. One boy instinctively ran to his hiding place when the critical time came. He then returned after the buses were gone saying, 'They didn't catch me. I'm smarter than they.' Karl fought with the driver and ran away shouting, 'I'll hang myself before I'll die like that.' Richard, who was paralyzed, knew he did not have a chance; with calm and purpose he gave his pocket money and watch to his closest friend. He discussed the situation with his housefather, and they prayed together as he made himself ready to die like a man with dignity. 'Cool' Emily calmly got into line on the day her name was called and walked to the bus. But, as she came near the door of the bus, she calmly walked right on by and nobody even noticed. Later, when the bus was gone, she returned to the institution and busied herself with her assigned task of scrubbing steps. All this points up how persons once overprotected may, can, will, and should respond to risk with full human dignity and courage.

It is my firm belief that we now need to ensure this dimension of human dignity for the handicapped and prepare them for facing real but prudent risk in a real world. Where many of us worked overtime in past years to find clever ways of building the avoidance of risk into the lives of our clients, now we should work equally hard to help find the proper amount of normal risk for every person. We have learned: there *can* be such a thing as human dignity in risk. And there *can* be a dehumanizing indignity in safety!

15 dignity and risk: a further reflection

In August of 1970, I guided a group of students in a 'Summer Work Experience and Training' program in mental retardation on a 1000-mile trip across the state of Nebraska. The purpose of this tour was to visit and study various community services for the retarded, and to take the students to one of their work-study assignments which was a summer residential camp for the retarded at Scottsbluff, near the borders with Colorado and Wyoming. On our way, we visited services in the town of North Platte, about two-thirds across the State. There, we also stayed overnight in the homes of parents of the retarded, and of the personnel operating the newly-developed community programs.

During the evening, there was a supper-seminar at which the coordinator of the regional mental retardation services gave a brief address. He read a letter which the director of the local sheltered workshop had just received from a mother whose two sons had perished in a fire which destroyed their home. One of the sons, a severely retarded young mongoloid adult, had been a worker in the workshop. The letter, exactly as written, follows.

Dear Mike & all
I was in North Platte on
a monday but the shop was
close.
I wanted to thank all of
you for every thing you had done
for Robert. He was so proud of
his job and the ability to do
things on his own.
I am very proud of him as
he went to the back room to
save his brother. He had
Donald from the head of the bed
to the foot. If he had only a
few more minites he would of
had Donald out – even tho we
know Donald was dead at
the time.
I am send ing his one
check back as they say it

A version of this paper by Wolf Wolfensberger has been published in *Of human courage and dignity*. MENTAL RETARDATION NEWS, 1970, *19*(9), 6. (b)

would not go thru the
machine. put the money in
your fund so your books
will balance.

to day was my first day
back at work. It was a long
day but I know I have to keep
busy. My two boys was my
whole life so now I have to
start over. My husband is very
under standing – was hurt
very bad also.

If I can be of any help
at any time please feel free
to let me know. I feel I
proved to the world a re-
tarded child has a place in
the world and can be a
use ful person.

Many thanks for the
picture. All of mine were
destroyed. I am very thankful
we had some taken the Friday
night before the Fire. the
Church was taking family
portait's. So I have some of
each boy.

Many thanks for every
thing.

as ever
(signature and town of residence)

The check the mother enclosed had been carried by the boy; it was burned at the edges, and that was the reason it would not go through the magnetic check-reading machine. It was for forty-seven cents.

The workshop director then spoke in an almost tear-choked voice; he stated that he would never relinquish this check, that he would keep it as a symbol of the courage of a retarded boy, and that he did not care if his books remained forever unbalanced because of this action.

Our students were deeply moved, and so was I. I was reminded of an early draft of what became the chapter on 'The dignity of risk', written by my friend, Bob Perske, when he was Chaplain at the Kansas Neurological Institute. We so rarely think of the mentally retarded as having certain positive qualities that are basic to humanness, such as courage, even though the ideology of normalization and our perception of the retarded as fully human would tell us that they should generally be expected to share all our human emotions – not merely our negative ones, such as fear. Robert's story reminded me forcefully that there is dignity in risk, and that it is dehumanizing to remove all danger from the lives of the retarded and handicapped. After all, we take for granted that there is risk and danger in our lives, and the lives of our nonhandicapped children!

Robert could have led a sheltered existence, perhaps in some residential haven for the retarded where no demands are imposed, and where risks are virtually eliminated. There, he might have lived to a ripe old age; but to me, in his charity-inspired and heroic death in the flames, he had found greater dignity.

C

special implementive strategies and mechanisms

16 some safeguards for integrative services

Contracting with generic agencies for service to special groups

Administrative safeguards for integrative services

- Major responsibility vested in a specialty 'point'
- Regulatory control
- Written agreement on program quality
- Funding tied to performance assessment
- Consumer representation
- Citizen advocacy
- Watchdog committees
- Placement of specialists into generic agencies
- Provision of external consultancy to cooperating agencies
- Back-up specialty services

Conclusion

Repeatedly throughout this book, maximal feasible integration of deviant persons into the cultural mainstream has been defined as a major corollary of the principle of normalization. Indeed, to many human management agencies, effective integration is one of the major challenges posed by the principle.

A large number of human management agencies are specialized for service to specific deviancy groups. Thus, we have specialized agencies for the retarded, disordered, poor, deaf, blind, epileptic, crippled, and so forth. Since specialized service often means segregated service, agency specialization raises some very problematic questions. To what degree must a special person be served in a special agency? To what degree is agency specialization necessary in order to meet special program needs? To what degree is specialization desirable because of socio-historical-attitudinal reasons? And when is specialization merely an administrative (though perhaps crucially important) expediency?

It is a well-established fact that specialized services have rarely developed as the specialized components of broad or even generic service schemas. Instead, many specialized services were established by small special-interest groups, often because generic services had failed to serve the special persons who were of concern to such groups. Thus, schools for the blind, deaf, retarded, *etc.* typically were founded for children excluded from public schools. Special clinics for the retarded developed because of the systematic failure of mental health and child guidance clinics to deal with the problem. The list could go on.

Clearly, where the service mainstream excludes persons with special problems and needs, special services must be created. And particularly where a special group is excluded or perhaps even persecuted for attitudinal reasons, the special service entity must not merely provide a needed service, but also function as an advocate and 'watchdog' for its special clientele.

In many cases in the past, as generic services increased, and as attitudes improved, special services allied themselves with generic services, or were even absorbed by them. Thus, in the last decades, many special programs for retarded children have been absorbed into the public school system, sometimes together with their buildings and entire staff. Increasingly, human services are seen as a right rather than a privilege; the generic societal service system is growing and broadening; and increasingly fewer conditions and persons are excluded. With this phenomenon in mind, Jaslow (1967), in a widely-quoted treatise, addressed himself to the issue of agency specialization. Though based on experience in the field of mental retardation, his discussion has much broader relevance.

Jaslow proposed a six-point program that would hopefully lead to a balanced as well as coordinated service system. Stated here in a generalized way, these six points were: opening of generic agencies as much as possible to special clients; provision to all generic workers of a broader orientation toward special conditions; redefinition of functions of special services, and evolution of clear criteria for their utilization; placement of specialists into generic services of adequate size; development of standards for training and service; development of coordinating mechanisms within communities.

An approach of the above nature would go a long way toward integrating special and mainstream services, and toward developing program quality. In this chapter, I want to take up certain strands contained in these suggestions, and elaborate upon them.

Contracting with generic agencies for service to special groups

Specifically, I will propose that a major integrating mechanism for special agencies can be the evolution of contracts which assure that selected potential clients of a special agency can receive appropriate services from specific generic agencies. In many cases, such contracts would imply a 'purchase of services', although other variants are also conceivable. The rationale of this proposal is that contracting would achieve integration, and that the special agency can function both as a back-up resource and a watchdog.

In many instances, such contracts would initially set up a trial arrangement, since much inexperience, uncertainty, prejudice, and mutual anxiety will have to be overcome, both on the specialty and the generic side. As these arrangements prove fruitful – as many or most of them should – contracts can be renewed and firmed up, and a regular renewal provision and procedure can evolve. Contracts can also contain cancellation clauses, and specifications regarding cancellation of services to specific persons rather than of the entire arrangement.

However, in order to make the proposed schema work, certain safeguards are needed. After all, there has always been some integration in the past, but often such integration has not worked out too well. For example, the retarded offender who is processed 'like any other offender' can be severely damaged. The disturbed child who is left to sit in a regular class without any special attention or provision may be integrated physically, but not socially; his needs – special or even nonspecial – are not well served. Thus, we must not merely strive to achieve physical integration, but also social integration; and we must institute certain safeguards that assure humane, appropriate, normalizing management – in some instances management of relatively higher quality than that received by the generic client.

Administrative safeguards for integrative services

Below, I will sketch ten conceivable mechanisms which – in various combinations – should greatly increase the probabilities that purchase of service and similar contracts and cooperative agreements will indeed result in normalizing services for special clients. Some of these safeguards are not specific to the contracting mechanisms, and can also be applied for the improvement of any service. Two safeguards (citizen advocacy and funding tied to performance) are covered in considerable detail in separate chapters. The chapter on 'Normalization via agency performance assessment and differential funding' will describe a new system (PASS) for objective assessment of service quality, and several of the mechanisms discussed below are among the attributes of an agency that are subjected to evaluation by PASS.

MAJOR RESPONSIBILITY VESTED IN A SPECIALTY 'POINT'

As long as our culture clearly identifies a group of clients as very special, there should be within a geo-political area and service system (*e.g.* agency, office, or function) one 'point' that is charged with a special concern for this group. This 'point' acts as a coordinator, watchdog, and back-up in regard to the special group. Many examples of such arrangements exist. For instance, a 1968 law restructured the Nebraska Office of Mental Retardation, and actually charged it with seeing to it that all the retarded who need services receive them. This responsibility can be met by this office in a number of flexible ways, by either providing direct services, by delegating them, by contracting for them, or by facilitating them. What is remarkable is that of these options, direct service has not been found necessary, and delegation of responsibility to autonomous regional offices has been quite successful. (For further description of the Nebraska system, see Wolfensberger & Menolascino, 1970a, 1970b.)

REGULATORY CONTROL

Laws or ordinances could subject the agencies that serve special groups to the regulations, standards, licensing, and surveillance of relevant (usually provincial- or state-level) specialty offices. These regulations might be made applicable only to those agencies that have a certain minimum number of special clients among its generic clientele; or they could be made applicable in any instance in which the regulating agency provides funds for service to a specific special person. For instance, in Nebraska, the above-mentioned law permits the State Office of Mental Retardation to impose its standards upon agencies which accept its money. Again, in order to facilitate the supervisory process, state or provincial regulatory powers might be delegated to local offices or even representative agencies, such as a local or regional specialty service system, or a 'point' such as described above.

WRITTEN AGREEMENT ON PROGRAM QUALITY

Where services to special individuals are contracted to a generic agency by a specialty agency or 'point', the contract should include specific written provisions that relate to the nature and quality of the services to be rendered. In other words, the contract must go beyond fiscal and administrative matters, and must be made contingent upon the meeting of certain program requirements.

FUNDING TIED TO PERFORMANCE ASSESSMENT

Written agreements are not enough; there must be ways to assure that agreements are kept. Many of the mechanisms enumerated below can address themselves to this task, but one is to apply objective performance criteria to an agency, and tie funding to this performance. If the agency falls short of acceptable goals, funding (which may include contracting) is terminated, and the service is purchased elsewhere. A tool for assessing agency performance is discussed in the chapter on 'Normalization via agency performance assessment and differential funding'.

CONSUMER REPRESENTATION

When a specialty agency contracts with a generic agency for the provision of services to its potential clientele, the contract should insist that the generic agency has built into its governance consumer participation from the specialty area concerned. If the contractor has a governing board, approximately half the board should consist of potential, active, or past consumers; and at least one of these should represent the interests of the involved specialty group. In some cases, one consumer could represent the interests of more than one specialty group. If the contractor does not have a governing board in the usual sense, or if it has a board which by law can consist only of public officials, then at least there must be an advisory board with approximately 50% consumer representation, including one person to represent the interests of each prominent specialty group served.

In many cases, both governing *and* advisory boards of the above descriptions are desirable. Especially in cases where a contracting generic agency offers several major services, or services at several locations, an advisory board for each type of service and/or perhaps for each service location will be needed in addition to the single overall governing board.

CITIZEN ADVOCACY

Children and impaired persons who are not in a position to strongly represent their own interests, and who do not have parents or spouses capable of representing their interests for them, should have these interests represented by a citizen advocate who is an unpaid volunteer and free from conflicts of interest. Such advocates should function on a one-to-one basis, and in any of a number of conceivable roles: informal friend, guide, counsellor, trustee, foster or adoptive parent, guardian, *etc.* Since 1970, citizen advocacy offices which set up and back up such advocacy relationships (but do not render direct advocacy services themselves) have been established in numerous states and provinces. Further details are found in the chapter on 'Normalization via citizen advocacy' later in this book, and in Wolfensberger and Zauha (being published).

WATCHDOG COMMITTEES

Specialty groups or agencies that purchase or arrange for services by generic agencies may appoint or arrange watchdog committees to conduct continuing surveillance over the generic agencies to whom service is contracted. Such committees may be appointed to monitor either specific agencies, or specific services contracted to more than one agency. For example, a committee might monitor all contracted developmental day care services, regardless of the number of generic agencies with which such day care may have been contracted; other committees might be concerned with vocational services, residential services, *etc.*

PLACEMENT OF SPECIALISTS INTO GENERIC AGENCIES

In accordance with Jaslow's (1967) suggestion, professionals with expertise in various specialties could be placed into consultancy and resource roles into those generic agencies which are expected to serve a sizeable number of special clients. Obviously, because of the shortage of such personnel, this option will only be applicable to larger agencies.

PROVISION OF EXTERNAL CONSULTANCY TO COOPERATING AGENCIES

Many generic agencies are so small and/or serve so few persons with special conditions that one cannot justify the employment of even one specialist. Such agencies might be provided with external consultancy by the contracting or coordinating specialty agency. In many cases, such consultancy could or even should be made available free of charge, in which case it should be viewed by the contractor or coordinator as part of the overhead of the contracting or coordinating costs. The consultant(s) could provide more detailed and sustained assistance than the envisioned advisory board, but also would be expected to work closely with it. In most cases, of course, the consultant(s) would assist a number of agencies, rather than merely a single one.

BACK-UP SPECIALTY SERVICES

Even with much good will and consultancy, there will be instances where, for a variety of reasons, generic agencies will not be able to cope with certain persons having very special needs. Therefore it is important in many service fields to have at least one specialty back-up service of each major type in every service system. For instance, in time, the mental retardation service system in an urban area may be able to contract out most of the needed developmental day care, and may meet most of the vocational service requirements of its retarded adults in industry-integrated work stations. Nevertheless, the system should probably operate at least one specialized developmental day care center, and at least one specialized vocational services center. In these specialty settings, difficult problems can be worked out, parental anxieties about integration can be reduced, specialists can be trained, *etc.* Also, the existence of such fall-back centers will reassure generic agencies, and may render them more willing to risk integration. Fall-back provisions can be included in the contracts.

Conclusion

Previous discussions of normalization and integration in this book have underlined the fact that integration can only be achieved if deviant individuals are dispersed widely within society, rather than congregated. For instance, a bowling alley, swimming pool, church, hospital, neighborhood, or camp can integrate a few stigmatized persons at a time, but not scores, hundreds, or even thousands of them. It is such congregation of hundreds or even thousands in the past that has made necessary the building of separate schools, camps, hospitals, churches, swimming pools, dance halls, skating rinks, movie houses, bowling alleys, *etc.*

Integrating programs and mechanisms, such as have been described above, are not new. In various versions, they have been sporadically developed and documented in Canada, the United States, and elsewhere. What must become new is the assimilation of such program goals into our ideology, and their *planned*, *systematic*, *routine* implementation in our service systems.

Prevailing local or even national ordinances, regulations, situations, and laws will constitute obstacles to the implementation – or at least the efficient implementation – of some of the things proposed above. Here, we must recall that program ideology and concepts lead the law, and not *vice versa*. If our ideology is good; we should and can change laws and regulations so as to comply with it; indeed, many are already overdue for revision, and consensus on the need for change is gathering as new community services are developing, and as building, fire, and program codes, regulations, and laws are found to be inconsistent with modern service concepts.

There should be no mistake about it: integration requires hard work, planning, consideration, sensitivity, and care. Segregation is a quick and easy way – like euthanasia.

17 normalization via citizen advocacy

Generally, a child in our society has one or two parents who provide for his physical and emotional needs, who socialize him into the larger culture, and who vigorously represent his interests. As time passes, and as the children grow up, parents retain deep emotional ties to their children, but the problem-solving oriented aspects of child-rearing become less and less a part of the parental role. As children become adults, our society expects them to function with competent independence, and to solve their own problems. Such functioning is perceived as 'normal'.

Inevitably, there will be children who do not have a living or functioning parent. In such cases, our society provides certain substitutes. Most commonly, these consist of adoptive or foster parenthood, or of various child-rearing institutions. But while society rather readily provides a substitute for those parental functions that are concerned with clothing, feeding, and housing the child, much less attention is paid to meeting the child's emotional needs.

When a child who does not have a living or functioning parent also happens to be handicapped or impaired, his needs are generally the same as those of nonhandicapped children in similar circumstances. In other words, much like any child, a homeless handicapped child should have a family willing to love him, provide him a home, and to raise him, either on an adoptive or foster basis. Unfortunately, it is much more difficult to meet these needs of a handicapped child who is in such circumstances.

The needs of handicapped and nonhandicapped children become less comparable as handicapped persons approach adulthood, even though the circumstances of a severely impaired adult often resemble those of a child without a living or functioning parent. Thus, a severely impaired adult may be in need of both emotional and practical problem-solving support to a degree as is ordinarily extended only to children. Yet, unlike a child he is usually not expected to be taken into a family home; if he cannot live by himself, he is expected to live in an institution, a nursing home, a boarding home, or one of the growing number of home-like hostels in the community. Even if a family could be found to take him in, we might prefer some type of group placement. As Nirje (1969) has pointed out, just as the normalization principle dictates that a handicapped child, like other children, should generally live at home, so should many handicapped adults live *away* from home because this is what is expected from nonhandicapped adults.

In the past, if a seriously impaired child, or an impaired adult who was not fully independent, came into a situation in which he did not have at least one parent who could help him meet the practical demands of everyday living –

and hopefully also his relationship needs – it was very likely that human management agencies would enter the case. In some handicap areas, such as mental retardation, the outcome until recently has almost invariably been institutionalization. Once institutionalized, a retarded person was virtually certain to be dehumanized. In many instances, he also became a ward of the state which, in many jurisdictions, meant that the institution superintendent became the legal guardian, even in those cases where the resident still had interested parents.

Today, we can legitimately wonder what might have happened if the involved agencies and professionals had had a commitment to a vigorous search for foster parents, adoptive parents, citizen-guardians, and citizen-friends for the dependent handicapped. Such a commitment might have been successful in achieving a higher level of functioning in many of the impaired, in keeping a significant proportion of persons out of institutions and nursing homes, in preventing their being dehumanized in the institutions, or in habilitating them back into the community. The fact is that such vigorous efforts were rarely made, in part because maintenance of many types of impaired individuals in the community was not believed to be in the best interests of society.

During the so-called 'alarmist period' mentioned several times in this book, when many of the handicapped were believed to be a major threat to society (*circa* 1890-1925; see review by Wolfensberger, 1969b), the perceived interests of society were given the most lopsided precedence over the interests of the impaired person or his family. As this period passed, feeble efforts stirred here and there to re-establish an equilibrium between these interests, and a number of plans were devised to aid in safeguarding impaired persons against neglect, abandonment, abuse, exploitation, *etc.* Many of the services that have sprung from these efforts have been subsumed under the concept of 'protective services'.

The concept of protective services covers a wide range of provisions. Among these are trusts, conservatorship, traditional forms of individual adoption and guardianship, and less traditional forms of public guardianship. Of all these, public guardianship has been widely supported as a mainstay of the protective services schema (Helsel, in press).

However well-intentioned, protective services (and particularly public guardianship laws and practices) have suffered from a number of major shortcomings. Among these are the unavailability or impracticality of many protective arrangements, the dull rigidity in which they are administered, the fact that conflicts of interest are built into the very structure and functioning of protective service agency personnel, the fact that agencies – again because of their very nature – can rarely provide the sustained individualized relationship so many clients need, and the inability of protective services to match protective measures to protective needs. Characteristically, a person who needed protection received either too little or too much.

Citizen advocacy was conceived in an effort to overcome the above shortcomings by recombining a number of old ideas, methods, and provisions; by adding new ones; and by uniting these into a coherent overall schema.

First of all, in citizen advocacy, competent citizen volunteers represent – as if they were their own – the interests of other individuals who are in some way impaired, handicapped, or disadvantaged. Secondly, this relationship is structured on an individualized one-to-one, or at least one-to-a-few, basis. Thirdly, many of these relationships will be established on a sustained and often life-long basis. Fourthly, the functions of the advocate will be highly differentiated in order to meet a wide range of 'protégé' needs, while only providing the minimal amount of protection that is needed. Fifthly, the efforts of the volunteer advocates will be coordinated and supported by a citizen advocacy office.

Advocacy roles can range from minor to major, from formal to informal, and from short-term to long-term or even life-long. Formal advocacy roles might include adoptive parenthood, guardianship, and trusteeship for property. Informal roles include friend, guide, and what we have called 'guide-advocacy'. Some advocacy roles emphasize close relationships, and exchange of affection and concern. Others are more involved with practical problem-solving. Many roles fulfill both types of need.

Perhaps the most 'perfect' type of advocacy occurs when a citizen chooses to adopt and perhaps even rear a handicapped and/or neglected child. A less demanding role would be to provide transportation, clothes, counsel, or other practical assistance to the handicapped child of a family who loves and accepts the child, but lacks the means to solve the child's problems. An advocate could make certain that a person gets the education, training, and other services which the community has a responsibility to provide. Advocates could sponsor children without (adequate) family ties by visiting them, giving them gifts, or taking them on trips or to entertainments. Handicapped adults can be assisted in such practical matters as managing money, finding and maintaining living quarters, securing jobs, and learning how to use transportation services. Citizen advocates can give friendship and emotional support to the lonely and neglected by offering companionship, and by sharing worship or the observance of holidays and special occasions.

There is a vast number of persons who are in particular need of individualized citizen advocacy: hundreds of thousands of residents of our mental, penal, and corrective institutions, and of homes for the aged. Many of these persons will also need individualized citizen assistance upon their return to open communities, as will almost all of those who reside in sheltered settings within the community, where even highly dedicated agency personnel must relate to so many persons. For example, an advocate for a young retarded adult or emotionally disturbed person can contribute much to the successful adjustment of his protégé, keeping him out of trouble, teaching him how to use his free time well, and offering advice and support in time of stress and crisis. In some cases, advocates and young persons of the same age who are being rehabilitated could live together in apartments, sharing skills and fellowship, and making more normal, adjusted living possible. (A small program similar to this is currently being operated in Omaha.) Persons once rejected by society for inappropriate action can be assisted to make acceptable social and job contacts in the community by their individual citizen advocates.

Many parents of retarded or physically disabled children look after the interests of their own child as long as they are able, but have great fears and misgivings about their child's future when they are no longer healthy or living. Citizen advocacy could be the means of providing attention to such a retarded or physically handicapped person, and of preserving the overall type and quality of life that he enjoyed with his real parents.

However, volunteer efforts of the citizen advocacy type will never play a major role unless coordinated and backed-up by a stable administrative mechanism. The advocacy office was therefore 'invented' to be this mechanism. This office attracts, selects, orients, guides, and reinforces citizen advocates; it assesses the needs of a person for advocacy, as well as the abilities of the citizen volunteer to contribute through advocacy. The office conducts advocate training, with emphasis on commitment to the concept; understanding of the protégé's condition; knowledge of laws concerning the rights of handicapped and disadvantaged persons, and of services of potential use to them; and many other areas of action. Furthermore, advocacy offices can provide practical assistance to advocates, and mediate legal and professional services that may be needed by the advocate and his protégé. An important point, though, is that the advocacy office does not conduct advocacy itself, but makes citizen advocacy possible and more effective.

When the advocacy schema was first articulated in 1966, leaders in the field rejected it as too idealistic and unworkable. Idealistic it is – but it is working nevertheless.

The first two advocacy services were initiated in Nebraska in late 1969 and early 1970. One of these is operated, primarily for retarded protégés, by the Capitol Association for Retarded Children in Lincoln, the capital of Nebraska. This office received one of the first presidential citations for volunteerism (January, 1971). It is currently funded jointly by federal social security monies and the Lincoln United Community Services, and was the prime feature of the latter's multi-media presentation which keynoted its 1971 fund-raising efforts.

The second advocacy service is a youth advocacy service which has recruited and guided approximately 180 young people from all over Nebraska to play advocacy roles to residents of similar age, and from their home communities, who reside at the state's institution for the retarded. One goal of this program is to provide continued support to these residents upon their anticipated return to the new community residential services.

Both of these Nebraska services have been widely imitated across North America. As of June, 1972, a total of at least 27 citizen advocacy offices have been initiated, including three state-level ones, 23 local ones, including four in Canada, and one other large youth advocacy service in St. Louis. Efforts to implement are underway in numerous other locations.

The fact that the advocacy schema was implemented first in the field of mental retardation is an historical accident, due probably to the reawakened dynamism in that field which is coming from way behind in setting the pace for certain other fields. From the first, advocacy was intended to be for anyone who needs it. While we can expect to see the development of advocacy offices serving specific groups, we will probably also see the initiation of generic advocacy offices.

On one point, the reader must be specially cautioned. Advocacy as sketched here is not the same as various other types of advocacy concepts and schemas which have recently been developed that imply advocacy by agencies and agency employees rather than by citizen volunteers (who are also free of conflicts of interest), that imply advocacy to groups of individuals rather than specific persons, and that do not rely primarily on sustained and individualized relationships.

The advocate's loyalty is to his protégé, not to an agency or even the advocacy office. Thus, he is a volunteer to the person, not the agency, and a very important part of his mission is implementation of the protégé's rights. Advocates see to it that protégés receive the services to which they are entitled, and are accorded the privileges of their citizenship. Pursuit of a protégé's citizenship rights may include such a basic symbolic act as seeing to it that he can cast his ballot at the polls. Advocate action may necessitate confrontation with agencies, and perhaps even legal action. In some ways, it implies consumer militancy with legal weapons, such as we have seen increasingly of late, and which has resulted in historic court decisions in Pennsylvania, Alabama, and elsewhere. Unfortunately, it was not possible to produce a chapter in this book on this very relevant topic of the role of the organized consumer movement in the implementation of normalization principles.

Because advocates will not always be viewed with favor by agencies, and because they must often become militant, it is of the highest importance that advocacy offices be funded and administered as independently as possible. Preferably, such offices either would be attached to voluntary agencies (such as chapters of voluntary associations in the field of cerebral palsy, mental retardation, *etc.*); be totally independent; be attached to the legislative branch of government, much like ombudsman offices; or be operated by Community Chest (Red Feather) conglomerates.

The citizen advocacy schema has received intense national and even international attention, and implementation is proceeding apace (Zauha & Korn, being published). This sketch here provides only the barest overview. Much like the description of PASS in the next chapter on 'Normalization via agency performance assessment and differential funding', this chapter is only intended to orient the reader to yet another way of implementing the normalization principle, and to entice him to study the advocacy schema in detail in another source (Wolfensberger & Zauha, being published). While advocacy activities can be described and interpreted in many ways, ultimately they imply a normalization of protégé functioning: to obtain for him, as much as possible, an existence comparable to that of other citizens.

18 normalization via agency performance assessment and differential funding

Table 1

Outline of rating elements of the Program Analysis of Service Systems – PASS

Appendix A

A sample rating from PASS

A sample rating from FUNDET

One reason why change has been so slow in many of our human services, and why service quality has often been low, is that in the past, we have neither been committed to an ideology of accountability in human services, nor have we had many accounting tools available to us. This is rapidly changing, due to the advent of new administrative concepts, new service orientations, and a new consumer activism. In this chapter, I will present a brief overview of a new human service accounting tool that has been developed in good part in order to implement the principle of normalization. Very arbitrarily, and admittedly with acronym considerations in mind, the tool has been labelled Program Analysis of Service Systems (PASS).

PASS consists of 41 'ratings', which are brief statements about various aspects of service quality. Each rating is scored on four to six levels, the lowest implying poor or even unacceptable service performance, the highest one implying near-ideal performance. Each level carries a weight (score), with the highest level of a rating carrying the maximum weight for that rating. Related ratings are grouped into subitems, related subitems are grouped into items, and so forth. The scores a service receives on all ratings are summated into a total score for that service, the maximum attainable score (for a near-ideal service) being 1000.

While the rating statements are very brief, each rating is accompanied by a lengthy narrative which states and explains its rationale, and which provides guidelines as to the scoring of the rating. In many instances, specific examples are given, illustrative of typical performance at different levels of the rating.

The weights or scores for each level and rating were determined on an *a priori* basis, and at this time, it does not appear that any other basis is really feasible or perhaps even desirable. In this fashion, it was arbitrarily decided to assign 840 of the possible points to ratings related to human management (especially normalization) ideology, with the other 160 points allocated to those ratings which concern themselves primarily with administrative matters. This approach contrasts sharply with that of other program assessment instruments that focus on superficial but more easily objectified elements such as window space, staff ratios, and number of lavatories and toilet seats. PASS attempts to make the important quantifiable, instead of the quantifiable important.

PASS has an interesting minor feature. The total score can be broken down into a program score, and a physical facility score.

It is not the intent of this chapter to provide a thorough knowledge of PASS, but merely to convey an appreciation thereof. A complete description of the system is available elsewhere (Wolfensberger & Glenn, being published). However, in order to facilitate the acquisition of this appreciation, *Table 1* is provided, listing the names of the ratings, their hierarchical organization, and the scores attached to ratings and rating clusters. Further, at the end of the chapter, one illustrative rating statement with its explanatory narrative and scoring guidelines is provided.

TABLE 1

Outline of rating elements of the Program Analysis of Service Systems – PASS

Code	Score	Element
PASS	(1000)	
1	(840)	Ideology
11	(670)	Normalization-related
111	(225)	Integration
1111	(95)	Physical integration
*R11111	(30)	Proximity
*R11112	(10)	Access
*R11113	(20)	Physical context
R11114	(35)	Size or dispersal
1112	(130)	Social integration
11121	(40)	Socially integrative interpretations
R111211	(20)	Program and facility labels
R111212	(20)	Building perception
11122	(90)	Socially integrative program structures
R111221	(30)	Deviant staff contact
R111222	(30)	Other deviant contact
R111223	(30)	Socially integrative social opportunities
112	(225)	Appropriate interpretations and structures
1121	(165)	Age-appropriate interpretations and structures
*R11211	(15)	Facilities, environmental design and appointments
R11212	(20)	Possessions
R11213	(20)	Labels and forms of address
R11214	(30)	Activities, routines, and rhythms
R11215	(35)	Autonomy and rights
R11216	(20)	Sex behavior
R11217	(25)	Personal appearance
1122	(60)	Culture-appropriate interpretations and structures

Maximum scores in parentheses. Ratings are prefixed with an R. Stars indicate ratings which yield a physical facility score.

Table 1 – Continued

Code	Weight	Label
R11221	(30)	Labels and forms of address
R11222	(30)	Personal appearance
R113	(50)	Specialization
114	(65)	Developmental growth orientation
*R1141	(15)	Physical overprotection
R1142	(15)	Social overprotection
R1143	(35)	Intensity of relevant programming
115	(105)	Quality of Setting
R1151	(25)	Physical comfort
*R1152	(20)	Environmental beauty
R1153	(35)	Individualization
R1154	(25)	Interactions
12	(100)	Administration-related
R121	(20)	Comprehensiveness
R122	(20)	Utilization of generic services
R123	(30)	Consumer & public participation
R124	(30)	Innovativeness
13	(25)	Various
R131	(15)	Ties to Academia
R132	(10)	Research climate
14	(45)	Regional priorities
R141	(20)	Deinstitutionalization
R142	(25)	Age group priorities
2	(160)	Administration
21	(35)	Manpower considerations
R211	(25)	Staff development
R212	(10)	Manpower development
22	(125)	Operational effectiveness
221	(80)	Internal administration
R2211	(25)	Administrative control and structures
R2212	(20)	Planning process
R2213	(35)	Program evaluation and change
222	(45)	Finance
R2221	(15)	Budget realism
R2222	(30)	Budget economy
3	(1000)	FUNDET
R31	(250)	Continuation of funding
32	(375)	Hardship factors
R321	(95)	Financial need
R322	(165)	Socio-ecologic hardship
R323	(115)	Geo-demographic hardship

Table 1 – Continued

R33 (75)	Newness	
34 (220)	Funder priorities	
	R341 (110)	Client appropriateness
	R342 (110)	Program appropriateness
R35 (80)	Consistency with Funder policies & standards	

PASS is administered by a team of trained raters (hopefully not less than three) who can be presumed to be objective and free of conflicts of interest; and it is administered to a service project much as a psychometric test is administered to a person. The raters base their judgments on written material submitted by the agency (program descriptions and documentation, brochures, operating manuals, fund application narratives, *etc.*); and on a site visit which includes a tour and interviews, perhaps with directors, supervisors, workers, clients, and possibly citizens of the neighborhood or community. Although the raters will usually share in all these experiences, they render their judgments independently. The scores are averaged for each rating after all the judgments have been made.

The raters are viewed as part of the instrument, much as psychometric test administrators are. Therefore, raters must become 'standardized', *i.e.* comparably highly skilled in normalization ideology, in perusal and interpretation of written program materials, and in site visit routines.

PASS was designed to have the following four characteristics

ability to quantitatively assess and compare the quality of the widest range of human services, regardless of the particular type of service involved (developmental day care, rehabilitation facilities, clinics, group residences, *etc.*); or the special human problem field involved (mental retardation, mental disorder, delinquency, physical or sensory impairment, *etc.*);

incorporation of normalization principles as major criteria of program evaluation;

sufficient objectivity to assure reasonable reliability across raters;

adaptability, so as to permit additions, deletions, or other changes, without impairing the total meaning of the assessment schema, and without losing comparability with other assessments performed at a different time or on a different service.

PASS is intended to be used primarily for four purposes

to establish a standard of normalizing human management agency performance;

to provide an objective means of assessing (either by internal or external evaluation) the quality of a human service, thereby to be able to assess quality change over time; compare the performance of different services;

to provide a rational means for allocating limited funds on a competitive basis;

to function as a teaching tool in disseminating the normalization principle.

The third purpose was actually the one that furnished the strongest initial impetus for the development of PASS. In 1969, the Nebraska legislature enacted a mental retardation community services bill that provided state matching for local programs. However, the initial appropriation was so modest that a way had to be found to disperse the money via a process that would be unaffected by political and other pressures, and in such a fashion as to make maximal impact.

To meet this demand, a cruder version of the present PASS was devised, and agencies applying for state matching funds had to undergo searching evaluations, some of these resulting in rejection of applications because of low quality or poor promise. One advantage of PASS is that it pinpoints strengths and weaknesses, and agencies will know exactly what they are expected to do in order to improve and be funded. For instance, one agency in Nebraska operated a home-like hostel for young adults, most of whom were in work training in a sheltered workshop. Although the hostel met most of the criteria of normalization, the PASS raters noted that the hostel was located on a country lane beyond the edge of town, and that this isolated location constituted a grave violation of the principle of physical and social integration. Therefore, the project was funded only on the provision that the hostel would be moved into town by a certain deadline, which was met. In another instance, a sheltered workshop was steered away from activities that had a childlike flavor, and directed toward more adult-type work. Thus, a resolute use of funding power can impose normalizing practices where inertia, lack of understanding of the normalization principle, or lack of commitment to it might perpetuate objectionable practices.

Among the educational functions of PASS is the development of a pool of raters sophisticated enough to use and apply the system appropriately. These raters soon internalize the normalization principle, and act as leaders in its dissemination and implementation in their other activities. Fortunately, one does not have to be a professional, or highly educated, to become a skilled rater; but one does have to be rather intelligent. Many knowledgeable non-professionals, such as sophisticated consumer representatives and members of self-help action groups, can become skilled raters.

PASS also becomes educational when agency personnel are asked to apply the system to themselves prior to an outside assessment. Especially where funding is at stake, and where an agency knows approximately whom and what it is competing against, such self-evaluation can result in drastic improvements – or in spontaneous withdrawal from the competition because the agency may realize that its quality or efficiency is too low. At any rate, self-evaluation is also intended to prepare the ground for program consultation aimed at improving those areas found to be weak by the raters.

PASS is concerned entirely with service quality, in the broadest sense. However, funding determinations must and should sometimes be based on additional factors, such as local needs. For this purpose, an optional subsystem was devised which is structured, administered, and scored analogously to PASS, but which contains ratings that concern themselves only with those non-quality factors that may have a bearing on funding merit. This system was called FUNDET, for 'funding determination'.

FUNDET can be used for making differential funding decisions in regard to those service projects which are of equal PASS quality, or which score above some predetermined PASS cut-off level. Also, a procedure has been worked out whereby PASS and FUNDET scores can be combined in a single score, called PASS-FUND, which can rank service projects on the combined criteria of the two systems. A sample rating from FUNDET is appended.

Almost concomitantly with the development of PASS, the Office of Mental Retardation in Nebraska developed a set of standards for community mental retardation services. These standards were probably the first ones that were based on the normalization principle in any human service area in North America. The standards are still evolving, but they and PASS were developed in such a fashion as to be consistent with each other, and complementary in some aspects. This interrelationship not only reinforces the teaching process, but also the process of implementation.

Actually, PASS is a very intricate system, and it specifies many details of normalization which are not even covered in this book. This chapter has merely provided a thumbnail sketch, in order to emphasize that the normalization principle is quantifiable, and that highly objective and administratively feasible tools can be used to implement it. Other tools and techniques might be found to serve as well or better, but here, at least, is one that appears to be unique in many ways, and that holds much promise. It appears to meet several contemporary needs, as well as a societal readiness to demand accountability in human services and to apply tough-minded administrative methods to that purpose.

appendix a

A sample rating from PASS

112 Appropriate interpretations and structures

What is appropriate within a culture is determined by many factors. For instance, there is tradition and religion; the natural environment and climate may play a role by setting certain limits; and often, personal characteristics, such as age or sex, will interact with other factors in defining acceptable norms for specific individuals within a culture.

How much esteem and dignity a person will be accorded will depend in large part upon the way he acts. His behavior will be judged by those around him in terms of its appropriateness for his age and for his culture. However, a person is also frequently judged on the basis of how *others* judge him and act toward him. Thus, a very important part of normalization is how a person is perceived by others.

Normalization implies that a person would be enabled to project an image that does not mark him as deviant in the sight of others. The rationale for this is twofold. First, as stated, how a person is perceived affects the way he is treated, and a person perceived as deviant is very apt to elicit pity, rejection, persecution, and other behaviors which tend to diminish a person's dignity, adjustment, growth, *etc.* Secondly, the way a person is treated by others will affect his self-image, as well as the way in which he will respond. It is well-known that a person perceived to be deviant is expected to act deviantly, and such expectations are often so powerful as to actually elicit the expected behavior, thus becoming self-fulfilling prophecies.

The two items areas following will concern themselves primarily with those social interpretations and human management structures which human managers and agencies may impose upon a client, and which may affect both the way in which he perceives himself, as well as the way he is perceived by others. The rater is reminded to remain alert to the fact that a human management measure may be appropriate and effective from a purely clinical viewpoint, *i.e.* if only the client and the manager were involved. At the same time, such a measure may be diminished in effectiveness, or even become counter-productive, because of the way it affects third parties, such as the family, other clients or managers, the public, *etc.*

The first item 'Age-appropriate interpretations and structures' will be concerned only with considerations based upon the client's age, while the second item 'Culture-appropriate interpretations and structures' covers a miscellany of other considerations which bear upon culture-appropriate social interpretation and human management structures. Aspects which are also concerned with personal development, but which are not as intimately tied to the medium of social interpretation, are covered in other elements. For instance, several such major considerations are subsumed under 'Intensity of relevant programming'.

R11221 **Culture-appropriate labels and forms of address**

The rater is reminded that age-appropriate labels and forms of address are treated separately under 'Age-appropriate interpretations and structures'. In the rating here, only those aspects of labelling and forms of address will be covered which transcend age, and which are generally applicable to persons of any age within the culture.

In *Level 1* projects, one encounters forms of address or labelling that are highly demeaning, devaluing, and implying inferiority and/or extensive deviancy. Such labelling may include reference to clients by numbers or as objects ('items', 'clinical material'); archaic and now generally derogatory classificatory and diagnostic terms ('idiots', 'dumb', 'lunatic', 'demented'); or use of highly inappropriate and stigmatizing nicknames and appellations (*e.g.* 'nigger', 'honky', 'kook', 'pig', 'freak').

Projects should be assigned to *Level 1* regardless whether the highly inappropriate labelling is used in addressing clients directly, or in speaking about them indirectly; and under the following two conditions:

a if such labelling is used by even a small number of key personnel, such as administrators, public relations personnel, *etc.*;

b if it is used by a significant minority of non-key personnel.

Level 2 projects would include the following.

a *Level 1* labelling may be encountered in only a few non-key members of the staff, in none of the key members, and the agency is making conscious efforts to remedy the situation.

b Other labels, appellations, and nicknames encountered by even a few key staff members, or even a significant minority of non-key staff, may be clearly but not totally inappropriate or outdated. For instance, staff unnecessarily may refer to clients with labels which denote their impairment, or they may label a person by his diagnosis: 'he is an epileptic' instead of 'he has epilepsy', 'retardate' instead of 'retarded person', 'convict Jones', *etc.* Also in this category fall moderately stigmatizing overtones or nicknames ('shorty', 'fatso', 'dago'), or calling clients by their surnames only.

In *Level 3* projects, staff typically make an adequate effort to address their clients in a way which does not connote deviancy. However, in at least a significant minority of staff, courtesy and respect may be forced, *e.g.* behavior of the staff may indicate that treating the clients as individuals and as human equals requires conscious efforts, while in other situations with non-impaired persons, the public, or personal acquaintances, such behavior would be almost automatic. Thus, while labels may be appropriate, the underlying feelings or the accompanying gestures carry the connotation that the client is being perceived as deviant, distant, inferior, or of lower value. Certain types of minor discourtesies and lack of sensitivity would also fall on this level, including the common custom of shouting at old people or at persons with limited command of English, as if to overcome a hearing impairment.

In *Level 4* projects, the attitudes and intentions of virtually the entire staff appear to be beyond reproach, and labelling is appropriate in all or virtually all aspects. Minor shortcomings may be due to slowness in adjusting to the most recent trends, or the implementation of well-intentioned rationales in a slightly unfortunate fashion. For instance, the term 'retardate' was a progressive term a few years ago, when it replaced more objectionable labels such as 'deficient' or 'feebleminded'. Thus, an agency may have been a little slow in adopting even more progressive labels, and may have used the term 'retardate' a few years longer than desirable, but with the best intentions and attitudes.

In *Level 5* projects, staff appear deeply imbued with the proper orientation, commitment, and attitude of human equality and dignity in the manner in which they address clients. Virtually all staff members bend over backward to use labels and forms of address which are not only appropriate and up-to-date, but which promote and enhance the status of clients to an optimal degree.

Note: The weights for the four levels of 'Culture-appropriate labels and forms of address' are −30, −12, 0, +24, +30 respectively.

A Sample rating from FUNDET

R31 Continuation of funding

The rationale for inclusion of this element is that a funding agent would, and should almost invariably, be concerned with the continued and long-term funding and operation of the service it supports. Also, almost any funding agent would encourage recipients of its support to seek additional and/or alternative funding from other sources. In many cases, funding agents specifically intend that their funds serve primarily as 'seed' or initiation money.

Evaluation of the likelihood of continuation of local, alternative, additional, matching, *etc.* funding for the operation of a project should include consideration of the following.

Level 1 projects appear to lack sufficient financial support of the above nature, perhaps indicated by:

a vague statements of financial backing, without tangible or meaningful documentation;

b initial matching funds coming from a one-shot contribution, without assurance of continued support;

c assertions regarding future financial support based on highly speculative conjecture or hope, or on unwarranted optimism.

Projects receive a *Level 2* score where community atmosphere and potential support sources appear such as to justify reasonable expectations of funding, even when there exist limited written documentations or assurances. To determine this, the rater should consider such points as:

a the existence and involvement of powerful, active interest groups, *e.g.* organizations, consumer associations, *etc.*;

b support from active civic leaders in the community;

c favorable opinion toward such programs on the part of public and potential funding sources;

d past actions of a favorable nature on the part of local civic groups, other funding sources, *etc.*;

e indications of strong (local) support in the news media.

Level 3 scores should be given to projects which are considered to have concrete, documented assurances of continued financial support. These would be accompanied by written authoritative letters of intent or assurance from governmental bodies, agencies, organizations, *etc.*

Level 4 projects would be those giving indications of unusually favorable support, for example, the existence of a legal-fiscal base for continued support such as:

existing, earmarked tax mill levies;

permanent endowments, with the amount of income reasonably stable, specific, and adequate.

Note: The weights for the four levels are —250, 0, +200, and +250, respectively.

19 miscellaneous other implementive strategies and mechanisms

Direct subsidy

As we reach the conclusion of this book, I regret very much that some strategies and mechanisms for implementing the principle of normalization have received little or no coverage. Perceptive readers will note that there should have been at least two additional chapters: one to explore the potential future role of organizations representing the interests of the handicapped and disadvantaged; and one to analyze the role and contribution of the law. Fortunately, the role of action groups is at least touched upon in the chapter by Bengt Nirje, but an analysis of the full relevance and potential impact of the law must await another occasion.

In this chapter, I wish to elaborate upon one administrative mechanism which is not major by itself, but which can be a most valuable tool in selected instances, and in combination with other approaches. I am referring to the utilization of direct financial subsidy of handicapped individuals or their families which would enable them to attain a culturally normative solution to their problems.

Direct subsidy

In our society, a highly valued and time-honored custom is to work out one's problems on one's own, and usually within one's own home or family setting. One may disagree with this cultural value, but one cannot deny its reality, nor its implication to the implementation of the principle of normalization.

One implication would appear to be that at least up to a point, human management structures should provide the type of service which maximizes a person's opportunity to resolve problems in traditional and valued ways. One such service appears to be the provision of direct subsidies.

Some forms of subsidy are quite traditional themselves; others may not be. Since the normalization principle is not only concerned with normative behavior and appearance, but also with normative means, those means should be favored which are well understood and accepted by the public.

Foster placement is such a form of family subsidy that is well understood and accepted: a family is paid to shelter or raise somebody else's child who has special problems, *e.g.* whose home is disordered or has dissolved. Only socio-political attitudes have prevented us from generalizing this option to include families who raise their own very special child. Perhaps only agency traditions and dynamics have prevented us from subsidizing the adoption of handicapped children, as discussed in the chapter on 'Additional implications of the normalization principle'.

These attitudes and traditions have cost us dearly. For instance, the cost of life-long institutional residence for a retarded person has been estimated to range between $100,000 and $300,000. In fact, even by 1969, the cost of capital construction of institutional space was in some instances as high as $40,000 per place, and as of June, 1972, the figure of $50,000 is being mentioned in the plans of one institution in the United States. A small portion of such sums applied to family subsidy may often suffice to serve a person within his home, or at least to avoid special residential placement. In many cases, this sum may amount to no more than a few hundred dollars at a time, or per year.

For instance, there are many cases where institutional placement is sought because of the stresses created by the fact that a wife or mother is overworked; here, a family subsidy might permit the purchase of a washer, a dryer, a dishwasher, and/or the hiring of a housekeeper for a half-day a week. In other cases, living quarters may be too cramped or inappropriate to accommodate a hyperactive child; a subsidy here might permit a move to more spacious quarters, the addition of a room, installation of a yard fence, and/or the purchase of some outdoor play equipment that affords the child constructive activity. In yet other instances, the direct or indirect cost of special treatment may threaten to impoverish a family; subsidy here might pay for such treatment, for special gadgets, special clothing, cab fare, *etc.* I have witnessed repeated instances where two weeks' vacation at $30-$50 per day would probably have been of as much, or more, help to a 'nervous housewife' than a month's residence in a psychiatric treatment center, at $50-$100 per day.

Direct subsidy to persons or families can be a powerful adjunct to the armamentarium of tools useful in implementing normalization. Its utility is maximal in a human management system or administrative structure where it can be combined with other new and old helping forms. However, it should never be proposed – as it sometimes is – as the single or even major means for service structuring. Used by itself, direct subsidy cannot assure that adequate planning, priority setting, manpower training, and other important systemic functions will be carried out.

Family subsidy is one of the most efficient service options imaginable. It already exists in many – often indirect – forms, as when certain treatment expenses of poor or dependent persons are paid by various public programs. The socio-political climate is now such as to permit expansion of this option, and the formulation of some new direct forms of subsidy. These forms should be applied not merely to the poor, but also to those middle class families where extreme management options, such as residential placement, are often invoked because of conditions which are actually alleviative by modest, perhaps even short-term, expenditure of money.

Direct subsidy carries with it certain dangers. Among these are abuse, and administrative chaos. Both of these can be minimized by the establishment of human management decision-making (*i.e.* option-offering) centers discussed in some detail elsewhere (Wolfensberger, 1969a). In brief, these centers would coordinate human services in a field or area, and offer clients, or their families, as many options as appear feasible and economic. One of these options might often be money, either in lieu of agency service, or in order for clients to purchase such a service on their own on the open market, as proposed in one model by Cooke (1969).

Especially within the context of new administrative structures and human management systems, direct subsidy can be combined with other new helping forms in developing a strong armamentarium for the implementation of the principle of normalization.

epilogue

The principle of normalization appears to be profoundly threatening to some individuals who have a strong or historical commitment to alternative human management ideologies, even if they may not recognize what these ideologies are. For example, those associated with dehumanizing programs will not identify very readily with normalization. However, more subtly, individuals who have been identified with relatively benign but paternalistic or pity-derived human service projects also have great difficulty adjusting to the demands of the normalization principle, such as those that call for a dignifying measure of risk, for granting autonomy and independence to impaired individuals and particularly adults, and for according full adult status to them.

It also appears that objections to the normalization principle frequently have both manifest and latent forms. In many instances, it may be objected that normalization requires conformity, that it does not furnish adequate emotional support, and so on, when at a deeper level there may be found motives such as those discussed above. Therefore, in concluding this book, I want to reiterate six points that are often misunderstood or advanced as objections when the normalization principle is discussed. All six points have been covered in the text, but their importance is such as to warrant their being restated here in such highlighted fashion.

ONE One reaction to the principle often heard is that it is not new. In a sense this is true, and in another sense it is profoundly false. At the very least, the normalization principle has not been systematically stated and explored, tied to sociological theory and empirical evidence, and spelled out in detail in a comprehensive fashion. Often those who claim that they have always practised normalization have not yet understood the principle; and in many instances, their clinical or systemic work is clearly inconsistent with it.

TWO Some individuals object to the use of the term 'deviant'. On occasion, they confuse it with 'deviate'. Actually, the term was borrowed from sociology where it has been found to have a great deal of theoretical utility. It certainly refers to a phenomenon that needs and deserves to be termed, and at present there exists no alternative label that has as much theoretical and explanatory power. However, the reader may have noted that throughout this text, pain has been taken not to make a noun out of an adjective; we have not made 'deviants' out of persons, but referred to persons as being deviant, and deviance has been clearly defined as being in the eyes of the beholder rather than in the person being perceived.

THREE The concept of 'normative', as used in the definition of the normalization principle, is a statistical one, or is at least idealized as one. However, there are behaviors which are normative, and yet which would be judged as being immoral by many people. Thus, we should assist a person to become capable of meaningfully choosing for himself among those normative options that are considered moral, and those that are not. If a person is capable of a meaningful choice, he must also risk the consequences.

FOUR The normalization principle does not imply gross imposition of conformity. It is true that there are certain limits which are forced upon all of us by society, and rightly so. But primarily, the normalization principle implies that we provide the conditions which eventually permit a person to function as normatively as possible unless he deliberately chooses to be deviant. If he chooses deviancy, we should practise as much tolerance as is possible in a well-ordered society.

FIVE Normalization does not mean that only normative human management tools and methods are used – merely that these be as normal as feasible. In many instances, there will come a point where extraordinary means are needed. This, the Scandinavians refer to as 'complementation', and it is similar to what Cobb (being published) calls an 'instrumentality' of support.

SIX Finally, the question often comes up whether the public will accept the implications of the normalization principle, especially those implications that have to do with integration. I believe that they will, especially because we are becoming an increasingly pluralistic society in which differences are no longer so apt to be viewed as deviances. However, I plan to explore this issue further in another context.

Wolf Wolfensberger
1972

references

Adorno, T. W., Frenkel-Brunswik, E., Levinson, D. J., & Sanford, R. N. *The authoritarian personality*. New York: Harper, 1950.
Albee, G. W. *Models, myths and manpower*. MENTAL HYGIENE, 1968, *52*, 168-180.
Anonymous. *The saint in our house*. NATIONAL APOSTOLATE FOR THE MENTALLY RETARDED QUARTERLY, 1970, *2*(3), 12-13.
Anonymous. *Hospital work stations for MR's*. REHABILITATION RECORD, 1971, *12*(2), 20-21.
Arieti, S. *Interpretation of schizophrenia*. New York: Robert Brunner, 1955.
Asher, J. J. *The total physical response technique of learning*. JOURNAL OF SPECIAL EDUCATION, 1969, *3*, 253-262.
Azrin, M. H., & Holz, W. C. *Punishment*. In Honig, W. K. (Ed.), OPERANT BEHAVIOR: AREAS OF RESEARCH AND APPLICATION. New York: Appleton-Century-Crofts, 1966.
Bachrach, A. J., Erwin, W. J., & Mohr, J. P. *The control of eating behavior in an anorexic by operant conditioning techniques*. In Ullmann, L. & Krasner, L. P. (Eds.), CASE STUDIES IN BEHAVIOR MODIFICATION. New York: Holt, 1965. Pp. 153-163.
Bank-Mikkelsen, N. E. *A metropolitan area in Denmark: Copenhagen*. In R. Kugel & W. Wolfensberger (Eds.), CHANGING PATTERNS IN RESIDENTIAL SERVICES FOR THE MENTALLY RETARDED. Washington: President's Committee on Mental Retardation, 1969. Pp. 227-254.
Bartlett, F. L. *Institutional peonage, our exploitation of mental patients*. ATLANTIC MONTHLY, 1964, *214*(1), 116-119.
Barsch, R. H. *Achieving perceptual-motor efficiency: A space-oriented approach to learning*. Seattle: Special Child Publications, 1967.
Bartlett, F. L. *Present-day requirements for state hospitals joining the community*. NEW ENGLAND JOURNAL OF MEDICINE, 1967, *276*, 90-94.
Bensberg, B., Colwell, C., Ellis, N. R., Roos, P., & Watson, L. S. *Report on symposium on environmental modifications for the profoundly retarded*. Albany: New York State Department of Mental Hygiene, 1969.
Berelson, B., & Steiner, G. *Human behavior: An inventory of scientific findings*. New York: Harcourt, Brace, & World, 1964.
Bower, E. M., Lourie, R. S., Strother, C. R., & Sutherland, R. L. *Project Re-Ed: New concepts for helping emotionally disturbed children: Evaluation by a panel of visitors*. Nashville, Tenn.: John F. Kennedy Center for Research on Education & Human Development, George Peabody College for Teachers, 1969.
Braginsky, B. M., Braginsky, D. D., & Ring, K. *Methods of madness*. New York: Holt, Rinehart & Winston, 1969.
Bricker, W. A. *Competence as a key factor in the study of children's deviant behavior*. MIND OVER MATTER, 1967, *12*(1), 16-23.
Bucher, B. *Some ethical issues in the therapeutic use of punishment*. In Rubin, R. D., & Franks, C. M. (Eds.), ADVANCES IN BEHAVIOR THERAPY, 1968. New York and London: Academic Press, 1969.
Bucher, B., & Fabricatore, J. *Use of patient-administered shock to suppress hallucinations*. BEHAVIOR THERAPY, 1970, *1*, 382-385.
Bucher, B., & Lovaas, O. I. *Use of aversive stimulation in behavior modification*. In Jones, M. R. (Ed.), MIAMI SYMPOSIUM ON THE PREDICTION OF BEHAVIOR: AVERSIVE STIMULATION. Coral Gables, Florida: University of Miami Press, 1968.
Buck, P. S. *The child who never grew*. New York: John Day, 1950.
Buddenhagen, R. G. *Until electric shocks are legal*. MENTAL RETARDATION, 1971, *9*(6), 48-50.

Bureau of the Census: *10th Census of the United States 1880, 21.* Washington, D.C.: U.S. Government Printing Office.
Cobb, H. *Citizen advocacy and the rights of the handicapped.* In W. Wolfensberger & H. Zauha (Eds.), CITIZEN ADVOCACY AND PROTECTIVE SERVICES FOR THE IMPAIRED AND HANDICAPPED. Toronto: National Institute on Mental Retardation, in press.
Colbert, J. N. *Philosophia habilitatus: Towards a policy of human rehabilitation in the post-institutional phase of disability.* JOURNAL OF REHABILITATION, 1969, *35*(5), 18-20.
Coleman, J. C. *Abnormal psychology and modern life* (2nd ed.). Chicago: Scott, Foresman, 1956.
Coll, B. D. *Perspectives in public welfare: A history.* Washington: U.S. Department of Health, Education, and Welfare, 1969.
Columbus, D., & Fogel, M. L. *Survey of disabled persons reveals housing choices.* JOURNAL OF REHABILITATION, 1971, *37*(2), 26-28.
Colwell, C. N. *The role of operant techniques in cottage and ward life programs.* Paper read at meeting of the American Association on Mental Deficiency, Chicago, 1966.
The Commission on Emotional and Learning Disorders in Children. *One million children.* Toronto: Crainford, 1970.
Conger, J. C. *The treatment of encorpresis by the management of social consequences.* BEHAVIOR THERAPY, 1970, *1*, 386-390.
Cooke, R. E. *The free choice principle in the care of the mentally retarded.* In Kugel, R. B., & Wolfensberger, W. (Eds.), CHANGING PATTERNS IN RESIDENTIAL SERVICES FOR THE MENTALLY RETARDED. Washington: D.C.: President's Committee on Mental Retardation, 1969. Pp. 361-365.
Cooper, D. *The death of the family.* New York: Pantheon Books. (Randon House), 1970.
Cruickshank, W. M. *Rehabilitation: Toward a broader spectrum.* PSYCHOLOGICAL ASPECTS OF DISABILITY, 1970, *17*, 149-158.
Cruickshank, W. M., & Quay, H. C. *Learning and physical environment: The necessity for research and research design.* EXCEPTIONAL CHILDREN, 1970, *37*, 261-268.
de Fuentes, P. *The conquistadors: First-person accounts of the conquest of Mexico.* New York: Orion Press, 1963.
Deutsch, A. *The mentally ill in America: A history of their care and treatment from colonial times.* (2nd ed.) New York: Columbia University Press, 1949.
Diaz del Castillo, B. *The discovery and conquest of Mexico: 1517-1521.* New York: Farrar, Straus & Cudahy, 1956.
Duncan, J. *Camerons at the castle.* London: Macmillan, 1965.
Dunn, L. K. *Small special-purpose residential facilities for the retarded.* In R. Kugel & W. Wolfensberger (Eds.), CHANGING PATTERNS IN RESIDENTIAL SERVICES FOR THE MENTALLY RETARDED. Washington: President's Committee on Mental Retardation, 1969. Pp. 213-226.
Dybwad, G. *Action implications, U.S.A. today.* In R. Kugel & W. Wolfensberger (Eds.), CHANGING PATTERNS IN RESIDENTIAL SERVICES FOR THE MENTALLY RETARDED. Washington: President's Committee on Mental Retardation, 1969. Pp. 383-428.
Eaton, J. W., & Weil, R. J. *Culture and mental disorders: A comparative study of the Hutterites and other populations.* Glencoe, Ill.: Free Press, 1955.
Edgerton, R. B. *Mental retardation in non-Western societies: Toward a cross-cultural perspective on incompetence.* In H. C. Haywood (Ed.), SOCIAL-CULTURAL ASPECTS OF MENTAL RETARDATION: PROCEEDINGS OF THE PEABODY-NIMH CONFERENCE. New York: Appleton-Century-Crofts, 1970. Pp. 523-559.
English, R. W. *Assessment, modification and stability of attitudes toward blindness.* PSYCHOLOGICAL ASPECTS OF DISABILITY, 1971, *18*, 79-85.
Fairweather, G. W., Sanders, D. H., Maynard, H., Cressler, D. L., & Bleck, D. S. *Community life for the mentally ill: An alternative to institutional care.* Chicago: Aldine, 1969.
Farber, B. *Mental retardation: Its social context and social consequences.* Boston: Houghton, Mifflin, 1968.
Fendell, N. *Israel's eternal children.* JOURNAL FOR SPECIAL EDUCATORS OF THE MENTALLY RETARDED, 1969, *4*(1), 19-22.
Franklin, D. S. *The adoption of children with medical conditions: Part I – Process and outcome.* CHILD WELFARE, 1969, *48*, 459-467.

Gangnes, A. G. *Architecture*. In Wortis, J. (Ed.), MENTAL RETARDATION: ANNUAL REVIEW. New York: Grune & Stratton, 1970. Pp. 150-177.

Gardner, J. W. *Educating for renewal*. OCCASIONAL PAPERS. American Association of Collegiate Schools of Business, 1965, No. 101.

Gardner, W. I. *Use of behavior therapy with the mentally retarded*. In Menolascino, F. J. (Ed.), PSYCHIATRIC APPROACHES TO MENTAL RETARDATION. New York & London: Basic Books, 1970. Pp. 250-275.

Gardner, W. I. *Behavior modification in mental retardation: The education and rehabilitation of the mentally retarded adolescent and adult*. Chicago: Aldine-Atherton, 1971.

Glover, E. *The technique of psycho-analysis*. New York: International University Press, 1955.

Goffman, E. *Asylums*. Garden City, N.Y.: Anchor, 1961.

Goffman, E. *Stigma: Notes on the management of spoiled identity*. Englewood, N.J.: Prentice-Hall, 1963.

Goldenberg, I. *Build me a mountain: Youth, poverty and the creations of new settings*. Cambridge, Mass.: MIT Press, 1971.

Goldfarb, W. *Psychological privation in infancy and subsequent adjustment*. AMERICAN JOURNAL OF ORTHOPSYCHIATRY, 1945, *15*, 247-255.

Goodwill Industries of America. *A report on the institute on sheltered workshop services for the mentally retarded*. Washington: GIA, 1961.

Gordon, G. A. *Roles, theory and illness: A sociological perspective*. New Haven, Conn.: College and University Press, 1966.

Gordon, K. (Ed.). *Agenda for the nation*. Washington, D.C.: Brookings Institution, 1969.

Governor's Citizens' Committee on Mental Retardation. *The report of the Nebraska Citizens' Study Committee on Mental Retardation*. Volume 1. Lincoln, Neb.: State Department of Public Institutions, 1968. (a)

Governor's Citizens' Committee on Mental Retardation. *The report of the Nebraska Citizens' Study Committee on Mental Retardation*. Volume 2. Lincoln, Neb.: State Department of Public Institutions, 1968. (b)

Greene, H. H. M. *The obligation of civilized society to idiotic and feeble-minded children*. PROCEEDINGS OF THE NATIONAL CONFERENCE OF CHARITIES AND CORRECTION, 1884, 264-271.

Group for the Advancement of Psychiatry, Committee on Therapeutic Care. *Crisis in psychiatric hospitalization*. New York: Group for the Advancement of Psychiatry, 1969.

Gruenberg, E. M. (Ed.). *Evaluating the effectiveness of community mental health services*. New York: Mental Health Materials Center, 1966.

Grunewald, K. *A rural county in Sweden: Malmohus County*. In R. Kugel & W. Wolfensberger (Eds.), CHANGING PATTERNS IN RESIDENTIAL SERVICES FOR THE MENTALLY RETARDED. Washington: President's Committee on Mental Retardation, 1969. Pp. 255-287.

Gunzburg, H. C. *The hospital as a normalizing training environment*. JOURNAL OF MENTAL SUBNORMALITY, 1970, *16*, 71-83.

Haffter, C. *The changeling: History and psychodynamics of attitudes to handicapped children in European folklore*. JOURNAL OF THE HISTORY OF THE BEHAVIORAL SCIENCES, 1968, *4*, 55-61.

Hamilton, J., Stephens, L., & Allen, P. *Controlling aggressive and destructive behavior in severely retarded institutionalized residents*. AMERICAN JOURNAL OF MENTAL DEFICIENCY, 1967, *71*, 852-856.

Hauck, P. A. *The forgotten concept*. JOURNAL OF REHABILITATION, 1971, *37*(6), 26-30.

Hayden, F. J. *Physical fitness for the mentally retarded: A manual for teachers and parents*. Toronto: Metropolitan Toronto Association for Retarded Children, 1964.

Hayden, F. J. *Learn to play center*. Washington, D.C.: The Joseph P. Kennedy Jr. Foundation, 1969.

Heather, D. *Design for play*. TEACHING AND TRAINING, 1970, *8*, 6-10.

Helsel, Elsie. *History and present status of protective services*. In Wolfensberger, W., & Zauha, H. (Eds.), CITIZEN ADVOCACY AND PROTECTIVE SERVICES FOR THE IMPAIRED AND HANDICAPPED. Toronto: National Institute on Mental Retardation, in press.

Hersch, C. *The discontent explosion in mental health.* AMERICAN PSYCHOLOGIST, 1968, *23*, 497-506.
Horsfield, E. *Mental defectives at the court of Philip IV of Spain as portrayed by the great court painter Velasquez.* AMERICAN JOURNAL OF MENTAL DEFICIENCY, 1940, *45*, 152-157.
Howe, S. G. *Report made to the legislature of Massachusetts upon idiocy.* Boston, Mass.: Collidge & Wiley, 1848.
Howe, S. G. *Third and final report on the experimental school for teaching and training idiotic children; also, the first report of the trustees of the Massachusetts school for idiotic and feeble-minded youth.* Cambridge, Mass.: Metcalf and Company, 1852.
Howe, S. G., in *Ceremonies on laying the corner-stone of the New York state institution for the blind, at Batavia, Genesee Co., N.Y.* Batavia, N.Y.: Henry Todd, 1866.
International League of Societies for the Mentally Handicapped. *International League of Societies for the Mentally Handicapped.* Brussels: ILSMH, 1969.
Jaslow, R. I. *A modern plan for modern services to the mentally retarded.* Washington, U.S. Government Printing Office, 1967.
Johnson, A. *Report of committee on colonies for segregation of defectives.* PROCEEDINGS OF THE NATIONAL CONFERENCE OF CHARITIES AND CORRRECTION, 1903, 245-253.
Joint Commission on Mental Health of Children. *Crisis in child mental health: Challenge for the 1970's.* New York: Harper & Row, 1970.
Kanfer, F. H. *Self-regulation: Research, issues, and speculations.* In Neuringer, C., & Michael, J. L. (Eds.), BEHAVIOR MODIFICATION IN CLINICAL PSYCHOLOGY. New York: Appleton-Century-Crofts, 1970. Pp. 178-220.
Kerlin, I. N. *Report of the committee on provision for idiotic and feeble-minded persons.* PROCEEDINGS OF THE NATIONAL CONFERENCE OF CHARITIES AND CORRECTION, 1886, 288-297.
Keyes, D. *Flowers for Algernon.* New York: Harcourt, Brace & World, 1966.
Kidd, C. B. *The nature of mental retardation in different settings: Some problems in cross-cultural study.* In Haywood (Ed.), SOCIAL-CULTURAL ASPECTS OF MENTAL RETARDATION: PROCEEDINGS OF THE PEABODY-NIMH CONFERENCE. New York: Appleton-Century-Crofts, 1970. Pp. 573-586.
Kierans, E. W. *Towards a new national policy.* CANADIAN FORUM, 1972, *51* (612-613), 52-55.
Kimbrell, D. L., Luckey, R. E., Barbuto, P. F., & Love, J. G. *Operation dry pants: an intensive habit training program for severely and profoundly retarded.* MENTAL RETARDATION, 1967, *5*(2), 32-36.
Kirkbride, F. B. *Types of buildings for state institutions for the feeble-minded.* PROCEEDINGS OF THE NATIONAL CONFERENCE OF CHARITIES AND CORRECTION, 1916, 250-257.
Klein, S. D., & Abrams, S. L. *Public housing for handicapped persons?* JOURNAL OF REHABILITATION, 1971, *37*(2), 20-21.
Kolb, L. C. *Community mental health centers: Some issues in their transition from concept to reality.* HOSPITAL AND COMMUNITY PSYCHIATRY, 1968, *19*, 335-340.
Kolstoe, O. P. *An examination of some characteristics which discriminate between employed and not-employed mentally retarded males.* AMERICAN JOURNAL OF MENTAL DEFICIENCY, 1961, *66*, 472-482.
Krasner, L. *Behavior modification, token economies, and training in clinical psychology.* In Neuringer, C., & Michael, J. L. (Eds.), BEHAVIOR MODIFICATION IN CLINICAL PSYCHOLOGY. New York: Appleton-Century-Crofts, 1970. Pp. 86-104. (a)
Krasner, L. *Critical notice.* BEHAVIOR THERAPY, 1970, *1*, 402-406. (b)
Kubie, L. S. *Pitfalls of community psychiatry.* ARCHIVES OF GENERAL PSYCHIATRY, 1968, *18*, 257-266. (a)
Kubie, L. S. *The future of the private psychiatric hospital.* INTERNATIONAL JOURNAL OF PSYCHIATRY, 1968, *6*, 419-433. (b)
Kubie, L. S. *A rebuttal in summary.* JOURNAL OF SPECIAL EDUCATION, 1969, *3*, 87-93. (a)
Kubie, L. S. *The educational process into a behavioral science.* JOURNAL OF SPECIAL EDUCATION, 1969, *3*, 45-57. (b)
Kugel, R., & Wolfensberger, W. (Eds.). *Changing patterns in residential services for the mentally retarded.* Washington: President's Committee on Mental Retardation, 1969.

Kuhn, T. S. *The structure of scientific revolutions.* Chicago: The University of Chicago Press, 1962.

Kurtz, R. A., & Wolfensberger, W. *Separation experiences of residents in an institution for the mentally retarded: 1910-1959.* AMERICAN JOURNAL OF MENTAL DEFICIENCY, 1969, *74*, 389-396.

Kushner, M. *Faradic aversive controls in clinical practice.* In Neuringer, C., & Michael, J. L. (Eds.), BEHAVIOR MODIFICATION IN CLINICAL PSYCHOLOGY. New York: Appleton-Century-Crofts, 1970. Pp. 26-51.

Lecht, L. A. *Goals, priorities, and dollars.* New York: Free Press, 1966.

Lecht, L. A. *Manpower needs for national goals in the 1970's.* New York: Praeger, 1969.

Lindsley, O. R. *Direct measurement and prosthesis of retarded behavior.* JOURNAL OF EDUCATION, 1964, *147*, 62-63.

Linton, T. E. *The European educateur program for disturbed children.* AMERICAN JOURNAL OF ORTHOPSYCHIATRY, 1969, *39*, 125-133.

London, P. *Behavior control.* New York: Harper & Row, 1969.

Lovaas, O. I. *Learning theory approach to the treatment of childhood schizophrenia.* In Mills, A. B. (Ed.), BEHAVIOR THEORY AND THERAPY. California Mental Health Research Symposium No. 8, Sacramento, California, 1968. Pp. 1-22. (a)

Lovaas, O. I. *Some studies on the treatment of childhood schizophrenia.* In Shlien, J. M. (Ed.), RESEARCH IN PSYCHO-THERAPY, Vol. 3. Washington, D.C.: American Psychological Association ,1968. Pp. 103-121. (b)

Lovaas, O. I., Freitag, G., Gold, V. J., & Kassorla, I. C. *Experimental studies in childhood schizophrenia: Analysis of self-destructive behavior.* JOURNAL OF EXPERIMENTAL CHILD PSYCHOLOGY, 1965, *2*, 67-84.

MacAndrew, C., & Edgerton, R. *On the possibility of friendship.* AMERICAN JOURNAL OF MENTAL DEFICIENCY, 1966, *70*, 612-621.

Margolin, R. J. *The concept of mental illness: A new look at some old assumptions.* COMMUNITY MENTAL HEALTH JOURNAL, 1968, *4*, 417-424.

Mendel, W. *Effect of hospitalization on rate and quality of remission from acute psychotic episodes.* JOURNAL OF NERVOUS AND MENTAL DISEASE, 1966, *143*, 226-233.

Mendel, W. M., & Rapport, S. *Determinants of the decision for psychiatric hospitalization.* ARCHIVES OF GENERAL PSYCHIATRY, 1969, *20*, 321-328.

Menolascino, F., Clark, R. L., & Wolfensberger, W. (Eds.). *The initiation and development of a comprehensive, county-wide system of services for the mentally retarded of Douglas County.* (2nd ed.) Vol. 1. Omaha, Nebraska: Greater Omaha Association for Retarded Children, 1968.

Menolascino, F., Clark, R. L., & Wolfensberger, W. (Eds.) *The initiation and development of a comprehensive, county-wide system of services for the mentally retarded of Douglas County.* (2nd ed.) Vol. 2. Omaha, Nebr.: Greater Omaha Association for Retarded Children, 1970.

Miller, L. C. Review of Hartmann, E., Glasser, B. A., Greenblatt, M., Solomon, M. H., & Levinson, D. J. *Adolescents in a mental hospital.* CONTEMPORARY PSYCHOLOGY, 1970, *15*(1), 52-53.

Mintzberg, H. *A framework for strategic planning.* CANADIAN FORUM, 1972, *51* (612-613), 46-48.

Mowrer, O. H. *Learning theory and behavior therapy.* In B. B. Wolman (Ed.), HANDBOOK OF CLINICAL PSYCHOLOGY. New York: McGraw-Hill, 1965. Pp. 242-276.

Mullins, J. B. *Integrated classrooms.* JOURNAL OF REHABILITATION, 1971, *37*(2), 14-16.

Murphy, H. B. M. *Professionals and the poor.* CANADA'S MENTAL HEALTH, 1969, *17*(3), 4-9.

Murray, E. J. *A content-analysis method for studying psychotherapy.* PSYCHOLOGICAL MONOGRAPHS, 1956, *70*(13, whole No. 420), 1-32.

Murray, E. J. *Direct analysis from the viewpoint of learning theory.* JOURNAL OF CONSULTING PSYCHOLOGY, 1962, *26*, 226-231.

National Goals Research Staff. *Toward balanced growth: Quantity with quality.* Washington, D.C.: U.S. Printing Office, 1970.

National Institute of Mental Health. *Mental health services for children.* (USPHS Publ. No. 1844) Chevy Chase, Md.: United States Department of Health, Education, and Welfare, 1968.

Nawas, M. M. *Wherefore cognitive therapy: A critical scrutiny of three papers by Beck, Bergin, and Ullmann.* BEHAVIOR THERAPY, 1970, *1*, 359-370.

Nawas, M. M., & Braun, S. H. *The use of operant techniques for modifying the behavior of the severely and profoundly retarded: Part I. Introduction and initial phase.* MENTAL RETARDATION, 1970, *8*(2), 2-6.

Neuringer, C., & Michael, J. L. *Behavior modification in clinical psychology.* New York: Appleton-Century-Crofts, 1970.

Nirje, B. *A Scandinavian visitor looks at U.S. institutions.* In R. Kugel & W. Wolfensberger (Eds.), CHANGING PATTERNS IN RESIDENTIAL SERVICES FOR THE MENTALLY RETARDED. Washington: President's Committee on Mental Retardation, 1969. Pp. 51-57. (a)

Nirje, B. *The normalization principle and its human management implications.* In R. Kugel & W. Wolfensberger (Eds.), CHANGING PATTERNS IN RESIDENTIAL SERVICES FOR THE MENTALLY RETARDED. Washington: President's Committee on Mental Retardation, 1969. Pp. 179-195. (b)

Nirje, B. *The normalization principle: Implications and comments.* JOURNAL OF MENTAL SUBNORMALITY, 1970, *16*, 62-70.

Norris, D. *The born fool: A study of attitudes in recent times.* FORWARD TRENDS, 1963-1964, *8*(1), 13-22.

Osmond, H. *The medical model in psychiatry.* HOSPITAL AND COMMUNITY PSYCHIATRY, 1970, *21*(9), 275-281.

Parsons, T. *The social system.* Glencoe, Ill.: The Free Press, 1951.

Parsons, T., & Fox, R. *Illness, therapy, and the modern urban American family.* In E. G. Jaco (Ed.), PATIENTS, PHYSICIANS AND ILLNESS. Glencoe, Ill.: Free Press, 1958. Pp. 234-245.

Pasamanick, B., Scarpitti, F. R., & Dinitz, S. *Schizophrenics in the community.* New York: Appleton-Century-Crofts, 1967.

Patterson, C. H. *Behavior modification in rehabilitation: A consideration of its values and limitations.* REHABILITATION RESEARCH AND PRACTICE REVIEW, 1970, *2*(1), 1-12.

Paul, G. L. *Chronic mental patient: Current status – future directions.* PSYCHOLOGICAL BULLETIN, 1969, *71*, 81-91.

Payne, D., Johnson, R., & Abelson, R. *A comprehensive description of institutionalized retardates in the western United States.* Boulder, Colo.: Western Interstate Commission for Higher Education, 1969.

Perske, R. *The dignity of risk and the mentally retarded.* MENTAL RETARDATION, 1972, *10*(1), 24-26.

Powell, J., & Azrin, N. *The effects of shock as a punisher for cigarette smoking.* JOURNAL OF APPLIED BEHAVIOR ANALYSIS, 1968, *1*, 63-71.

President's Committee on Mental Retardation. *MR69: Toward progress: The story of a decade.* Washington: U.S. Government Printing Office, 1969.

President's Committee on Mental Retardation. *MR68: The edge of change.* Washington: U.S. Government Printing Office, 1968.

Provence, Sally, & Lipton, Rose C. *Infants in institutions: A comparison of their development with family-reared infants during the first year of life.* New York: International Universities Press, 1962.

Rabkin, R. *Inner and outer space: An introduction to a theory of social psychiatry.* New York: W. W. Norton, 1970.

Rachman, S., & Teasdale, J. *Aversion therapy and behavior disorders: An analysis.* Coral Gables, Florida: University of Miami Press, 1969.

Raush, H. L., & Raush, C. L. *The halfway house movement: A search for sanity.* New York: Appleton-Century-Crofts, 1968.

Reiff, R. *Mental health manpower and institutional change.* AMERICAN PSYCHOLOGIST, 1966, *21*, 540-548.

Reports from states. *Proceedings of the National Conference of Charities and Correction, 1890*, p. 329.

Ricke, H. K., McDaniel, M. W., Stallings, V. D., & Gatz, M. J. *Operant behavior in vegetative patients II.* PSYCHOLOGICAL RECORD, 1967, *17*, 449-460.

Roberts, C. L., & Perry, R. M. *A total token economy.* MENTAL RETARDATION, 1970, *8*(1), 15-18.

Roos, P. *Development of an intensive habit-training unit at Austin State School.* MENTAL RETARDATION, 1965, *3*, 12-15.

Roos, P. *Current issues in residential care with special reference to the problems of institutional care.* In International League of Societies for the Mentally Handicapped, SYMPOSIUM ON RESIDENTIAL CARE FOR THE MENTALLY RETARDED, Brussels, Belgium: International League of Societies for the Mentally Handicapped, 1969. (a)

Roos, P. *Residential care for the mentally handicapped.* Brussels, Belgium: International League of Societies for the Mentally Handicapped, 1969. (b)

Roos, P. *Opening address.* In NATIONAL CONFERENCE ON RESIDENTIAL CARE. New York: National Association for Retarded Children, 1969. (c)

Roos, P. *Normalization, de-humanization, and conditioning: Conflict or harmony?* MENTAL RETARDATION, 1970, *8*(4), 12-14.

Roos, P., McCann, B., & Patterson, E. G. *A developmental model of mental retardation.* Paper presented at the 1970 Annual Convention of the National Association for Retarded Children.

Roos, P. *Misinterpreting criticisms of the medical model.* MENTAL RETARDATION, 1971, *2*(1), 22-24.

Rosen, J. N. *Direct analysis.* New York: Grune & Stratton, 1953.

Rosen, B. M., Kramer, M., Redick, R. W., & Willner, S. G. *Utilization of psychiatric facilities by children: Current status, trends, implications.* (USPHS Publ. No. 1868) Washington, D.C.: United States Government Printing Office, 1968.

Rosenberg, A. D. *Appropriateness of the continued institutionalization of the state school population in New York state.* Buffalo: New York Department of Mental Hygiene, 1969.

Rosenthal, R., & Jacobson, L. *Pygmalion in the classroom: Teacher expectation and pupil's intellectual ability.* New York: Holt, Rinehart & Winston, 1968.

Rowland, G. T., & Patterson, E. G. *Curiosity: An educational key to change.* EDUCATION AND TRAINING OF THE MENTALLY RETARDED, 1971, *6*, 92-97.

Rubin, R., & Balow, B. *Learning and behavior disorders: A longitudinal study.* EXCEPTIONAL CHILDREN, 1971, *38*, 293-299.

Rubin, R. D., & Franks, C. M. (Eds.). *Advances in behavior therapy, 1968.* New York & London: Academic Press, 1969.

Sabshin, M. *Theoretical models in community and social psychiatry.* In Roberts, L. M., Halleck, S., & Loeb, M., (Eds.), COMMUNITY PSYCHIATRY. Madison, Wis.: University of Wisconsin Press, 1966. Pp. 15-30.

Sabshin, M. *The anti-community mental health 'movement'.* AMERICAN JOURNAL OF PSYCHIATRY, 1969, *125*, 1005-1011.

Saltsman, M. *A national plan.* CANADIAN FORUM, 1972, *51*(612-613), 56-58.

Sarason, S. *The creation of settings.* In R. Kugel & W. Wolfensberger (Eds.), CHANGING PATTERNS IN RESIDENTIAL SERVICES FOR THE MENTALLY RETARDED. Washington: President's Committee on Mental Retardation, 1969. Pp. 341-357.

Schaefer, H. H. *Investigations of operant conditioning procedures in a mental hospital.* In Fisher, J., & Harris, R. E. (Eds.), REINFORCEMENT THEORY IN PSYCHOLOGICAL TREATMENT: A SYMPOSIUM. Sacramento: Department of Mental Hygiene, Research Monograph No. 8, 1966.

Schorer, C. E., Lowinger, P., Sullivan, T., & Hartlaub, G. H. *Improvement without treatment.* DISEASES OF THE NERVOUS SYSTEM, 1968, *29*, 100-104.

Schwitzgebel, R. L. *Survey of electromechanical devices for behavior modification.* PSYCHOLOGICAL BULLETIN, 1968, *70*, 444-459.

Science Council for Canada. *Towards a national science policy for Canada.* Report No. 4. Ottawa: Queen's Printer, 1968. Pp. 13-18.

Senate Special Committee on Science Policy. *Science policy for Canada: Report of the Senate Special Committee on Science Policy.* Vol. 2. TARGETS AND STRATEGIES FOR THE SEVENTIES. The Honourable Maurice Lamontagne, Chairman. Ottawa: Queen's Printer, 1972. Pp. 374-375.

Shatto, G., & Keeler, C. *Rehabilitation in San Blas.* JOURNAL OF REHABILITATION, 1971, *37*(2), 10-13.

Shotwell, A. M., & Shipe, D. *Effect of out-of-home care on the intellectual and social development of mongoloid children.* AMERICAN JOURNAL OF MENTAL DEFICIENCY, 1964, *68*, 693-699.

Smith, M. B., & Hobbs, N. *The community and the community mental health center.* AMERICAN PSYCHOLOGIST, 1966, *21*, 499-509.

Spitz, R. A. *Hospitalism: An inquiry into the genesis of psychiatric conditions in early childhood.* THE PSYCHOANALYTIC STUDY OF THE CHILD, 1945, *1*, 53-74.
Spitz, R. A. *The role of ecological factors in emotional development in infancy.* CHILD DEVELOPMENT, 1949, *20*, 145-156.
Staats, A. W., Minke, K. A., & Butts, P. *A token-reinforcement remedial reading program administered by black therapy-technicians to problem black children.* BEHAVIOR THERAPY, 1970, *1*, 359-370.
Stedman, D. J., & Eichorn, D. H. *A comparison of the growth and development of institutionalized and home reared mongoloids during infancy and early childhood.* AMERICAN JOURNAL OF MENTAL DEFICIENCY, 1964, *69*, 391-401.
Stimson, C. W. *Physiatry in state institutions for the mentally retarded.* ARCHIVES OF PHYSICAL MEDICINE AND REHABILITATION, 1967, *48*, 227-228.
Suraci, A. B. *Reactions of Puerto Rican and non Puerto Rican parents to their mentally retarded boys.* (Doctoral dissertation, New York University) Ann Arbor, Michigan: University Microfilms, 1966. No. 67-4930.
Sutherland, J. D. (Ed.). *Collected papers of Sigmund Freud.* London: Hogarth Press and the Institute of Psycho-Analysis, 1957.
Szasz, T. S. *The myth of mental illness.* New York: Hoeber, 1961.
Talbot, Mabel E. *Edouard Seguin: A study of an experimental approach to the treatment of mentally defective children.* New York: Bureau of Publications, Teachers College, Columbia University, 1964.
Talbot, J. A. *Community psychiatry in the army: History, practice, and applications to civilian psychiatry.* JOURNAL OF THE AMERICAN MEDICAL ASSOCIATION, 1969, *210*, 1233-1237.
Tarjan, G., Brooke, C. E., Eyman, R. K., Suyeyasu, A., & Miller, C. R. *Mortality and cause of death in a hospital for the mentally retarded.* AMERICAN JOURNAL OF PUBLIC HEALTH, 1968, *58*, 1891-1900.
Tarjan, G., Eyman, R. K., & Miller, C. R. *Natural history of mental retardation in a state hospital, revisited: Releases and deaths in two admission groups, ten years apart.* AMERICAN JOURNAL OF DISEASES OF CHILDREN, 1969, *117*, 609-620.
Tate, B. G., & Baroff, G. S. *Aversive conditioning of self-injurious behavior in a psychotic boy.* BEHAVIOR RESEARCH AND THERAPY, 1966, *4*, 281-287.
Teufel, W. *Das Schloss der Barmherzigkeit.* Stuttgart: Quell-Verlag, 1960.
Thorne, F. C. *Principles of personality counseling: An eclectic viewpoint.* Brandon, Vermont: JOURNAL OF CLINICAL PSYCHOLOGY, 1950.
Tiffany, F. *Life of Dorothea Lynde Dix.* Cambridge, Mass.: Riverside Press, 1891.
Truax, C. B. *Reinforcement and nonreinforcement in Rogerian psychotherapy.* JOURNAL OF ABNORMAL PSYCHOLOGY, 1966, *71*, 1-9.
Ullmann, L. P. *Institution and outcome: A comparative study of psychiatric hospitals.* London: Pergamon Press, 1967.
Ullmann, L., & Krasner, L. (Eds.). *Case studies in behavior modification.* New York: Holt, Rinehart, & Winston, 1965.
United States Department of Health, Education, and Welfare. *Toward a social report.* Washington, D.C.: U.S. Government Printing Office, 1969.
Vail, D. J. *Dehumanization and the institutional career.* Springfield, Ill.: Charles C. Thomas, 1967.
Vanier, J. *Eruption to hope.* Toronto: Griffin House, 1971.
Wahler, R. G., Winkel, G. H., Peterson, R. F., & Morrison, D. C. *Mothers as behavior therapists for their own children.* BEHAVIOR RESEARCH AND THEORY, 1965, *3*, 113-124.
Wallace, G. L. *Plan and construction of an institution for feeble-minded.* JOURNAL OF PSYCHO-ASTHENICS, 1924, *29*, 256-270.
Wallner, T. *Sängliggande utvecklingsstörda: Resultat av en enkät.* Unpublished manuscript, Stockholm, Sweden, 1970.
Watson, L. S. *Applications of behavior-shaping devices to training severely and profoundly mentally retarded children in an institutional setting.* MENTAL RETARDATION, 1968, *6*(6), 21-23.
Watson, L. S., Jr. *Behavior modification of residents and personnel in institutions for the mentally retarded.* In Baumeister, A. A., & Butterfield, E. C. (Eds.), RESIDENTIAL FACILITIES FOR THE MENTALLY RETARDED. Chicago: Aldine, 1970. Pp. 199-245.
Weinberg, A. M. *The axiology of science.* AMERICAN SCIENTIST, 1970, *58*, 612-617.

subject index

name index

Other publications of the National Institute on Mental Retardation

Citizen Advocacy and Protective Services for the Impaired and Handicapped
W. Wolfensberger & H. Zauha

Describes the concept and rationale as well as providing concise guidelines for the implementation and operation of protective services, and specifically, Citizen Advocacy. Relevant to workers in mental health, developmental disabilities, aging, poverty and other social services.

1973 soft cover 290 pp. $7.50 *in Canada* $8.50 *outside Canada*

PASS – Program Analysis of Service Systems, 3rd edition. A system for the quantitative evaluation of human services.
W. Wolfensberger & L. Glenn

Based largely on the principle of normalization, this unique instrument is applicable to virtually any type of human service and permits comparisons between entirely different kinds of services. Also included is the description of a similar instrument FUNDET, which develops criteria for funding decisions.

1975 soft cover 2 volumes $9.50 *in Canada* $10.50 *outside Canada*

Orientation Manual on Mental Retardation, Revised Edition

An overview of mental retardation for a wide audience, including parents, volunteers, and students. Can be applied to other disability groups, and, in part, focuses on the concerns of all handicapped persons. Used extensively in community college courses.

1977 soft cover 118 pp. $4.00 *in Canada* $4.50 *outside Canada*

Residential Services: Community Housing Options for Handicapped People

A manual to assist people engaged in planning community residences for mentally retarded persons. Identifies principles and common elements that go into developing and operating a high quality residence within a system of residential services.

1975 loose leaf binder 142 pp. $5.00 *in Canada* $5.50 *outside Canada*

Prevention of Mental Retardation
J. B. Fotheringham & M. Morrison

A valuable text in the education of medical, nursing and public health practitioners, which can also be used as a program handbook by provincial and municipal health and social service agencies. Contains "Action Steps" for use by voluntary associations and other citizen groups. Examines biomedical and environmental causes of mental retardation.

1976 soft cover 142 pp. $1.25 *in Canada* $2.00 *outside Canada*

Orders and requests for further information should be addressed to:

Publications
The National Institute on Mental Retardation
Kinsmen NIMR Building, York University Campus
4700 Keele Street, Downsview, Ontario, Canada
M3J 1P3